Say Nothing

Josephine Duthie

Say Nothing

The Harrowing Truth about Auntie's Children

EDINBURGH AND LONDON

First published in Great Britain in 2012 by
MAINSTREAM PUBLISHING COMPANY
(EDINBURGH) LTD
7 Albany Street
Edinburgh EH1 3UG

ISBN 9781780575193

A catalogue record for this book is available from the British Library

Printed and bound by
CPI Group (UK) Ltd, Croydon CR0 4YY

1 3 5 7 9 10 8 6 4 2

Contents

Acknowledgements

Thanks to my dear devoted husband, for his never-ending support and encouragement; for the many times I have distracted him from his own work to listen to my story and for the advice on how to continue; for the affectionate hugs when I needed them most and for the confidence he has brought to my life and the decisions I have had to make along the way. Without his valuable input and his tremendous patience, this book would never have been written.

For the support of my three darling children, who have listened to each stage as the book progressed. In their midst, I learnt how to play, how to perceive life from a child's point of view; they filled a vacant gap in my whole make-up, which in turn healed the hurt in me and made me a better person.

For the four beautiful grandchildren they have given me to love with all my heart.

A warm thanks and a special tribute to my first husband, who died suddenly in 1988, for without him I would not have three children to love and cherish or four adorable grandsons to carry the family into the future.

A special thanks to Harry, for his encouragement and advice. I have immense admiration for the continued and dedicated support he gives to survivors of historical abuse in Scotland.

Thanks also to *The Northern Scot* for permission to use the article 'Sorry Plight of Moray Crofters' and for the publicity they are willing to give this book.

A warm-felt thanks to the grown-up children and neighbours of the crofts mentioned, for their encouragement and verification of many details that I couldn't readily recall and for supplying me with several photographs in this book; to the fond memory of the shepherd and his caring family, and the special black-and-white collie Flogal who followed me everywhere and made life on the croft somewhat bearable.

Preface

The day I decided to visit the past, to bring some sense to the nightmares that once dogged my living hours, was the day I truly began to heal. When I was sent to live with 'Auntie', as we came to know her, I was just eight years old. I was a vulnerable child, confused and hurt by the break-up of my family. A lifetime has passed since that day in 1956 that changed my life forever.

It was at Coxton that I spent my childhood in constant fear of pain and punishment, my stomach tight with tension and worry, my mouth dry as sandpaper. It was on a rural croft, in an idyllic spot, some might say, that I spent many hours afraid of the hopelessness, afraid of powerful adults, afraid of the night and the monsters that lurked in the dark, and afraid for the safety of my siblings; sometimes just afraid of what each day might bring. I feel distant and disconnected now; it's as if I am writing someone else's story.

The political climate in the early 1950s, when my story begins, influenced how social-work issues were handled. Barely eight years after the end of the Second World War, the excess of children in urgent need of home placements due to different aspects of parental and economic failure resulted in a general acceptance of any offer to house these unfortunate children outside the control of residential care homes. This, in turn, left the system wide open to misuse. The four of us – two brothers and two sisters – were vulnerable and trusting, in the care of a welfare system that assessed our situation solely in terms of keeping us together as a family unit. This system failed to recognise the simple need to provide us with a stable environment that was monitored carefully and regularly. It also failed to correctly assess this particular inexperienced adult and how she could cope with the complexities of childcare and the management of four lively city kids.

While writing this book has been part of a greater healing exercise, I also want to use this opportunity to voice my support for abused children, especially those like myself who were – and still are today – fostered into the hands of inexperienced carers, and show how the effect of abuse in all its forms can have an adverse effect on the lives of those involved.

The time is right to correct the wrongs of the past and to help prevent situations like mine from destroying the lives of all future generations. Within my story, I have tried to emphasise the need for a child to be listened to by friends, neighbours and local authorities.

I have tried to use humour, where possible, to lighten the darkness that hung over my childhood: remembering the events as they happened was emotionally painful and I found I could express myself with more ease assisted in this way.

For my own benefit psychologically, I have incorporated several of my poems within the text. As a child, writing these poems created a sense of euphoria, an anaesthetic that eased the pain of continuous neglect and punishment. I loved the power of words, how they could capture a moment in time and help to diffuse any violent thoughts I had against Auntie. I found I could tell the world how I felt without fear of being accused of telling lies or inventing stories: I could paint pictures with a pen and lose myself in a reality I could understand. Poetry has become a healing matrix for me and has helped to release the trauma of the years at Coxton. I wrote 'If', the following poem, on a brown-paper bag while curled inside a potato sack under a canopy of fir trees. My determination to develop my own strength of character is clearly evident in its words.

If I had a summer breeze
for every breath I took,
I'd calm the waves of fury,
subdue the ground that shook.
The winds of change I'd capture
and blow across the land,
to cool the steaming deserts,
to fertilise the sand.
If I had the distance
for every step I made,
I'd bear the hottest climate
to find the coolest shade.
The footsteps I would follow
along the Sands of Time,
to gather in the harvest,
to make the sweetest wine.
If I had a parchment
for every word I wrote,
I'd print the words of wisdom,

and read the wisest quote.
The book of life I'd study,
the knowledge I would gain,
to push the pen of freedom,
to lift the mist of pain.
If I had a moonbeam
for every star that shone,
I'd shine the beam of wonder
across the rising dawn.
The sunrise I'd take captive,
inhale its golden charm,
to have the light of many,
to make me what I am.

I came across the article below, published in 1959 in *The Northern Scot*, describing the local community where I spent my childhood years. It gives some sense of place and hopefully a clearer image of that landscape. Although the area mentioned is the Moss of Barmuckity, the area where the croft was situated, Coxton, was close by.

> Sorry Plight of Moray Crofters
>
> A little beyond the eastern outskirts of Elgin and tucked away in a quiet backwater lies a remarkable community. Moss of Barmuckity is a gathering of crofts and smallholdings where television helps the hardy residents to pass away the winter nights yet where for some an open, muddy ditch is their only source of water . . . Situated only a few hundred yards from the busy Aberdeen–Inverness trunk road, it is hidden from the eyes of the general public.

Preface

A picturesque corner, The Moss supports some seventeen smallholdings and more than 50 people. Some have a few cattle and poultry; others an acre or two to till and a cow to keep; a few pigs. For the answer to what life on the Moss is really like, I went to 79-year old but very active Miss Jane Winchester, who has lived there all her life. Miss Winchester has a five-acre croft. 'There's just me, my heifer, a piggy and six cats,' she told me. 'I was born and brought up here and I like it fine' – that coming from someone who has little or no amenities and who has daily to trudge with her water from a ditch, little more than a hole in the ground.

'I've never had water in the house,' she said, 'and never drink it on its own. I'll show you why,' she offered. Having seen it, I cannot blame her. For her domestic supply, it is a brown sandy-looking concoction. 'If I want a drink,' she said, 'I usually have lemonade, as this stuff has to be boiled before it can be used.'

Prologue

I felt the thick cord slip through my hands as the simple coffin slid slowly into the hole in the ground and rested with a dull thud on the bottom. A black cloud broke the sunshine and a chilly breeze swept past our faces, as the grass stirred and the trees rustled. A small cluster of bowed heads watched in silence as a few final words were spoken. A handful of earth drizzled lightly onto the highly polished lid and a black beetle scurried into the shadows. I could imagine Auntie lying there clothed in her favourite nightdress, her body lying to attention, the eyelids closed over expressionless eyes; her violent, shaking hands, pale and lifeless, pressed neatly into her sides. Her screaming mouth permanently closed, free from cigarette ash. Her grey hair neatly combed into place.

The funeral was over. Auntie was lying in a six-foot hole, alone. How would I remember her? Would it be as a cruel, unfeeling foster mother or rather the lonely old lady who died with no one around except medical staff who didn't really know her?

Looking back, Auntie's evil seemed invincible; our time at

Coxton would leave us with memories we'd rather forget. We were vulnerable and confused and at the mercy of an individual whose rage was the result of a confusion I don't believe she understood herself.

We were living with the trauma of knowing our parents had betrayed us. The consequence of this was that we expected every adult to treat us the same way. We harboured a deep inner pain that we could not express; this was compounded by a sense of being let down by a welfare system that, in retrospect, was naively ignorant.

Our perception of the older generation was directly influenced by Auntie's behaviour: everything we did or said seemed to be wrong. From this stemmed a raw helplessness that made us aware of our failures, the effect of which gave us nightmares and brought on depressions, anger and insecurities in later life.

I stood for several minutes at the graveside with my own thoughts. My brothers were not there and I was alone with the memory of Auntie. I was afraid to lift my head, to look at the small group of people around me, frightened of what they were thinking, how they were judging me as a foster daughter, as a person.

I missed my brothers: they would never forgive Auntie for what she had done to them, what she had done to our baby sister Mary. But I was ready to understand her failures and put aside the bitterness of the past, though I too could not forgive and forget. She had made my life as a child seem complex and difficult to understand.

I fought back tears with a stout determination that Auntie would not make me cry any more. But I was shaking uncontrollably. I focused on the birdsong that reverberated in the silence like an army bugle indicating the end of day.

When they inevitably came, my tears were not for Auntie, not for the present, but for the childhood we had missed, and for the need to understand the piercing ache of sadness that still existed within me.

A firm, reassuring hand shook me from my reverie and affectionately clutched my shoulder. It was the shepherd whose comforting friendship had helped me to endure ten long years at Coxton. He offered to drive me out to the croft one last time, to say goodbye to a time and a place where the sound of sobbing children filled the air and where life now stood still and at peace.

The building had died the minute Auntie had been taken into care, its worn facade now crumbling to the stony ground. This was a sad place – a sad, tired old house. I saw Auntie sitting at the head of the table, her steel curlers rolled tightly round the ends of her hair, a half-smoked cigarette stuck to her bottom lip, a long trail of ash, ready to drop onto the table below, her flower-patterned overall pulled tightly across her ample breasts. Her mind was in a perpetual haze of chaos, wanting to do the right thing but not knowing the right way to do it. It should have been a happy home, a home filled with love.

It was time to leave before I broke down completely. I had done my duty, as the eldest child, to Auntie and to the croft. I walked down to the car where the old shepherd was patiently waiting. He removed his hat as I climbed into the back seat, smiled, then said in his warm north-eastern accent, 'Ye'll be awa hame noo, will ye, ma quine? Aye, bless yer wee sowel.'

I whispered goodbye to Coxton. I had to leave the memories behind, the ghosts to slumber in their coffin of shadows. They were only shadows, after all, and shadows could not hurt me. Everything had changed.

I watched the house on the hill grow smaller; it seemed to cry out as the car drove further and further away. A greyness surrounded the croft and hung above it like a cloud of depression. I wanted to knock the building down, rebuild it and fill it with children's laughter, bathe it with a type of love that only a family devoted to one another and the ground around them could give. I wanted to give it a hug. It deserved that.

I felt the tears run down my cheeks. I wanted to stand with my brothers and sister in the middle of the croft, hold hands and shout at the world. I wished I could tell everyone we were all right, that we had survived, but I couldn't. My brothers were emotionally damaged, my little sister dead, and my head was full of a sadness I found difficult to shed.

It was time to go home, back to Aberdeen, back to nursing and my family. The train left on time and headed east. I looked for the croft as the train sped past. The dullness of the building was more pronounced than ever. It looked naked, with all the outhouses gone and the fields empty of cows and sheep. What would become of it? Would the elements finally destroy the building and bring it to the ground, to be forgotten along with the children it housed, their cries forever silent?

I hoped so.

1

Earliest Memories

I am a little girl of five again and desperately alone. My mother has left the house without telling me and I am hungry and lost. I have a yearning sense of something missing, something misplaced, an aching kind of vacancy that needs to be filled. I have come out of the toilet and my dress is in disarray. I am cold and wet. The outside door is open and I wander into the tile-covered close, my hair blowing in the strong breeze that whistles through the tenement building. My little brother Robert is chewing on some old newspaper, his face covered in black printer's ink and dry crusted tears. He wants his mummy and so do I. It is getting dark and the gas-lit street lamps are flickering quietly in their glass prison. I hear the siren sounding from the shipyard close by and know that it should be teatime. Where is she? I need her.

I had spent the day before with my mother, standing at the kitchen window, watching a small plane circle above the tenements. A long brightly coloured banner celebrating the coronation of Queen Elizabeth II trailed behind the aircraft. I didn't know who this Queen was, but by the tone of my mother's voice I understood she was of great importance. An empty cot sat in the corner of the dimly lit room, awaiting the birth of a new baby, and Robert and George, who was only a year old, were taking a nap on the threadbare settee in front of an unlit fire.

Although our family's disintegration probably happened over some months, looking back it feels as if in that moment the foundations of our happy life began to crumble. One minute we were a normal family, with a loving, attentive mother; the next, she was gone. I remember once looking in all the rooms for her, wondering why she was hiding from me, not realising that she wasn't in the house.

Then one morning my mother arrived at the house with our new baby sister. I was very excited – I wanted to hold her, to hug my mother, but I was pushed aside as if I no longer existed. A coldness arrived with my sister Mary and never left.

But within weeks of coming home from hospital, my mother had vanished again, leaving my ten-week-old sister lying in her cot. Her hungry cries alerted the neighbours and the neglect was soon reported to the authorities. Robert, who was four years old and the eldest of my two younger brothers, and I were bundled into a van and taken into care.

I remember very little of the time I spent in this children's home, as it wasn't long before we were back in the relative comfort of familiar surroundings. However, a short time later the neglect and desertion by both our parents resumed. What was once, as I remember it, a happy household was now full of chaos and confusion. Clothes seemed to be lying everywhere. Mealtimes were a biscuit or a slice of toast left on the kitchen table. Any sense of our daily routine had vanished, as day became night and night became day.

I felt a loneliness I couldn't comprehend. An emptiness had

broken into the house when we weren't looking and stripped us clean of everything we once knew. We became afraid of the changes taking place in our lives and felt that the love that was once evident in our home was slipping away and we were powerless to stop it.

During the day we yearned for one of our parents to be at home and give us some sign of reassurance, a sign that never came. No one was around any more when a grazed knee or a sore finger was in desperate need of sympathetic treatment. The soothing understanding we always received from the parents we loved with all our hearts seemed to be gone. Parental hugs disappeared and a sense of fun vanished from our lives. Instead we were left all day to fend for ourselves.

Every afternoon, rain or shine, I could be seen pushing one of my younger siblings up and down the street in an old pram in a futile attempt to keep the baby from crying. A bottle, either empty or full, sagged from the baby's mouth. Every now and then I stopped and adjusted the covers. I was so small that my head was the only part of my body visible above the main structure of the pram. I continued to walk up and down the street until my father came home and took the pram inside. I would follow him inside, eat my toast and go to bed.

Robert and I were often seen wandering aimlessly round the street, holding hands and looking lost. We were always together – sometimes we were crying, sometimes chatting like two frenetic sparrows – but there didn't seem to be anyone who was very interested in where we were or what we did. We could be seen standing under the street lamps waiting for our father to come home. I don't know if he had to work late to make extra money or he just didn't want to come home, but I would like to believe that my father tried his best until things got on top of him and he couldn't cope any more. His mounting financial worries and the continual absence of our mother probably robbed him of valuable sleep and destroyed within him all form of normal reasoning. His gentle personality had changed, and a sense of impatience and irritation replaced it. A strangeness, which none of us could understand, seeped into the house, soaked our everyday life and altered the way our parents treated us. Our father's attitude became erratic and uncaring. He made me feel I had done something wrong, that my mother's absence was somehow my fault. He was finding it increasingly difficult to deal with the needs we had as children and as each day passed we saw less and less of him.

For the first time in my life, I was on the receiving end of a rolled-up newspaper bouncing off the side of my face, a sudden, impatient push. There was a growing feeling of total rejection from a man I once thought was my friend and protector.

Bedtime became the most confusing time of all. It seemed to be whenever we got tired or crawled under the covers seeking comfort from the uncertainty around us. With no mother to tuck us in at night or get us up in the morning, we depended solely on the amount of light coming through the house windows or the sounds of hustle and bustle outside to determine the order in which our day was to be ruled.

I can't remember exactly how I felt during that time, but looking at children of the same age today the sudden change in our family must have affected each one of us in a very traumatic way. I was nearly six years old, the eldest of four children.

My parents, who were both in the forces when they married during the Second World War, were for many reasons finding it impossible to stay together. This resulted in the disintegration of their relationship and led to the inevitable breakdown of their marriage. Although I knew things were not right at home, I did not understand why. I was aware of raised voices and frequent absences on my mother's part. When they were arguing, I became confused and didn't know which parent to turn to for comfort and reassurance. Many times I found myself standing between them, watching the anger in their eyes and aware that they didn't know I was there. They didn't seem to notice when I was crying and failed to respond when I touched them. It always ended with one parent leaving the house, usually my mother, and sometimes it was the next day or several days later before I saw her again.

One night, I became so upset at the thought of her leaving that she put my coat on and took me with her. We ended up sitting in a relatively empty railway station café eating ice cream. I don't remember what she said to me, but when we eventually returned home, everything appeared back to normal, and I presume I was put to bed. I wanted to hug my father and say sorry for leaving him, but I didn't, and for a long time I regretted this. I can still see the look of hurt on his face when I drew back from his outstretched arms, turned my back on him and went to my room. I was sticking up for my mother, a normal decision for a little girl of six to make, and I still feel bad about it.

Some nights would be quiet, but as the days wore on I heard them shouting more and more as I lay in bed. Every time my bedroom door opened, I hid under the blankets and pretended to be asleep. I crouched in the foetal position and hugged my knees for comfort, wishing I could hear my parents laugh like they used to, wishing I wasn't so scared and sad. What was happening to our family? Would my parents leave us one day and never come back?

My father had been demobbed from the navy in the early 1950s and then took a job as a fishmonger in Govan, Glasgow. Although I can still see his shop floor covered in sawdust and remember him cutting off the heads and tails of fish, which he gave to his elderly customers to make soup, I don't remember the true relationship I had with him. I recall his friendly smile and his very tall height. I have vivid recollections of sitting on his shoulder and having to duck down sharply as we entered the tiled close; this entrance led directly to our ground-floor accommodation. I remember his infectious laughter as he swung me off his shoulder and the friendly pat on the back to let me know that he had had enough and it was time to go and play.

I remember the day, and my excitement, when he brought home my first kilt, those numerous pleats spreading in a splendid fan-like apparition as I spun round and round in a soporific glee. There was a time when happy chatter permeated the house as supper was cooking and bedtime stories were read as we huddled together before lights were switched off for the night.

Many times I sat beside him at the kitchen table watching as he worked on black-and-white pencil drawings of battleships and submarines, fascinated by the effect his pencil had on his blank sheet of paper and how easy he made it look as each picture came alive and recognisable. I wanted to be able to draw like that and somehow I sensed his passion as each picture took shape. The closeness I had with my father disappeared quite suddenly and left me with a sense of desperate isolation. I had been robbed of his care, his company and his love.

I know very little about my mother's situation, other than from the minimal amount of information supplied to me by the welfare department. The details state that she misused bank books and money from the family allowance and was consequently charged and arrested for fraud and forgery. Her mental health was fragile and unstable, and because of this she was placed in the care of the Salvation Army, where she remained for some time.

There are small things I recall, however, such as her favourite songs – 'Cruising Down the River' and 'The Black Hills of Dakota'; her whistle as she arrived home so our father would know it was her at the door; the smell of roses as she flitted past; her presence at my hospital bed after a tonsillectomy, pulling up the covers to keep me warm.

One winter's night, after we had returned from our brief stay at the children's home, she held me up to the window to watch the snow fall onto the grass at the back of the tenements and told me that the biggest snowflakes she had ever seen fell on the day I was born. I felt comfortable again, reassured, the bond with my mother seemed strong. This kind of relationship was meant to last – why wouldn't it? – but I had a feeling something was wrong. There was an unhappiness about her, a sadness in her body language and an uncertainty in the tone of her voice as she spoke. It was a feeling I did not understand. I remember looking into her eyes and seeing they were full of tears. Looking back, I believe it was the moment she decided to leave us.

Did she not want me any more because of my baby sister? Was she fighting with her conscience that evening? Was she trying to say goodbye? Did she find it easy? As far as I can recall, that was the last day I saw her in that house. Suddenly she wasn't there. I didn't see her leave and couldn't understand why I couldn't find her. She was my life; she was my mother.

I remember standing outside every day in the close entrance looking for her to come home and feeling excited when I thought

I could see her silhouette appear round the corner; I remember thinking I will be very good today and maybe she will stay this time, but it was not to be and I eventually stopped looking.

I have often wondered how she could leave us behind. Were we not worth her love? What was going on in her mind, what was she really thinking? Had depression stolen my mother's mind so much that she didn't want her children any more? Love is the most important thing a child needs – love strengthens their emotional and physical growth; it builds self-confidence, which prepares the child for a secure step into adulthood. I don't think I will ever understand her decision to leave or why she didn't ask for us back when her life returned to normal.

Both of my parents are now deceased, leaving me with so many unanswered questions, feelings of regret and even guilt at the thought that we might, in some way, have been the cause of their break-up.

Less than one year after we were removed from our home in Glasgow, our parents went on to have another two girls, one they also named Josephine. It was as if they wanted to wipe out the memory of the children they already had, allowing them to start again with a clean slate. This renewed relationship did not last and it was not long before they were separated for the final time. The two girls themselves struggled through life with an unstable mother forever searching for a better life.

There is no photographic evidence of my infant years before their separation and I have been able to trace very few pictures of the childhood I so desperately seek to understand. Some memories make little sense: I remember one night finding myself lying on the bed covered in newspapers – why newspapers? – a coal fire burning furiously in the grate, listening to my father telling me how lucky I was because outside in the wind and rain there were many people who did not have a home to stay in or a bed to sleep in.

I remember getting a row for flooding the kitchen floor by leaving the tap running, but I don't know why I did it. I can see myself lying in bed, unwell, with a sock filled with hot salt held against my ear; another time I am hiding under the kitchen table with my mother as a siren goes off, probably from some works yard. I remember it being very loud and not understanding why my mother was so scared, not knowing that the war years and the bombing raids had affected her greatly and that, like other women of that era, only time would turn the sound of those sirens into something less threatening.

I recall sitting on the pavement trying to tie my shoelaces and feeling pleased with myself when I eventually succeeded; visiting a dark place with hundreds of coloured lights and running water, a fairyland of wonder and music somewhere underground. Where was it, and who was I with? There are memories of being lifted up onto the stage after a performance. A woman dressed as a man took my hand and bowed to the audience. One of many acts in the flourishing music-hall traditions in Glasgow during the 1950s, no doubt.

One day someone put me on a tramcar and told me that my mother would be waiting for me at the terminus. I must have been five or six at the time. For some reason, she didn't turn up and I remember wandering about in a strange place feeling very frightened and alone until I was found and taken home. I felt my mother had forgotten me. I was beginning to have this feeling more and more as the days progressed and I didn't like it. It made me feel scared and lonely and, most importantly, very lost. Robert and I seemed to be together more often and I do remember not feeling safe unless he was in my company.

Robert and I used to sit on the window ledge in the bedroom as darkness fell and watch the Leerie light the gas street lamps. He carried his ladder to each light and carefully placed the pole inside the glass panel and lit the flame. He never forgot to wave and smile at us; one night he brought us a bag of home-baked cakes, which we both ate ravenously. I don't remember giving any to George, or what was happening to our baby sister. In fact, I don't recall what they were doing during those periods at all. Both must have been very quiet babies, and probably rather sickly, but we were too young ourselves to realise they might need help.

For some reason, we did not have electric lights – or maybe we were just too little to reach the switch – but I do however recall the warm glow from the street lamps that shone into the room where we sat and how safe and secure this light made us feel.

A number of candles were stuck to odd pieces of furniture and we used to scrape the candle grease off the wood and eat it. Whether it was because we liked the taste or because we were rather hungry, I'll never know.

It's hard to say what we did on a day-to-day basis, and even harder to envisage how we survived those times. Some of the most pleasant memories remain the most vivid and this probably helped to dampen the desperate months we lived through, when our parents stopped loving us and no longer wanted us in their lives.

Once a week Robert and I looked forward to the rag-and-bone man, who came round our area on a horse and cart. His clothes looked like the ones he had in his wagon, his soft hat sat at an angle on his head and a blue-knotted scarf stuck out like a ribbon from his neck. He whistled all the time while he patted his old horse on the side of its leg. I couldn't understand why this horse had covers over its eyes and I remember asking this kind man if the horse was blind and why didn't it have a white stick like the man at the foot of our road? He smiled, held me up to the animal's head and pulled back the blinkers to show me that the horse's eyes were working normally. He always seemed pleased to see us and never failed to hoist us up to sit amongst musty old clothes and bric-a-brac. His pockets were filled with lollipops and balloons, which he dished out to any child who came forward with bits and pieces for his cart. We often stayed with him for the whole afternoon. Before he finished for the day, he would present us with a handful of goodies to eat and drop us safely back to our door.

My seventh birthday came and went unnoticed, and although our family unit was deteriorating we were innocently unaware of what was actually happening to our lives. We had got used to fending for ourselves during the day and getting ourselves to bed at night. It wasn't hard to find friends to play with and if we were lucky a sandwich or a biscuit was shared by all.

Over a period of months, several strange visitors – some pleasant, others not so pleasant – came back and forth regularly to the house. They tried to keep us inside most of the time, but once they left Robert and I ventured onto the streets again.

The neighbours were aware that something was wrong, though at the beginning no one was willing to inform the authorities – maybe they hoped our parents would work it out for themselves – but some of the residents became so concerned by the lack of parental attention we were receiving that they contacted the child welfare services. Our mother had disappeared several weeks previously, leaving us in the care of our father and a white-haired woman. I don't remember who she was, but she came into the house from time to time and gave us something to eat. One day I saw an ambulance sitting outside our flat when I came home from school. After that I never saw this woman again.

As far as any schooling was concerned, my recollections are very vague for this period of time. The one memory that sticks in my head is being called to the teacher's desk and the date 5.5.55 being written across the blackboard in white chalk. I am not sure if it was my last day in that class and my teacher was trying her best to explain something to me, something that was going to change the future of our whole family, or there was some connection to the ambulance parked outside my home and the sudden absence of our white-haired friend.

You left before I came home from school.
I never saw you again.
My parents split up,
sent me to a home.
I never saw them again.
Were you my grandmother or a friend?
Did you know me at all?
Your hair coloured white
is all I can see.
In memory I recall.
I hope you always felt proud of me,
of this I never will know.
I hope you loved me
and taught me to read,
but no one can tell me so.
Did you die on the fifth day of May?
This date stands out in my mind.
Were you at home when the ambulance came?
The day I was left behind.

A few months after this, however, along with my two brothers, aged six and three, I was taken into care by the local authorities. My last recollection of home, before being strapped into a white van, was of my father standing on the doorstep holding Mary, who was two years old and too young at that point to come with us. My father looked as if he was crying and was leaning heavily against the wall of the house. Mary was asleep in his arms and he was looking down at her. We called to him for some kind of reassurance that everything would be all right and tried to say goodbye to him, thinking, like the rag-and-bone man with his horse and cart, that this van would bring us back before bedtime, but he didn't look up as the door of the vehicle closed and the moment was lost forever.

The windows of the van were blacked out and we couldn't see where we were going. All we were told was that our mother and father were not able to look after us any more and we were going to a children's home for a while. I remember Robert crying as the vehicle moved away from the house and I didn't know what to say to him to make him feel better.

Life had become very confusing. We did not know what was happening, and no one was there to hold our hands and explain anything to us when we needed it the most. Who would take the place of our parents to heal the hurt from this sudden break-up of our family and who would be there to care one way or another? I, for one, felt really scared and extremely lonely. All I wanted was my mother and father to be together again.

The van travelled a short distance and before we knew it, or Robert had a chance to stop crying, we had arrived at the first children's home, where we were stripped and piled into a large bath filled with warm water. Our hair was oiled and combed rather savagely, then we were dried, a pink sticking plaster bearing our name and number being placed on the back of our necks. We were quickly clothed in fresh-smelling pyjamas and told to sit down at a small table. After eating a plate of vegetable soup, Robert and I were taken to a room with several beds in it. We were the only children there and took comfort in the fact that, for the moment at least, the two of us were together; the nurses had taken George away.

We didn't sleep very well that night. We lay for a long time listening to heavy footsteps walking up and down the passageway outside our room, hoping it was our mother and father coming to take us home. As we lay in the darkness, I started telling Robert a story about a teddy bear with big floppy ears, but he found it hard to concentrate in the strange room. It was bigger than we were used to and odd-shaped shadows flickered across the walls. A small light hung from the ceiling and we stared at it for quite a while, waiting for it to go out.

Robert kept asking me when we were going home. He sobbed into his pillow, calling repeatedly for his mummy, when I said I didn't know. After some time, our eyes closed and before we knew it morning had arrived, with the sun streaming in through the large multi-paned windows. The brightness hurt our eyes. Sleep had swept away the memory of the day before and for a few moments I didn't remember where I was. I looked across at Robert; he was very quiet and staring at me. We sat up in bed just as a nurse appeared with some porridge. Once we'd eaten, Robert and I were dressed and put into another van. I didn't want to leave this home without George; I couldn't understand why they had to keep him. I think I must have been making quite a noise about it, as a woman spoke to me rather firmly as the door of the vehicle closed. We would not see him again for some time. According to notes I acquired in later years, he was so malnourished it was thought he would not survive.

The van dropped us, along with a female escort, at the railway station. She told us that we were being moved to another home with lots of children our age and we would have to stay there until our parents wanted us back. She was very kind and Robert seemed to be much happier and more at ease. She made a fuss of him, and his sad eyes seemed to brighten. When I asked what had happened to George, she said we would see him again soon.

A few hours later, we boarded the *Waverley* paddle steamer and headed across the River Clyde to Dunoon on the Cowal Peninsula. It was the first time I had seen or been near water like it and I distinctly remember the sun dancing on its surface. As we approached Kirn Pier, just outside Dunoon, it started to rain. I watched the raindrops beat on the river, creating a fine mist that crept across the surface.

Wind blows through greying clouds
and listens for the rain, and the rain comes.
Streaming down sky-spirit pathways,
tick-tocking down, beating on and on.
For the stars are leaking,
dumping their tears in falling chaos.
Tap-tapping on blue muslin
like drumbeats on soft calf leather.
With trembling skins of shimmering light,
they dive into graves of silvered water,
into underground pools of hidden secrets,
and melt into the tomb of a great river.

In the distance I could make out the small hills we had left behind and I remember wondering if I would ever see them again. Would our mother and father be able to find us? Would they be able to come on this boat, too?

It is strange how immature minds work: the naivety of any reasoning prevents them from analysing things logically. Their lack of experience means they depend solely on what is seen and heard, with the expectation of instant results and easy answers. Would the boat go back for them? Who will tell them where we are? I was frightened they might never find us again. I could feel myself being hypnotised by the rhythmic beat of the paddles as they splashed into the water and the steady chug of the engine as the steamer neared its destination. Subdued conversations played with my ability to hear, resembling the noise of a seashell held close to your ear. I felt light-headed and unsteady, and grabbed for the rail.

Our female escort brought me back to reality when she took hold of our hands as we stepped from the ferry. A black car was waiting at the end of the pier and a nurse came towards us. Her black shiny shoes splashed in the small puddles that had formed on the road. I noticed that one of her laces was flopping about and distinctly remember thinking that perhaps no one had taken the time to teach her to tie them. It crossed my mind to bend down and fasten them for her, but she began to speak to our escort and I forgot all about it. She appeared friendly and made us feel comfortable by asking our names and if we had enjoyed the journey. She then ushered us into the car and within minutes we had arrived at a large, well-built house set among trees of all shapes and sizes. Their leaves were beginning to change colour and the golds and browns lit up the garden with a warm autumnal hue. It was 1955 and the end of two years of parental neglect.

* * *

I was used to living in Glasgow, a city full of hard-working people, renowned for its shipyards and famous football parks, where work and play seemed to thrive together in perfect balance with nothing but sandstone buildings to look at, fine architectural buildings built to house the working class, erect and standing to attention like an army of disciplined soldiers. Many were left to deteriorate into derelict slums, with back gardens full of flapping washing. There was very little vegetation of any kind, which gave our new environment a picture-book appearance, creating a fresh sense of place that I would come to love.

When we arrived at the home, we were immediately fed and dressed in clean nightclothes, whereupon another nurse took us into a small dormitory, where several children were already in bed. It had been a long, tiring and uncertain two days since we had left our father's house. We clung together, hoping that we could stay in the same room, but for the first time in our lives Robert and I were separated. The nurse spoke softly to us and explained that girls and boys usually slept in different rooms. We must have trusted her, and what she was saying, and settled down quickly in our allocated beds. Before she switched off the lights she assured us that we would see each other again at breakfast time in the dining hall. I listened for a while to the other girls speaking in whispers until I drifted into an exhausted sleep.

I awoke to friendly laughter and a hive of activity as the nurses prepared us all for a new day. Once I was washed and dressed, all the girls were led in single file down the corridor to the hall for our breakfast. I found Robert there already tucking in. The hall seemed huge and all the children were speaking together. Nurses were walking up and down between the tables, keeping everything under control. We were very hungry and I greedily tucked in to a large bowl of cornflakes and several slices of toast. I was given a green plastic mug filled with my first-ever drink of warm, sweet tea. I looked around and watched everyone eating. They looked happy and at ease.

Once breakfast was over, the hall emptied quickly, leaving Robert and me sitting alone uncertain of our next move, but it wasn't long before a friendly nurse came and took us round the home, showing us a large playroom filled with toys of all shapes and sizes. The smell of clean plastic and the visual brightness of multicoloured playthings caught our attention and lost us in a world of exploration and wonder. We were left there for a short time, to let us explore the room and its contents in great detail. After some time, the nurse reappeared with our shoes and coats and, once clad in our outdoor wear, she led us up a small hill towards our new school.

When all the introductions were over, we were left in the classroom with our new teacher and classmates and encouraged to make ourselves at home. We easily made friends with the rest of the children and settled into a more secure family unit where our well-being and psychological health were fully maintained. Each day was filled with new experiences, and Robert and I were beginning to discover what it was like to live in close relationships with other people, something that had been lacking at home for some time.

The only confusing incident I remember occurred when I was sitting happily on one of the swings at the back of the home. A smiling nurse came up to me and proceeded to ask some questions, which I answered to the best of my ability, except for one that I did not understand. She asked, 'Are you a Protestant or a Catholic?' I had never heard those words before and because I couldn't get my tongue round the word Protestant, I innocently replied, 'Catholic.' I liked the sound of this word and was pleased with my answer. Next day she approached me again, this time without a smile, and lightly slapped me on the face, informing me that I was a Protestant. I still did not know what the word meant. She did not have anything to do with Robert or me after that. I can only guess she was a Catholic herself and would have been happy to look out for us if we had been of the same faith.

When our first Christmas away from home came round, and parties were in full swing, the fact that our parents weren't around any more became less and less important. Many children there had no relatives and this helped us to fit in better and not feel left out. I was encouraged to join a small percussion band and was given a triangle as my musical instrument. The matron gave me a soft blue dress with a lace collar and a pair of red, strapped shoes for the Christmas show and I felt special. When Santa arrived, I opened my present – nestled inside was a beautiful doll with large blue eyes. I couldn't stop hugging her. I named her Rosebud – this word was engraved on the back of her neck and I automatically thought this was what I should call her! I didn't realise I could keep her, so when the party was over I carried her to a nurse and tried to hand her back. She smiled and told me that the doll was mine to keep always.

My eighth birthday was greeted with an excitement that filled the whole dinner hall. A large cake lit with several candles was wheeled into the room and I was encouraged to blow them out amid squeals of laughter and applause. The January afternoon was dull and dreary, but the coloured paper stuck to the windows brought a cheeriness to the hall. Robert stood behind me in anticipation of the biggest slice. This remains one of my happiest memories.

There were many good times in this home. I specifically remember watching the wedding in 1956 of Princess Grace and Prince Rainier of Monaco on a black-and-white television, surrounded by excited children and kind, understanding nurses. I remember thinking how beautiful she was and wondering if anyone could become a princess. I would have lots of beautiful dresses and a prince for my best friend. I thought if I worked very hard at my lessons, one day maybe I would be one, too. Biscuits and juice were passed round and the evening went by very quickly.

It was a good home: not only were we introduced to a healthier environment but we were also encouraged to have fun and play together. We planted flowers and fed the many birds that inhabited the area, especially in winter, making us aware of nature and life in general. I was given little jobs that made me feel important, for example keeping the bird tables clean and helping the nurses on duty to put clean clothes on everyone's locker on Saturday nights. I always seemed to be in a hurry, as if time was somehow too short, running everywhere and doing everything at top speed. This resulted in limitless knee plasters and a grazed forehead. The special attention I received after each fall made things so much better and I began to feel wanted again.

The time I spent in this children's home was to be the best of my young life. Little did I know what was in front of me.

Robert and I developed a special relationship with a Nurse Guy and because of her name I became convinced that she was related to the infamous Guy Fawkes. She took advantage of this and proceeded to invent, to my great pleasure, a plethora of believable tales. Once a week she spent time with both of us, helping Robert and me to feel more comfortable in our new surroundings, taking us on walks along the shoreline and letting us run about the sand until it was time for supper.

Our parents came to visit us in the children's home just after Robert's seventh birthday. We couldn't wait to see them again. We were anxious to hear that they wanted us back, that everything was going to be all right, that we would be a complete family again. We ran towards them, expecting to be swept off our feet and welcomed with open arms, but they treated us like strangers and remained distant, speaking to us from afar. The affection we were expecting did not materialise and the much-longed-for cuddles did not come. Instead, Robert and I walked together behind them as they argued continuously. We followed them round the grounds of the home, then our mother fell down a small hill, grazing her knees, and made a fuss about it.

We felt unwanted and wished they'd never come. It was the last time we saw them. We both cried as we watched them disappear down the small path. Without a goodbye wave or a final embrace, they walked out of our lives forever. We stood there feeling helpless until one of the nurses took our hands and gently led us inside.

Several months later, we were told that we were going to live on a croft with a lady who looked after some animals. We all assumed that this would be temporary – almost a holiday – still thinking that our parents would come for us eventually. The nurses gave us some books with lots of colourful farmyard scenes to look at. Even the pigs and cows looked happy and well fed. The staff looked pleased as they described the place to us and appeared excited for us. Everything about it appeared bright, clean and cheerful, so we began to warm, rather apprehensively, to the thought of a new adventure.

Our little brother George, now four, arrived to join us several weeks before we left on our journey north to the croft. It was nice to see him again, but he had forgotten us and it took some time for him to realise that he was part of our family and that we were not strangers. His reaction to us was difficult to understand. We tried very hard to get to know him again, to regain that special bond the majority of siblings have. Unfortunately, we had been apart for so long that this bond never fully returned. Robert and I played with him every day and when school was finished we took him out to the playground until suppertime. He remained very quiet and unsure of us, but as the days went on he began to relax a little and was beginning to smile more often. We did everything we could with him and felt pleased when at last he accepted hugs from both of us.

The morning finally came to leave the home and we rose early to help the nurses pack our clothes into small suitcases. We took George's hands and sat down together at the breakfast table for the last time. Robert was very quiet and tearful. We both did not want to leave this place and the people who had looked after us so well. We felt very sad and helpless. We seemed to have no control or choice over what happened to us and even though we pleaded with the nurses to let us stay, our cries were sympathetically but firmly dealt with. Once breakfast was over, we gathered together our belongings and sat at the front door to wait for our escort. It wasn't long before we saw a black car drive slowly towards the home. A smart-looking lady stepped out of the vehicle and came inside to collect us. After saying our tearful goodbyes to the matron, staff and our new friends, our journey began.

2

The Journey to Coxton

Once safely aboard the paddle steamer to cross the River Clyde, we settled in to what was to be a long and tiring day. It was raining softly and a slight breeze brushed against our faces as the boat moved forward.

Since the last time I had crossed this river, a vessel had sunk and the masts were still sticking out of the water. I remembered seeing pictures in the newspaper and reading the details of the sinking of the boat. The nurses had woken us up that night, saying, 'The sea is on fire!' The home was near the water's edge and because of this the staff and police had thought we might have to be evacuated. We had gathered in the dining hall and the nurses helped to put our outdoor coats on top of our pyjamas, but the emergency passed quickly and after a hot drink we were soon tucked back in to our warm beds.

I couldn't take my eyes off this sinister image in the water. I imagined the ghost ship rising from the depths and reaching out to touch us as we passed, but before I could let my imagination run wild the moment had gone and it had disappeared into the distance.

We arrived at the ferry terminal shortly afterwards. I glanced across the river but could not see the home; we were too far away. I knew I would never see it again and felt very sad. When we eventually arrived at Glasgow railway station, it was crammed with people and luggage, dashing this way and that. A porter came to greet us and seemed to take a special interest in our welfare. He spoke to our escort and then proceeded to sit us on top of our suitcases, where he fed us with sweets and entertained us until the northbound train arrived. I couldn't sit still because I felt very excited and was looking forward to our new life in the country. This kind gentleman remained near and kept a close watch on all of us in case we slid off the pile of bags onto the platform.

After waiting some time, the steam train puffed into view and daylight from the overhead canopy reflected on the black-painted steel, sparkling on the brass trimmings. It seemed impatient to leave and intermittently hissed at us as we gingerly boarded and found our reserved carriage. The seats were soft and spongy and we settled down quickly. We were given a small bag of sandwiches and a bottle of milk, which we consumed immediately. I was beginning to feel better and less scared and I'm certain Robert and George felt the same.

Our time spent in the children's home had been a healing experience, both mentally and physically, from the lonely days of an ever-absent mother and a father who was not interested in keeping the family unit together. I cuddled deeper into the padded seat, seeking comfort from the warm fabric as I thought about leaving my new friends behind. I was very apprehensive of a future I knew nothing about.

I didn't know what to say to Robert and George. I was scared in case I couldn't answer the questions they asked, especially ones stemming from the feelings of uncertainty we were now beginning to experience about a future we could not predict or imagine.

The train whistled loudly as it moved slowly forward and the platform filled with steam. People were running alongside our carriage, waving, and I waved back. I relaxed a little as the train pulled out of the station, leaving black, dirty tenements behind. The scene outside the window changed from large tall buildings, then scattered houses, to trees and fields. Signposts that seemed to be stabbed into the edge of each platform caught our eyes as our heads flicked back and forth, dizzy with the motion of the train. The journey became a blur of confusion, a mixture of whirling emotions I couldn't control. I wanted to hug my brothers, but they were asleep, so I fell asleep too, clutching my doll Rosebud.

Metal clinking, wheels a-clanking, chugging down the line,
passing grey old architecture clothed in twisted vine.
Gentle spasms slowly shiver reaching to a pitch,
rapid thrust increases as we leave without a hitch.
In a station, out a station, held in constant sway,
rounding corners, up and downwards, trundling on our way.
Burrowing through the underpass, like frantic, furry moles,
thundering in the darkness, towards our future goals.
As minutes tick the journey and each second slips away,
daylight wakes euphoric worlds where dreamers' minds
  can play,
till forward motion ceases and the sequence of advance,
terminates direction and wakes us from our trance.
Our senses seem to shudder as we skip along the track,
reaching to a future, with no hope of turning back.

As I was the eldest, I was sure I had let my little brothers down, and my sister, who I felt was lost to us at that time. Our parents did not want us and the nurses had sent us away. Why could they not have sent someone else to this farm? We had been happy in the home and everyone seemed happy for us – but maybe we didn't fit in as much as we thought. I was confused and suddenly felt lonely again. Had I done something wrong? I thought the people at the home had been fond of us and I did not understand their decision to send us away. I had tried to behave myself and do everything I was told, but maybe I had not worked hard enough. Had I failed miserably as a big sister, as a person? Doubts whirled in my mind.

We had been hungry and cold, and I am sure quite dirty, when we were taken from our home in Glasgow; now we were hungry and emotionally cold again. Could things really get better? What would become of us? Where would we end up? Would we really find someone who wanted to care for us, who wanted us as part of a family? It felt too good to be true.

All these questions rushed through my head in a confused state of uncertainty. I wanted a hug from someone I knew and trusted, some reassurance that everything was going to be all right. Luckily for me, the swaying movement of the train and the rhythmic rattle of the carriage kept us asleep for most of the journey and prevented me from getting too stressed out and worried about our future. I woke up several times as the train stopped at the stations along the way and each time I was ready to pick up my doll and leave the carriage, having watched the passengers frantically scramble to get out, hoping it was our stop. The chugging of the engine went on and on in a never-ending cycle, hypnotic in its deliverance, and sleep came again and again.

It was late afternoon by the time the train pulled to a stop and we were told to get off. There seemed to be an angry disagreement between our escort and a man in uniform and we waited patiently on the platform until it was resolved. It turned out we had travelled too far north and had arrived at Inverness instead. Our destination was Elgin, so we had to wait some time for a taxi to take us there. This added another two hours to our journey. It was still raining and everything was coated in a glistening film of water. Robert and George headed for the puddles and began to splash about. 'Just like silly boys,' I thought, as the child officer quickly steered them the other way. When our transport eventually arrived, we climbed into the back seat. I lay back against the cushion and became hypnotised by the numerous woods we saw along the way. Tree after tree flashed past, blinking green and brown through the tinted-glass windows. Robert and George had fallen asleep again and I had no one to talk to, so I just stared out of the car window as town after town sped past. Every croft or farmhouse I saw was our possible destination. I couldn't wait to meet our new foster mother. Would she like us? Should I give her a big hug when I see her? Would she like my doll? Maybe she would help me make new clothes for Rosebud. I hugged my doll tighter. I adjusted her blue-knitted hat and told her that we were going to be all right soon and we could sleep now.

Just as my eyelids became heavy, we turned down a side road and travelled for a short distance. The lady in the front seat pointed to a long, one-storey building with a light-coloured roof sitting high above the road. I immediately thought, 'I don't want to stay here.' My mother had told me stories from the war, about planes, bombs and moonlit raids and how they would aim for light-coloured roofs. There was another house at the other side of the road with a dark slate roof and I hoped she would change her mind and take us there instead, but our future was mapped out. The choice had been made for us.

Our journey was finally at an end: we were tired, hungry and sore from sitting all day, trying hard to behave like good little children. It was nice to be somewhere at last.

The taxi turned into a small, steep driveway. Ducks, geese and hens seemed to be everywhere and a long stone building, clad in whitewash, sat neatly at the top of the brae. It was early evening in mid-May 1956; the sky was a silver-grey. It had been raining and water was dripping from a low corrugated-iron roof. A green double wooden door opened and an old woman shuffled into view, her head covered in red frayed cotton. Her huge nose burst from inside this scarf. A patterned apron hung loosely from her non-existent waistline. Her feet sat in pom-pom'd slippers that looked as old as she did. I couldn't help staring at her left leg. It was straight and thicker than the other one. Every time she moved, the leg scraped across the ground. She seemed to sway from side to side and each step ended with an exaggerated thump on the cement slabs that led to the house.

She turned towards a black-and-white collie crouched timidly near the front door, growling quietly. 'Flogal, inside now,' she said. The dog rose and crept into the dark interior. I looked around and felt small and insignificant. I had never been in open country before and the vastness scared me. It seemed to be everywhere, on all sides. The sky was huge and towered above me. There was no hiding place and no way to escape this place to which, it seemed, we were now condemned.

I held my two little brothers' hands as we were reluctantly led towards the front door. I could feel the boys shaking as they drew closer to me. I turned and looked back at the car. I was torn between the safety of this vehicle and the uncertainty of the stranger standing in front of us. But I was pulled forward by the social worker whether I wanted it or not. My eyes glimpsed a sparkle of wet rain on the tiny windows set deep into the walls. I remember thinking: how could anyone see out of them, they're so small?

I looked at this woman in her red headscarf and searched for a hint of a smile on her face. I found none. Maybe she is scared, too, I thought. I wanted to hug her and let her know that I wanted to be her friend. I gingerly moved towards her and she instantly stepped back. I held out Rosebud to show her, but she completely ignored me. I looked round and saw nothing familiar. I felt like crying. A sudden feeling of absolute helplessness flooded my whole being: I wanted my mother and father, but they weren't there. All I could see was a strange house and a massive sky.

This was our new world, a world where nothing looked as if it had changed for decades. This horizon of woods, of small hills where perpetual rainbows skirted the mist-covered edges in the early morning as the sun rose, and of a railway line under whose bridge we would fill our hungry stomachs and finish our homework before going to school, was to be the limit of our world. It was to be a branding time of experience that would affect us for the rest of our lives. I was afraid of it.

The door swallowed us into a dark and dingy room smelling of old floorboards, musty rags and burning wood. The brown ceiling hung in suspense, threatening to crush us. There was no evidence of any lights. Two small four-paned windows set directly opposite each other allowed daylight to squeeze in and no more. The tiny room held this darkness and hid the corners and their contents from sight. Thick handmade rugs dressed a linoleum floor and plates of smelly cat food lay under a plastic-covered kitchen table. A log fire crackled from a blackened open fireplace and a soot-covered kettle whistled its presence from a hook somewhere within the chimney breast. From every nook and cranny came cats of all colours and sizes. The air stank of a strange miasma that clung to everything and everyone who entered the place.

I hugged my brothers and cried for Mary, who had been left behind in an infants' home until she reached the age of three, when she would be able to join us. What were we expected to do and say? We were very tired – could we sit down? No one was telling us what to do, so we just stood closer together and waited. I stopped crying and began to look around again, suddenly realising that this was going to be our new home. Up against the far wall stood an old wood-wormed dresser filled with Coronation cups. A set of cracked willow-patterned plates, scattered among various *objets d'art*, lined the other shelves. It didn't seem to matter what colour anything was: greyness overpowered it all. There was a feeling of total disconnection from the bright, clear world outside; inside it was like an old discarded paper bag, its contents forgotten and its usefulness outlived. I was trying to stay positive, but nothing seemed to welcome us here.

I watched a watery sun creep across the faded wallpaper and struggle to stay alive within this small stifling space where light seemed afraid to enter. We had come to a house in the country, as was promised. We should have been happy and at ease, but I was suddenly aware of how vulnerable we had become. I was unsure of this woman, a total stranger, who was going to be our guardian.

We stood patiently and quietly in the corner for some time, waiting to be welcomed into this woman's home, but she continued to avoid us. The black dog moved towards us and licked my hand.

I bent down to pat it and the woman pointed to a rug under the table. With its tail between its legs, the dog slid underneath.

The social worker brought us forward and tried to introduce us, saying we were a little nervous and shy. She gave our names and ages and talked a little about our likes and dislikes, but our foster mother didn't seem to be very interested; she just nodded her head. She appeared to be more concerned about getting the formalities over and done with as quickly as possible and ridding herself of this unwanted stranger.

Once the necessary paperwork was completed, our female escort left. I watched the taxi as it disappeared down the steep hedge-lined brae. George, only four years old, had begun to cry and I felt helpless. This time I could not make his monsters go away. I had to get outside into the fresh air for a few moments; I needed time to think, to look for an escape of some kind, to make sure we would be safe if there wasn't one. I also wanted to reassure myself that the car had not returned for us – was this place indeed our final destination?

I moved out into the daylight where geese were parading their authority among scratching hens and waddling ducks. The contrast was extreme: on one hand, stone tenements, Leerie-lit lamps and Glasgow street playgrounds; on the other, this fresh, open environment which felt somehow clean and new, yet so alien. There was so much for us to explore, to learn about nature in all its glory, to get the help we needed to develop and heal our minds and bodies from the uncertainty we had left behind. I looked around, still hoping that the taxi would come back for us, but deep down I knew it wouldn't.

I noticed that several wooden outbuildings circled the main house and a path, nearly hidden by tall unkempt grasses flirting in the wind, appeared to lead towards a thick wooded area about half a mile away. There were large fields filled with sheep and cows, where I noticed a man walking with two black-and-white dogs by his side. He was skirting the edge of the wood and continually shouted orders at his dogs, to which they seemed to react instantly. He was wearing a flat cap and was carrying a stick, which he raised in acknowledgement when he saw me waving. I watched him as he disappeared slowly over the hill towards the trees. He was to become a great friend and would give me substantial support in the years to come.

A strange feeling came over me as I stood and stared at this large wood. What was on the other side? Was this what you called a forest? It looked quite sinister. I looked up at the huge sky and wondered what my mother and father were doing now. Did they see the same clouds as me? Would I ever see them again? I felt anchored to the spot and didn't know which way to turn. I couldn't run down the brae because I had nowhere to go; I couldn't leave my brothers behind anyway, so I stood there numb and confused.

It was now early evening and daylight was slowly fading when I was called back into the house. We were shown our bedroom and told to unpack our things. It was another very small room, with a distinctive sour smell and a heavy dampness that caught our breath. Once our clothes were neatly folded by us and placed into drawers that were very stiff to open, we headed for the living room, hoping for something to eat. George was desperately needing the toilet and, as we couldn't see one, I asked where it was. Our foster mother's immediate reaction was one of surprise: we had not asked permission to leave our room! She proceeded to tell us in no uncertain terms that this was not to be repeated. She sent us back to sit on our beds until we were called through for supper and she handed me a bucket for my little brother to pee in.

We felt rejected and a little bit scared. She didn't seem to be happy to see us, so we decided to sit on the bed until she was ready for us. After a short while, she called us through to the table and told us where to sit. We began to chatter and I suddenly noticed her fingers tightening on the edge of the table. Her body tensed and her breathing seemed to quicken. I watched as she carefully straightened her apron and ordered us to be quiet. She looked around, taking each one of us in, clasped her hands together and bowed her head. We were asked abruptly to do the same and she said Grace. We were then allowed to eat some sandwiches and drink a glass of milk. When supper was over, we rose quickly from the table and prepared to go outside and explore, but she clapped her hands loudly and ordered us to sit down. There was no welcome chat or conversation of any kind. The only thing she said to us was to remember to say excuse me before leaving the table. If we didn't, we would be left there all day, if need be, until we complied. Minutes later we were told to go to bed and to do so quietly and quickly.

George was crying again because he didn't want me to dress him in his nightclothes. I got him as far as his vest and he ran for the outside door. Before I could stop him he had run out into the half-light wearing a tiny vest and nothing else. He was confused and unsure what to do next, so he huddled against the hedge and waited for reassurance. I saw that our foster mother had no intention of going to help him, so I would have to coax him back into the bedroom myself. I was expecting her to come and help George with his pyjamas after that, especially as he was so little, but she didn't and I had to put him to bed myself.

Robert and I took our positions in the bed on either side of

George to give him some comfort and we snuggled down together. Once we were under the covers and the lights were out, this woman appeared above us, her metal curlers rolled tightly in her hair clinking in the darkness, and her face, deep in shadow, forming a sinister outline of unknown malice. We felt no warmth, nor did we sense any form of friendship. Her shadow hovered above us for a few seconds, leaving us with a feeling that we were unwanted and suddenly alone in a strange and unfamiliar place. We took comfort in our own togetherness and because of sheer exhaustion instantly fell asleep.

Next morning we woke to a cacophony of strange noises coming from outside. I had never heard birds chirping so loudly or such a mixture of animal sounds all at once. We wanted to rise and explore our surroundings immediately but, because of the reaction to us the night before, we decided to lie in bed and wait to be told to get up. She was some time in coming through to see us; so long, in fact, we thought she had forgotten we were there. In the end, we decided to move of our own accord. We put on the same things we had worn the day before and sat on our beds, waiting to be called for breakfast.

I didn't want to make her angry and I thought if I saved her some work by getting everyone dressed and ready for the morning she would be nice to us. After what seemed like forever, she appeared, pushed us out of her way, inspected the bedsheets and made us strip naked. A basin of soapy water, a facecloth, a towel and a bucket for our toilet were placed in front of us on the floor. She grabbed Robert by the ears and whacked him across the neck; I didn't hear what he had said to make her angry. I stood and looked at this woman and felt like crying. Without a second glance in our direction, she threw clean clothes on the bed and walked away. Before she left the room, I asked if we could come through for breakfast when we were finished, but she said we would have to wait until she was ready for us. It seemed as if she didn't know what to do with us or how to approach us.

After we had eaten our toast, we were put outside for most of the day and were allowed in for meals only and nothing else. I could see we were making her feel very uncomfortable.

She flitted in and out of the house, watching us as we wandered about, but not a word of comfort or a smile came our way. We were feeling confused and vulnerable and wanted more than anything to be welcomed into her life with open arms. If we picked up a stone or a stick, she shouted at us to replace it. What did she want us to do? There was nothing to play with and nobody to guide us in this strange place. We explored our immediate surroundings and did not venture past the first fence.

For the first two weeks, we darted around like frightened chickens, wanting to play and investigate everything, but not knowing how to go about it. The faster the chickens ran, the faster and noisier we became. It was fun when the geese chased us into the shed and the hens clucked in annoyance. I guess, in our own way, we were trying to adapt to and understand our new way of life. We darted in and out of the sheds, running after one another, kicking the straw in the henhouse and poking at the hissing geese with small pieces of stick. We didn't realise that we were upsetting her animals or harming them in any way. For weeks after that, she blamed us every time a hen didn't lay and threatened us with a stick if we ventured near the henhouses.

One day during these first weeks at the croft, George was sliding on the loose stones scattered on the ground as his little legs desperately tried to keep up with Robert and me. As he passed the front door, our foster mother rushed out of the house, grabbed him by the hair and slapped him on the face. She shook him until he began to cry and screamed at us to behave. Robert and I were shocked into silence and stood to attention like obedient soldiers. Flogal had wandered outside, dying to run about with us, but she grabbed the dog by the collar and dragged her inside. We wanted to pet Flogal, to play with her, but she would not let us.

Our guardian had established herself as 'Auntie'. She remained rather distant towards us and there was always a noticeable lack of affection. Every day we hoped that our parents would come for us and take us home, but they never did. We didn't know it then, but our parents were not aware of our whereabouts, probably for our own protection.

Letters from our mother came regularly at the beginning – no doubt she was encouraged by social services to keep up contact with her children, but they were impossible to read, as most of the content was blotted out with black ink. One particular letter stated that she had given birth to another baby while we were in the children's home and named her Josephine. I couldn't understand how I could have a sister named after me. Did she not want me any more? Had I been so bad? I felt totally rejected and it became very difficult to find anything nice to say in the letters I wrote back. By the end of the first year, her letters had stopped altogether. My father never wrote to us and so contact with both of our parents was lost for the rest of our childhood.

At the beginning of our stay, I was haunted by those strange tales my mother had told me, of enemy planes and accurate bombing raids. I remember her talking about the war years and the fears of a city dweller, especially on a clear night. In my mind, the light colour of the croft roof could be seen very easily from the air, making the croft house an easy target. This fed my immature imagination to the point where, even in daylight, I would lie down on the ground, face up, so I could watch every plane that flew overhead, always in readiness to escape a bombing scenario. I tried to talk over these upsetting dreams with Auntie, but she was not able to sympathise or even attempt to understand why I was having them in the first place.

Those disturbing war tales continued to fill my sleep, with soldiers running through mud carrying rifles, me becoming that soldier. Every dream was the same: I tripped against a sharp wire fence and, just as I was in the process of being shot, I woke up. One night, I managed to stay within that dream and allowed the shot to reach me. There was no sensation of pain, but I remember seeing a red flash and then nothing. I saw myself, the way we do in dreams, moving amongst noise and dirt. Moving slowly, much more slowly than we can in real life, the other soldiers, a blur of grey floating mist. I was running from something or someone who was chasing me and then falling, falling. I looked down at my body and saw a red blotch on my clothes and in that blotch the reflection of an old woman's face scowling back at me. She stared at me from within my jacket and her voice chilled my blood. 'You're bad, you're wicked,' she screeched. I looked down at my hands and noticed they were covered in chicken feathers. Had I eaten her hens? It wasn't possible because I was still hungry.

My dreams were the result of listening to and not understanding my mother's fears and uncertainties and the psychological effect of my foster mother's insensitive and strange behaviour as she flitted between quiet, unresponsive moods to extreme ones, when she screamed and shouted at every move we made. These scenarios, mixed with the unsettling months of family trauma, brought all these past images to the fore in a jumbled mishmash of events.

Those dreams gradually disappeared and, as the weeks progressed into months, I felt that the hallucinations of the past, or my monsters, were slowly being put to rest, only to be replaced by strange new ones with creaking floorboards, the step and shuffle of Auntie's dead leg scraping across the floor, and the night creatures she said would come and swallow us whole, deliberately sketching into our minds terrifying ideas as a form of control. All of these I was determined to conquer.

Every task our guardian gave us was an order rather than a request. She shook visibly when she communicated with us and looked as if she was expecting us to refuse to do what she'd asked. There was no calm approach or any attempt to work with us in an adult-to-child manner. It was as if she was unsure of the method to use. She was abrupt and lacked any understanding of the way she treated us.

Our new environment was hard to get used to and Auntie did not seem to understand this. She expected us to adapt overnight, not to be afraid of cows and sheep and know exactly how to handle life on a croft after being shown only once to do something. A step-by-step introduction in the transition from city to town living did not cross her mind. Instead she reacted to our misunderstandings with aggression and confusion. If we hesitated or became uncertain as to what she meant, her anger and impatience exploded around us. Anything she could lay her hands on became a flying missile, which she aimed at us. Her favourite expression from the first few weeks we were there was 'You buggers of hell.'

3

The Nightmare Begins

Within the first few months of arriving at Coxton, we had experienced anger and violence beyond any of our imaginations. Life with my father had eventually become painful, emotionally and physically, but while his newspaper on the back of my head had seemed a great outburst of agitation at the time, compared to the abuse we suffered in the isolation of our rural foster home, cut off from the kind of community we had got used to, initially in Glasgow, then at the home in Dunoon, it seemed almost forgivable.

By the end of that short summer, everything we did or said was taken the wrong way. We were either shouted at or physically bullied. She would push us up against a wall with her stick if we put a foot out of line; often she would grab us by the hands and drag us outside, rain or shine, and leave us to stand together until she calmed down. It was as if she couldn't even look at us, so out of control had her life become. She just couldn't cope.

Looking back, I think Auntie was struggling to do the right thing. Her inexperience with children prevented her from communicating with us and she became frustrated by this, as far as

I can work out. Her impatience to control us and make us behave as she wanted us to was relieved only by violent outbursts – verbal and physical. I am quite sure that she had not anticipated this outcome when she had offered herself as a guardian, and perhaps her disappointment at failing in her attempt to do good became a pronounced chip on her shoulder. This in turn made her behaviour towards us more and more vindictive and erratic.

Very early on in our stay, I was asked by Auntie to take a letter to one of the nearby crofts. I was still unaccustomed to the area and to living in the country, but when she asked me to deliver the note I said I would. I could see the main house, where I was to make the delivery, sitting amongst dense shrubs and bushes, and I could see the front door, but I could not see a road leading directly to it, so asked Auntie if she could tell me how to get there. Her reaction frightened me: instead of explaining my route, she pointed to the road, calling me a 'stupid ignorant child', and pushed me roughly down the brae. I slid on the loose stones and scraped my knees on the ground. I wanted her to pick me up and kiss them better, but she walked away. I couldn't understand why she was so angry and agitated.

Hoping that I could get back on her good side by delivering the letter as she'd asked me to, I decided to start walking along the rough path, which she insisted would lead to the house. It began to veer to the right, away from the place I was supposed to be heading for, and I felt a little uneasy. I was worried in case I got lost and couldn't find my way home. I noticed a wooden gate at the side of the road, which opened into a field of grass. I felt this must be the way because I could see the house very clearly, but the further I walked, the muddier the ground got. The wild grass disappeared and I was soon stumbling through a ploughed field, dressed in neat rows of green leafy plants. I reached the fence at the other side and climbed over. This led me straight to a half-open door. I was delighted with myself – I hadn't got lost, after all, and I could still see Coxton from the hill. Auntie would be pleased.

By the time I reached the door, my thin sandals were coated in mud and my white ankle socks were grey and mottled. The farmer's wife took me into her porch and, with a smile, took off my dirty, mud-covered socks, cleaned my shoes and gave me a couple of plain biscuits to eat on the way home. She looked like Auntie – the difference was that I felt comfortable in her presence. She reacted in a kind and motherly way; she did not scold or chastise me.

She asked my name and if I liked living at Coxton. I hung my head and didn't answer. I wasn't happy, but I didn't know what to say. If I said no, would she tell Auntie? If I said yes, I would be telling a lie.

I felt the warmth of her body as she hugged me. I wanted to stay in her arms, in this cocoon of love I so badly needed. I wanted to live with her, I wanted her to be my mother, but she gently removed her arms and pointed me in the right direction for a safe return journey.

I wanted her to come with me – I was unsure of the way home because the rough road ran away from the croft – but when I turned round to look at her, she waved me on. It wasn't until I reached the bend that I saw the house. I followed the winding road all the way round and was soon walking up the brae. Would Auntie be in one of her quiet moods? I hoped so.

As soon as I reached the door, Auntie appeared and I handed over my dirty socks. She threw them back at me and ordered me to wash them in a bucket of cold water. I told her that the lady had given me some biscuits and she held out her hand, expecting me to hand them over. I shook my head and said, rather meekly, that I had eaten them on the way home. I let her know that I was sorry, but I didn't know I had done something wrong. She stared at me for a moment and then spoke to me in a raised voice: I was stupid and greedy and selfish. She grabbed my hands and rubbed them together so savagely that her nails left scratches on my fingers, then she told me I would not need any supper because I had eaten all the biscuits myself.

She stood over me as I frantically scrubbed the socks clean. With tears streaming down my face, I rubbed until my hands hurt. Every time I stopped she found another spot of mud, then, without warning, she kicked the bucket against my legs and walked away.

I hung my socks over the fence and went inside to get clean ones. I told her my feet were cold, but she ignored me and said that if I wanted to wear socks for the rest of the day I would have to put on the wet ones. Maybe I would think twice before making decisions on my own in future, she snarled.

I watched her swaying body march to the front door, her straight leg dragging at the ground as she moved forward. I walked slowly behind her and slid quietly into my bedroom. What had I done that was so wrong? I wanted to speak to her, to say sorry, but the living-room door closed and I was afraid to disturb her.

Robert and George were sitting on the double bed playing with their pillows and I sat beside them. We wanted a hug, so we hugged one another. Auntie had switched on the wireless and the sound of band music filtered through to the bedroom. Auntie was quiet. We were quiet.

This small escapade – me having trouble finding a country path rather than my punishment for muddying my socks – became one of the many stories she enjoyed telling visitors to the croft. As long as we played along with her when other people were in the house, and smiled as we gave her a hug, Auntie appeared relaxed, revelling in the praise she received from these people. She was determined to give the impression that, although our understanding of country living was very limited, she was training us well. We were obviously grateful for all her efforts, emphasising this gratitude with an affectionate, albeit perfunctory, embrace. I could sense her withdrawing at this bodily contact – it was as if she were fighting some inner conflict.

Throughout these early months, apart from sudden unpredictable outbursts, Auntie was in her quiet time, as we called it. We received visits from many curious neighbours who came to the croft to meet us. Auntie was distracted by these guests, always wishing to make a good impression to the outside world.

During the summer afternoons, children from nearby crofts came to play and we were lulled into a false sense of security. Maybe, I told myself, these isolated incidents of violence would pass. But as the summer drew on, I began to catch glimpses of Auntie peering out at us through the small living-room window, watching us as we played. She scared me with her strange looks. Her eyes were hard and dead: they seemed to hold a calculating malice in their stare. The greyness that stalked the croft inhabited her eyes: it seemed to bore into us, into our very souls. I did not like the feeling she gave me.

As the weeks passed, I sensed fear when she touched me. I recognised her body language and learned when to expect consequences for earlier actions. Soon, after our friends left, she would call us in and accuse us of preferring their company to hers. She twisted our hair or nipped our arms, forcing us to say that we wanted to work for her instead of playing with our friends. She continued this abuse until she was satisfied with the answers we gave. Each day was the same and soon every afternoon resulted in an unpleasant confrontation.

One day I noticed her staring continuously at me through the small window. I stopped playing and tried not to look as if I was having fun. Our new friends had become aware of her watching all the time, too, and one by one they eventually left and never returned. I remember once sitting on the old cement flagstones that surrounded the front entrance after our playmates had left, trying to come to terms with a wilderness of emotions, not knowing whether we should try to be happy or pretend not to be. I sat outside for a very long time. I knew I would have to grow up emotionally if both my brothers and I were to survive in this environment. Her lack of love prevented us from being in tune with her; in fact, I was beginning to see that it was a real effort for her to feel anything for us. You need imagination to put yourself in someone else's shoes and she seemed to have neither. She didn't seem to understand anything we did or said, and she was not able to communicate at a level we could understand.

Without friends to occupy our afternoons, Auntie's prophecy came true and we were soon working on the croft rather than exploring our new surroundings, quenching our thirst for knowledge, and making friends with children our own ages. Auntie so easily crushed our spirits. It seemed the only way she could cope with us. Work was all she knew; her imagination had long ago been dulled by the grey-damp of the croft, and so we were to be used as a way to gain extra income for the household.

Her first scheme involved us making mealie jimmys – or white puddings, as they are best known in Scotland. They consist of sheep intestines, soaked in salt and water, washed and scrubbed, inside and out, then filled with a stuffing of oatmeal, chopped onions, roasting fat and seasoning. Once full they are tied at both ends with string.

We provided the labour for Auntie's enterprise, having first to prepare the intestines when they were returned from the slaughterhouse. We didn't want to touch the wriggly tubes we called guts and at first refused to pick them up. Auntie became impatient, though, and threw them over our heads. The long, slimy skins, covered in sawdust and clotted mucus, smeared our faces and hands. We gingerly fingered them, frightened in case somehow they would attack us. Washing the outside was relatively easy, but turning them inside out to clean them was very difficult, as our small fingers lacked enough coordination to handle them to Auntie's satisfaction. She would become very angry with us when we couldn't do it, slapping us with the skins, stinging our legs and arms. After receiving a painful thrashing, we worked out a way to push the skins onto a spurtle (a wooden stick normally used for making porridge), then quickly flip them back onto a funnel, filling them with the stuffing, which made it easier to complete the task set for us.

The finished products were fat lumps of different-sized puddings not fit for any butcher. Each time Auntie discovered a misshapen product, she squeezed the tube empty and gave it to us to refill. As the day progressed, our attempts improved slightly, but our failure to produce a quality item forced Auntie to abandon this project after two weeks, much to our relief.

Another of her schemes involved us making butter and cheese. Our milk supply came from the main farm and apart from its daily use, it went to make small quantities of these dairy products. For this, the milk was left to stand in earthenware basins for a few days in the milk house until the cream rose to the top. This was skimmed off to be made into butter. We would place the cream in a churn, which looked like a barrel, and turn it for 15 to 20 minutes. A glass lid allowed us to see when the butter process was complete. Buttermilk was then drained off and given to the cats, then the butter was mixed with wooden spatulas, salt gradually being added in, then it was shaped into rounds ready to be stamped with Auntie's identification mark – a swan. This design was pressed into the finished pat, then each one was covered in greaseproof paper. Any milk left over was heated in a pot and rennet stirred in to curdle the milk. It was left standing until it solidified. During the day, from time to time whey was poured off, then removed from the pot and kept in a strainer until enough was collected for making a cheese. This mass was then broken up, salt added, then squeezed until it resembled a smooth paste.

This process took a long time and by the end of the day our hands and arms were aching. The paste was placed into a small barrel with lots of holes in the bottom and round the side, allowing whey to drain off quickly when the cheese press was used. After a few days it was taken out of the barrel and left on a shelf in the milk house next to the window to dry out. The grocer collected it and stored it in his premises until it was ready for sale.

These tasks involved in making this produce were numerous and exhausting. Auntie stood over us and watched our every movement throughout. Each of us was scrutinised and verbally assessed. By the end of the day, at least one of us had been slapped in the face or prodded with her stick. Often I would watch Robert as he bit his lip, trying to keep his temper under control. He knew that if he retaliated in any way I would be punished along with him.

Although this work was time consuming, we were only able to make small quantities at any time due to our lack of experience, and because of the tiny amounts of ingredients Auntie purchased. As a result, Auntie did not make enough from the sale of these goods to continue and her displeasure was obvious. It occurred to me, even then, that she expected too much from us. It never occurred to her to mix work with play. We were just young children, after all.

The age of eight became a milestone for me: my childhood ways and feelings disappeared forever. We were innocent victims of a raw society recovering from years of conflict and a naive social awareness. Any professional support for us and our foster mother from outside the croft dwindled away and our life among the rawness of nature became a never-ending exercise in trying to please a woman from whom no praise or encouragement ever came, only condemnation, pain and grief.

We longed to be loved by someone who really cared.

The days became full of rules and strange rituals, with endless things to remember and responses to rehearse, which we forgot on pain of punishment. The forever-ticking grandfather clock and the smell of damp clothes, the stink of wet cat fur and a cloying coldness stuck to us all and permeated deep into our senses.

I was finding it increasingly difficult to settle in and often thought back to the colourful pictures shown to us by the nurses at the children's home. They were nothing more than a child's fantasy. They didn't resemble our new environment in any shape or form. I felt we were in danger of losing what we had gained over the previous year. The care and attention given to us in the home would soon be forgotten; we were drifting back to the years of neglect, when our parents were never there when we needed them.

I complained to Auntie about everything, from strange-tasting jams to the lack of electricity. The dull brown colour of her sour rhubarb jam made me feel sick. Every time she spread a slice of bread with it, it stuck to the knife like a piece of curdled mud. Pieces of green mould slid round the blade and dropped back into the jar. It was disgusting and I told her so. I objected to the smell of paraffin used to light the tilly lamps. I hated the smell and tried to sneak out of the room every time she filled the lamp. I asked why there was no electricity, and why she did not have a tap for water. I didn't like the low, dark wooden ceiling. It felt oppressive and threatening, as if it was going to fall down and crush me. I was a normal eight-year-old child removed from her familiar way of life and I was questioning why it was so different there. I had become accustomed to certain things and didn't like the change. But Auntie did not understand my curiosity and instead of explaining to me why things had to be different, she made up a list of my grievances and presented me with this during supper one evening. I was made to go through each item on this list and asked to explain the problem I had with it. She wanted to know why it was proving so difficult for me to accept things. If my reply or reaction was not to her liking, she thumped the table and shouted until I agreed with her. A couple of times I absentmindedly placed my fingers on the edge of the table, where she tapped them sharply with her stick. Robert and George sat very still, watching Auntie conduct this exercise as if she was directing a piece of music. She jumped and screeched in unison – if we had not been so afraid of what she might do, it would have been quite funny.

She kept her list until I no longer protested, reluctantly accepting what she placed in front of me for dinner or what she had available in her cupboard, making mealtimes less stressful for everyone.

Every thump of the table or crack of her stick had an adverse effect on all of us. We jumped at the slightest noise and cowered into a corner when her voice increased in volume. When we saw that she was showing the signs of agitation and was likely to explode, we ran for the front door. Auntie soon realised what we were doing, however, and barred our escape. If we managed to get outside, we were not allowed in until bedtime, no matter what the weather was like or how hungry we became.

It didn't matter how hard we tried to get everything right or how nice we were towards her, our efforts were greeted with contempt. It was our presence in her house that brought about this onslaught of abuse, so we were helpless to stop this cycle of torment.

We were automatically accused of stealing when Auntie misplaced or lost one of her personal items. We would be told to sit around the green-and-white-covered table where every day we would eat the porridge I made for breakfast and the inquest would begin.

This table was used for everything from cleaning shoes on a Friday to plucking chickens and pigeons, and skinning and gutting rabbits ready to give to the butcher, as well as our homework. It was the centre of any activity and in most houses the life and soul of the family – a place where love flourished, arguments were settled and the problems of home life resolved. But for us, over the coming months and years this dinner table became a place for recriminations and lectures.

Once Auntie had established who the culprit was, we were either made to punish one another with a stick or a belt, or it would be quite normal for any of us to be grabbed by the hair by Auntie, dragged around the sheds, through the stinking midden, and left cringing and trembling on the ground. We often lay there sobbing, covered in dirt and human waste, which we had to wash off before we were allowed into the house. If there was any trace of this dirt when we went inside, it was smeared over our mouths before we were pushed outside, soaking wet and shivering, to clean ourselves thoroughly. We soon learned that no matter what we did or said, we were never right.

There were no services attached to most of the crofts or holdings in the area during this time, so all our fresh water was brought up from an underground well several times a day. This well was approximately a quarter-mile away from the main building. During the summer months, a multitude of flies gathered on the surface and had to be removed before taking the water bucket into the house. Never at any time did the water dry up; it was crystal clear once the green scum was skimmed off the surface, and refreshingly cool. Every autumn when the water was at its lowest and the inlet was visible, Robert and I had the job of cleaning it out. Auntie blocked this small hole with a rag of cloth held in place with a stone and got us to empty the well, bucket after bucket. As the water level dropped, we had to climb down into the mud residue that had settled on the bottom. It was very slimy and slippery and there was very little room to move about. Our rubber boots immediately sank and filled with mud and water, becoming very uncomfortable, but we were not allowed to climb out until it was cleared. The plug was then removed and the clear water flowed once again.

We dreaded this task. Although we tried to follow her orders, we invariably got something wrong, year in, year out. Auntie expected it to be done perfectly, and quickly, and would push us back down into the well, screaming and shouting as we slid backwards, whenever we carried out this task.

Her actions were all about absolute control, with no allowances for our young age, ranging at that time from four to eight. She would get agitated by our childish chatter and lack of concentration and had no time for failure; nor did she understand our physical limitations, meaning we were often unable to do this type of work with any success. She pushed us until we were exhausted.

During one of the first years we carried out this task, I remember she threw a bucket of mud back into the well to shock us into focusing on the task in hand. This dark mud fell all over me, covering me in a cold, gooey mess. I got such a fright I could only stand and stare at her. Before long, I was shivering violently, trying to climb up the side, but she would not let me out of the well until the job was finished.

Without warning, Robert, who had become my protector, grabbed the bucket she had thrown in, filled it with more mud and scrambled out as fast as he could, emptying the whole contents over her. I didn't know whether to laugh or cry; my stomach was in knots. I was hoping she would take it in good spirits, but she didn't.

She froze to the spot, dead quiet, looking like a chocolate soldier melting in the sun, a bent cigarette dangling from the edge of her tight-lipped mouth. Torn shards of tobacco flaked onto her chin and dripped earthwards. The metal rollers round the edge of her hair held the mud in clumps before it too slithered onto her shoulders, down her body and onto her crêpe stockings, snaking its way onto her tartan slippers. Only one hate-filled eye was visible, unblinking and staring.

Robert burst into a fit of nervous laughter, then ran for his life towards the woods; I didn't see him again until early morning. George crouched deeper into the long, dry grass, hoping Auntie would forget he was there. While I was cleaning up the mess, I carefully leant towards my little brother and advised him to sneak back to the croft in the hope that he would not be involved in the row afterwards.

Once I was finished and the job was done, Auntie caught hold of the collar of my jumper and screamed into my ear. I was thrashed with the spade's wooden handle for our undisciplined behaviour and put to bed without supper. I tried to tell her that we were sorry and that it was an accident, in the hope that Robert's punishment would be less severe when he eventually returned home, but she didn't seem to hear me.

I kept watch for him because I knew that by this time he would be cold, hungry and frightened to face Auntie. I wanted to warn him to be careful, but eventually tiredness took over and I fell asleep. I was wakened in the early hours of the morning by a frantic rapping on my bedroom window. Robert had come back and wanted inside; he looked cold and scared. Auntie had hidden the keys for the outside door and the window wouldn't open wide enough to pull him in. I was frightened she would hear us whispering, so I handed him one of my blankets and told him to sleep in the henhouse until breakfast, hoping that her anger would subside by daylight.

In the morning before I dressed, I heard Auntie go outside looking for Robert. At first I heard her talking loudly and then screams and shouts followed. I watched helplessly from the window as he was dragged inside and smacked with her stick before being shut away. I could hear him crying but couldn't get near him to give him some comfort. I knocked quietly on the wall and he eventually heard me. We used this wall as a way to communicate with one another and to act as a soothing agent when we were recovering from a severe beating.

Trips to the well in the dark of night were fraught with uncertainty. Going to the well was easy enough, as long as you kept hold of the fence posts that lined the path, but once you let go to lower the bucket into the water it was practically impossible to find the posts again in the blackness. It felt so thick it seemed to press against your face as you ploughed through the long grass.

I always walked with one hand thrust out in front of me to keep me from banging into the fence. Very often I took a wrong turn and found myself at the edge of the burn near the wood's edge, or fell over scattered stones from the ruin of an old shepherd's cottage. One night, after taking the wrong turn, I wandered further into the field than I intended, missing the path home. I was going in the right direction but found myself in a field of cows. I kept walking towards the main gate, which I knew was at the top of the hill. At every step, I bumped into a cow; it was as if the field was crowded with the animals. They pushed and shoved my bucket, ignoring my every protest. I could hear lapping and slurping noises: they were drinking my water!

By the time I reached the gate, my bucket was lighter than it should have been. I didn't want to go back to the well and just hoped that I had saved enough to satisfy Auntie. As I climbed over the gate, the moon shone briefly through the thick cloud and my hopes were immediately dashed. There was just a small puddle in the bottom. I had no choice but to go back down to the well. I opened my eyes wider in an effort to see anything against the heavy darkness.

My journey had taken twice as long as it should have done and I knew Auntie would be annoyed. Just as I reached the henhouse on my return from the well, the door of the croft opened and I could see Auntie framed in the lighted doorway. Her silhouette oozed menace – it seemed to swell as she stepped aggressively towards me. I couldn't see whether she was scowling or smiling and was afraid to step into the light, to come face to face with this unpredictable woman.

She screamed something incoherent at me and pushed me away from the door. I stood quietly and listened until I knew she had calmed down, then I began to walk towards the house. She grabbed the bottom of the bucket and threw the contents and pail in my direction. I was soaked to the skin. The metal bounced off my forehead, as she screamed, 'I thought I told you to fetch water from the well!'

I tried to tell her what had happened and said I was sorry, but she wasn't listening. I picked up the discarded pail and, without another word, went to the well for a third time.

By the time I returned, she was in bed and the house was in darkness. I set the full bucket carefully by the side of the sink. I could hear her snoring and knew she was already asleep. It was with immense relief that I crept into my bedroom, undressed and slipped beneath the covers.

Not only did we have no running water in the house, but our toilet was a small shed at the end of the last outbuilding. It served its purpose, the only problem being that the contents drained into the field at the back and seeped into the grass. One morning, a strong wind blew this shed down. Robert had just gone inside when all four sides collapsed outwards, leaving this wee boy sitting like a king on his throne. I heard him shouting and ran down the path to see if he was all right. When I saw him sitting there, I thought it was the funniest thing I had ever seen and I started to laugh, then I realised how scared he really was. He tried to stand up, but then he noticed a herd of cows walking slowly towards him. He was terrified that these beasts, with their long, wet tongues, would lick his bare bottom.

I climbed over the fallen planks of wood to reach him, waving my arms to shoo the cows away, but they wouldn't move; in fact, the more I waved and the more Robert cried, the more the cows were attracted to the shed. He was screaming and crying both at the same time and I was beginning to feel uncertain myself about how to help him. Then Auntie appeared. I looked at her to see if she was smiling, but she looked agitated and annoyed. She walked quickly down to the shed and grabbed Robert by the arm, pulling him up the path, his trousers still round his ankles. He was sobbing and kept shouting, 'I'm sorry, Auntie,' his free hand shielding his face in readiness for one of her vicious slaps. Even though it was the wind and the poor condition of the shed that were responsible for its sudden demise, Robert expected to get the blame and prepared himself for punishment. She threw him in my direction and told me to sort him out.

He was very upset, but after we talked it over he saw the funny side. We hid behind the house and giggled, as I pulled up his trousers and pretended to look for a tongue mark on his wee bottom. No other toilet facility was ever built to replace this one and we had to get used to crouching in the open air in the croft's midden among the hens' waste and rotten vegetation.

Auntie's lack of humour throughout our childhood didn't mean that we had to do without. We were children, after all, and could see the funny side of things. Looking back, I remember these intimate times when Robert and I could share a laugh. These isolated instances brought some light-heartedness to our days and cheered up the dark hours.

One morning after breakfast Auntie brought a dirty, battered old bucket and spade, covered in rust, with a broken splintered handle, to the front door of the croft and gave Robert and me instructions to collect potatoes from the field. We stood for a few minutes, waiting for her to tell us where to find them, and when the information did not surface I decided to ask her myself. She grunted impatiently and pointed to the field behind us, then slapped us both on the back of the neck and told us not to be so stupid. With bucket and spade in hand, we went – not very confidently and rather confused – to look for the beautiful, white eatables that we were used to seeing on our plates. No matter how hard we tried to find them, we could not see any potatoes lying anywhere. Everything looked so dirty; I couldn't understand why they would be lying in this dirt anyway. Maybe someone else had been here before us and taken them away? Or were we in the wrong field? We trudged up and down, falling into deep ruts in the ground, our hands and boots sinking continuously into the soft, sticky mud. We began to laugh at each other as we stumbled about like clowns. For a few delicious moments, we forgot about the task in hand.

We could see Flogal watching us from the gable end of the house and every time we looked at her she wagged her tail. I could see she wanted to join in our fun, but we were afraid to call her. After about half an hour of unsuccessful searching, Flogal disappeared and Auntie came out to see what we were up to, wondering why we were taking so long. When she saw our empty pail and our muddy appearance, there was a short silence. Then her face tensed. We knew what was coming.

I tried to tell her that we had looked hard for them but couldn't find any potatoes. We didn't know we were already standing in the middle of the potato field. To us, they were just green plants set out in neat lines. We didn't realise that we had to dig them up and that the potatoes would be covered in dirt and still attached to the roots of this plant. She was shouting and screaming at us, her anger at our ignorance sending her into a fit of rage.

We were confused by her reaction. She snatched the bucket from my hand and swung it at both of us. I stepped back quickly from the swinging pail, but it struck Robert on the shoulder, knocking him flat on his back. I stood there mystified, with a mixture of horror and anticipation, expecting any moment for her to turn and swing the pail at me. When this didn't happen, I began to smile, thinking somehow that she must be playing with us. Suddenly, she turned towards me and bent forward threateningly. I couldn't understand what was happening, yet I felt frightened. She slapped me across the face and pushed me down onto the ground. Scared to move, we stayed there until she had stopped shouting and screaming at us.

Such was our innocence, when she walked away we grabbed the bucket and spade and frantically started to dig for our potatoes, hoping to please this 'impossible to please' woman. Once we understood how potatoes look in their raw form, we hurriedly filled our bucket with mud and potatoes, and ran apprehensively back to the house. We proudly presented the contents of our buckets, delighted with ourselves.

Of course, praise was a thing of the past. Auntie beat us out of the house, still carrying the bucket, shouting at us to wash the potatoes and ourselves in the rain barrel until everything was spotlessly clean. When we had done this, we dried ourselves as best as we could with sacks lying in the shed and carried the wet, dripping potatoes back into the house, afraid to put them back into the filthy bucket. She pointed, without speaking, to a metal basin sitting on a stand and we threw them in without looking at her, beating a hasty retreat outside so as to keep out of her way.

Whether our mistakes were forgivable or not, beatings for the slightest wrongdoing were becoming common practice. It didn't matter how hard we tried to be good, Auntie was permanently frustrated. Her only outlet or relief for this was attacking us. We craved attention and wished she would listen to us without hitting us, and for once give us a reassuring cuddle when we were hurt.

When she was in her quiet moods, she sat very still, her eyes darting all over the room, as if she was searching for something. We were able to talk to one another, but we dared not laugh or giggle, as this would immediately provoke a serious reaction from her. Her hands would slap the table and her screams shook us into silence. Sometimes we wanted her to speak, to ask us if we were all right, but she seemed unable to understand our need for comfort, understanding and forgiveness.

4

Mary's Arrival

As August 1956 drew near, preparations were under way for the arrival of our little sister. I was very excited and couldn't wait to see her again. She was three now and I didn't know what to expect. Would I still recognise her? Would she remember us? The last time I saw her, she was sleeping in my father's arms. Where had she been all this time?

On the morning Mary was expected, we were pulled out of bed at 5.30, bleary-eyed and full of anticipation. I looked at Auntie, hoping she felt the same, but she deliberately avoided my gaze and completely ignored any questions I asked. She looked nervous; her hands were shaking as she handed me a bucket of water and a scrubbing brush and ordered me to clean the floor until it was spotless. She emptied the contents of the drawers onto the bed and gave me clean newspapers to line them with before putting the freshly folded items back in. The bed was stripped, and the covers turned and put back on. When the room was cleaned and ready for Mary, my brothers and I were sent outside and ordered to finish our jobs early, then dress in our Sunday clothes.

We knew we had to do what she told us, and do it well. We were still adjusting to our new life with Auntie, trying to understand the harsh way she spoke to us and doing our best to come to terms with the difference between her quiet moods and her aggression. We were either ignored or allowed to speak with her permission, and when we were over-talkative or inquisitive, she became angry and impatient. We worked quickly and quietly and crept into the house to change our clothes.

The living-room door was slightly open and we peered through the gap to see what Auntie was doing. She was muttering to herself and flicking through sheets of paper. I wanted to ask her when Mary was coming, but we decided to leave her alone and go back outside.

We stood at the end of the house, watching for the car. We were afraid to play in case we got into trouble, so we huddled together and tried very hard not to look excited. When we thought she wasn't looking, we decided to play a quiet game of noughts and crosses in the mud with sticks, all the while watching for the slightest indication that the door might open. When the door-latch clicked, we stood still, standing to attention like a miniature army. She didn't need to speak to seek obedience; she stuck her head round the door and we reacted immediately, her face cracking into a supercilious smile, one that showed contempt and conveyed control.

Our meagre lunch of cold boiled eggs was set on the flagstones outside the front door. We took water from the rain butt to drink and sat on the ground to eat. Just before teatime, we noticed a black car driving slowly up the narrow road towards the croft. We knew it was Mary.

I became nervously excited and found it difficult to calm down.

I began to tremble; butterflies bounced in my stomach and I wanted to jump up and down and shout at the sky. I ran inside to tell Auntie, but she grabbed me before I reached the living-room door. She squeezed and nipped my arm so much that she left nasty nail indentations on the surface of my skin. She stared into my face and marched me outside so fast that my feet barely touched the ground. She hissed into my ear that we were not allowed into the house until we were asked, shaking me violently until I responded.

'Yes, Auntie. Sorry, Auntie,' I replied meekly, as she dropped me heavily on the ground, grazing my knee on the loose gravel in the process. She closed the door behind her and we waited.

As the car turned into the brae, we couldn't contain our excitement; we danced and giggled and hugged one another. We were going to be a complete family again and maybe, just maybe, Auntie would accept us more.

The green door opened the same way it had done the day we had arrived three months previously. I glanced at Auntie's annoyed face as she emerged from the house and decided to calm my brothers, knowing what would happen to us once the car left. She had given me precise instructions to keep things under control and I knew I had to obey her. Auntie appeared nervous and wasn't in the mood to cope with our excitement.

As the car drew to a stop, I watched her facial expression change from complete displeasure to delight. Her smile brought a warm welcome and an assured understanding to her visitors. It was as if a mask had been flashed in front of her face and her persona automatically adjusted to suit the moment.

Mary was bigger than I had expected. I could tell she had been crying. She was walking and seemed a small independent being, no longer the helpless sleeping child I remembered. She glanced at us as she was led inside and I could see by her expression that she did not know who we were. I watched as she nervously approached in her pretty dress and wondered if she would feel the same cloying dampness we'd felt the first time we'd entered that house. We tried to look into the window without Auntie seeing us, but a white cat was sprawled across the windowsill, making it impossible to see anything.

After what seemed forever, we were called into the house for the child welfare officer to complete her report on how we had settled into our new home. She asked us several questions about living in the country and how we were getting on with the animals. She did not ask if we were happy or if we wanted to stay. We were compelled to look at Auntie before giving what we thought were the right answers – we were afraid *not* to look at her. We needed to get her approval. As long as Auntie was smiling, we felt reasonably comfortable and fairly confident that everything we said was correct and our behaviour was acceptable.

All the while I wanted to touch this little girl, to let her know that I was her big sister. I bent down to pick her up, as any big sister would do, and in my excitement overbalanced, knocking her against the hot range. The welfare officer grabbed hold of her and reassured me that no harm had been done, but I knew I was in trouble. In my haste to show affection towards my sister, I had made a big mistake. I had not behaved as Auntie expected. She had warned us about acting impulsively and I had done just that. I had shown the visitor a complete lack of respect and, in Auntie's mind, I was showing a failure in her ability to control us.

Auntie grunted and groaned as she listened to the visitor and shifted continuously from one foot to the other. I knew I would be punished later and moved closer to Robert for comfort. I saw the visitor look in my direction, but she didn't speak. I wanted to let her know that I was afraid to stay here, that I wanted my parents, that I wanted to go home, but the fear of punishment was too great.

Once the forms were signed and the visitor had left, I was pushed roughly into my bedroom, falling onto the floor in the process. She kicked my legs and stood on my foot. She then pushed me against the bed and twisted my hair. The door was then locked and supper was forgotten. I did not see Mary again until bedtime. She had been washed and was dressed in her pyjamas when Auntie brought her through to the bedroom. We felt strange and awkward together at first, and all the things I'd planned to tell her seemed to disappear in the moment. But out of sheer desperation for some form of comfort, Mary relaxed, snuggled in beside me and, after talking together for a short time, we fell asleep.

Auntie treated Mary reasonably well at the beginning and seemed to want to spend time with her. Her attitude to us was less severe and, as long as we did our work, she practically ignored us. She didn't want us in the house other than at mealtimes and bedtime. We wanted to see Mary, but she kept her indoors and away from us.

This behaviour lasted until the health visitor had been to see her. This woman came once more, then never returned. No further visits from anyone in authority were made to check our progress until the next official call during Easter 1957.

After several weeks, we heard Mary crying inside. It wasn't a quiet cry but a heartbreaking sob. It went on and on until the door opened and Mary was pushed outside. I picked her up and asked her what had happened. She said Auntie wanted her to rub her leg and when she had refused, Auntie had smacked her across the face. Mary was now one of us.

Although she cried a lot at the beginning, we gave her hugs and helped her with everything she had to do for herself. She began to accept us as part of her family. We were left to look after her and, if Mary's needs were beyond us, or we were taking too long to finish a task, Auntie took over. We were beginning to realise that life was not going to be easy with this woman, but we did not know what to do to improve it. We could not relax without being pushed and shoved, and when we didn't understand what she was telling us to do, she threw whatever she was holding in our direction. If we didn't move immediately when she asked us to, she physically manoeuvred us into what she thought was the correct position. She used the belt and stick freely to hit us and treated us with utter contempt.

Auntie moved out of her bedroom to give the boys a place to themselves. It was a very small house and she ended up sleeping on a bed settee in the living room. My bedroom, which I now shared with Mary, was dark and dingy. A narrow, dirty four-paned window, set deep into the faded, papered wall, cast a dusty light into the room, suffocating the colour already there. A black-tiled central fireplace, never lit, even on cold winter nights, dominated one side of the room. A deep cupboard in the far corner next to our bed was full of mould and dead-spider crusted webs. Strange noises emanated from inside this hole, especially at night, probably coming from the chimney breast. We were afraid to open this door because of the monsters Auntie had created, ones that would eat 'bad' children – and of course we were bad. She repeatedly used our fear to her advantage, in this case to discourage us from getting out of bed at night.

Once the lights were switched off, Mary and I chatted quietly. We told each other stories and talked about our day; we confided in each other about Auntie. Sometimes we could hear her outside the bedroom door, listening. We would stop talking and lie quietly until she went away. Other times she would knock on the door and tell us to be quiet.

If we continued to talk, the door would burst open and she would grab us and push us into the cupboard. She called it the Devil's Home. It was cramped, dark and claustrophobic. We were terrified to open our eyes in case we saw something terrible and jumped at the slightest squeak or rumble. Mary shook and sobbed uncontrollably on those occasions, holding onto my arm with a vice-like grip that numbed my fingers. The thought of spiders' webs trembling in the draught, hidden from sight, frightened me more than any sinister monster that might be crouched in the darkness beside us.

It always seemed like hours before she returned to let us out. She would ritually grab our hair, twisting and pulling it as she shouted and screamed into our faces. She then dragged us roughly across the room, knocking us onto the floor with her foot. After several minutes her anger slowly subsided and she released her hold, our heads burning at the hair roots, our eyes blinking from the moonlight filtering through the small window, our bodies shaking with emotion and fear. She dumped us onto the hard bed and slammed the door behind her. We crumpled together and sobbed into each other's shoulders.

The old mattress was stuffed with horse hair. It had never been renewed and was flea-ridden, probably due to the large number of cats roaming freely around the house. We often woke in the morning with flea bites on our arms, necks and legs. We were too young to worry about this at the time, but as we grew older gym days at school became quite embarrassing and we did all we could to hide these bites from our school friends. Although the mattress was hard and felt cold and damp on the skin, it was nearly always our island of sanctuary in the middle of chaos, a safe place to hide at night.

> I lie curled in maternal warmth,
> floating on an island of sanctuary.
> A sea of invisible grotesques distort the darkening
> shadows all around me and before me.
> I lie deeper into my wombed mantel,
> hiding from self-made demons.
> They haunt my mind and stab each nerve
> as fear creeps through my cocoon, and I feel threatened.
> An irredeemable urge tugs at my senses,
> begging me to reveal myself to the night and its monsters.
> I lift my head and open my eyes, the darkness pours in,
> and I sense the demon is near.
> I sink deeper into the cold mattress, and wait for the sunrise.

From the very beginning, we felt safe from Auntie and her monsters as long as we'd stayed under the covers. Our bedroom was the best place to escape her unpredictable moods and, as long as we were quiet and kept out of sight, we were conveniently forgotten about – to the extent of starvation, on some occasions – until she required us to fulfil any needs she might have.

One night this sense of security was broken. I had just fallen asleep when suddenly I felt myself being dragged out from under the blankets by my hair onto the cold bedroom floor. Auntie was screaming, her face a contorted, grotesque mask of hate; her spit was spraying my face in spurts as she spoke. The words came out fast and incoherently, so fast I found it difficult to understand her.

She pushed and shoved me into the small lobby beside the front door, my bare feet slapping on the damp floorboards as I tried to keep my balance. She threw me against the door handle and walked away, leaving me in the unlit hall.

It was cold and dark and I couldn't stop shivering. My skin crawled at the thought of cobwebs dangling from the low ceiling and the hairs on the back of my neck stood erect with visions of forky-tails and spiders creeping over my bare feet and falling in between my toes. I shuddered and wiggled them about until I got tired. I knocked several times on the living-room door and asked if I could please go back to bed, but she ignored me. I kept asking what I had done wrong, but I got silence in return.

There was no sense of time in the dark passageway: all I could hear was the ticking of the grandfather clock, quietly marking its own minutes and seconds. It was as if it knew that time waited for no one, especially if you lived in this house.

I heard Auntie shuffling about as she prepared for bed. I was too afraid to go back to mine. I knew I would be punished severely if I moved from the spot, so instead I tried to think of something pleasant but couldn't. I wrote poetry in my head and invented a tune to go with it. The words came easily. My melancholic mood created a melody that seemed to fit the sadness in my heart and soothe the anguish of daily life. Poetry and song created a sense of euphoria that numbed the pain of existing in the stressed environment that was Coxton. They helped me cope during those lonely days, hours and years.

I had come to the edge of my world,
I heard her screaming and scratching.

Nothing else moved, even the stars had gone out.
I could not see or speak, and a stillness
I did not like settled around me.
I shrank into the walls,
to sleepwalk among the dead,
hoping she would not find me.
I felt my feet rise from the floor
and float across the room, my hair
caught in a vice-grip of hate.
An invisible force swung me to and fro
like the grandfather clock ticking in the hall.
My knees cracking off stones and mortar
and slapping onto coarse handmade rugs.
She released her frenzied hold
and fled to her sanctuary.
I cried among night vapours
half-numbed and cold.
I felt the wetness of my bloody knees
and sank into the nearest corner.
The darkness clothed me in its arms,
I inhaled its comfort
and slept till morning.

Every noise I heard seemed louder than it actually was. The darkness became darker – a musty-smelling, oppressive darkness. I was scared and very tired. I heard Flogal sniffing under the door. She knew I was there; she scratched at the rug that Auntie laid out to stop the draughts at night and whimpered until she was ordered to her bed under the table.

When I thought Auntie was asleep, I lay down on the bare

floorboards and rolled into a ball to keep warm, tucking my bare feet into the bottom of my pyjamas. Every time I heard her moving, I jumped up and stood to attention because this was what we were expected to do. I was left there for several hours until she remembered about me. Without any rational explanation, I was ordered to bed.

This became a regular occurrence and after a while we all began to dread bedtime. At one stage, nearly every night one of us was dragged out of bed, pulled by the hair, either to stand in the porch or to listen to a lecture about something or other. She had a habit of waiting until the moment when we were on the point of sleep before pulling us out of bed; she must have worked out that by this stage we would be too tired to argue and too groggy to object or struggle.

It was bitterly cold in that porch; the wind whistled through the many cracks in the outside door and the darkness was overwhelming. Often as I was standing in the cold, I could see the glowing embers flickering in the grate through the half-open living-room door and desperately tried to imagine the warmth coming from it.

Auntie would often forget we were there and when she finally awoke and remembered, she pushed past, completely ignoring whichever child was there, knocking him or her against the wall, her straight leg scraping along the stained floorboards in her hurry to get away from the annoying situation that made her feel uncomfortable. She would be muttering to herself, waving her clenched fists at monsters we could not see.

The croft was a severely cold place in winter and if we were lucky a paraffin heater would be lit, giving out very little warmth. It created a haunting blue vista, adding a sinister aspect to the already chilling atmosphere. The walls and ceiling were drenched with a misty half-light from the burning fuel, filling the room with shadows of dragons, or serpents with forked tails and scaly backs. As the flames died down during the night, I could hear them sighing as the wood around me cooled. Water streamed down the window and dripped onto the floor. I lay for what seemed hours watching the blue flame slowly burn out, leaving a heavy, stale smell in the damp air. I listened to Auntie shuffling about in the living room and waited for any telltale sound that might mean she was coming to disturb us.

It soon became apparent to us that Auntie's animals, especially the domesticated ones, were top of her list as far as welfare was concerned. She treated them with the utmost respect: they were fed better than us and allowed to sit round the fire at night. Many times Robert was so hungry he ate out of the cat bowls under the table, but no matter how famished I became I couldn't bring myself to do the same. There was a strong smell of fish and something sour which filled the room, and that was enough to discourage me from trying. Why her affection towards these animals did not stretch to the young children she had decided to foster is beyond my comprehension.

Several cats were kept on the croft to help to control the mice that come with country living. Kittens were born regularly in the barn and sheds, but only a select few were allowed to live. The rest were drowned in a bucket of water before their eyes were opened at six weeks old. This was normal practice and deemed to be the most humane time to carry out this procedure, but I hated it and refused to take part, even on threat of punishment.

One of my favourite tomcats was called Rory O'More. He was multi-striped, similar to a Scottish wildcat but with a very placid nature. He caught rabbits regularly from the surrounding woods and whenever I saw his head bobbing up and down among the grasses I knew another catch was coming home. Due to the size of this prey, he often found the carcass difficult to handle. By the time he had killed it, he was exhausted and wasn't able to eat it.

At the beginning, it wasn't unusual to find a dead rabbit or pheasant halfway between the wood and the croft. He eventually learned that if he brought it back to Auntie she would pull it apart for him. She couldn't use the rabbits herself – this was the time of the myxomatosis outbreak of the late '50s, early '60s, when rabbits were dying in vast numbers after a highly infectious pox virus was introduced into the country by the government to help control the rabbit population. Farmers used it completely indiscriminately to devastating effect.

The only time we saw Auntie amused was when one of her pets did something silly and it was the only time we could stand beside her without fear of rejection. We would watch Rory O'More's determination as he dragged his well-earned meal nearly a quarter of a mile home. If anyone approached with the offer of help, he growled furiously and clung onto his catch with super-strength. We learned very quickly that it was best to allow him to drag the rabbit himself, the journey often taking nearly an hour to complete. Auntie would inspect his meal and if it looked free of the virus he was allowed to eat it.

All the other cats in the house were unique in their own right. Queenie was white with one blue eye, the other green. She was a Persian breed and lived up to her name. She lay all day, every day, at the living-room window and only came down to feed and to see to her toilette. She did not allow any other cat to take her window position, becoming very noisy if any tried.

Sasha, also white, was much thinner and very docile. One of her ears was missing and this made her look very odd. Buffer, my second favourite, was a black Persian, very fluffy and eccentric in nature. She lay on the floor with her hind legs resting halfway up the wall. It was as if she objected to sitting on the bare floorboards. She hated alarm clocks and every time one went off, she attacked it with terrific energy. Auntie enjoyed playing with the clock and the cat, and on those occasions we enjoyed the few minutes of relative peace.

The other five cats spent most of their time outside in the barn and came in at night to eat and sleep. Sometimes we were very envious of them because they always had pride of place in the house and never wanted for food, but we never did them any harm.

When any one of the ten cats that lived in the house and outbuildings failed to return by evening, Robert or I were sent out to wander the fields in the dark in search of the missing animal. We were not willingly allowed in until the cat appeared safe and sound.

On one occasion, when she caught us playing round the ruined bothy beside the wood instead of looking for her cat, she thrashed us both and never sent us out together again. She wanted the job taken seriously and was only interested in the recovery of her cat. Hours, not minutes often passed as one of us paced the fields calling the cat by name, cutting our legs on various rough grasses and sinking into boggy holes in the ground, which were hard to see because they were hidden by clumps of dark-green rushes. We were terrified to return without the cat; often she would refuse us food or dry clothes if it had been raining, and if we arrived home empty-handed, there would be the ubiquitous whip of her stick as punishment.

It was on dark nights out in the fields that we were scared the most – not because of any strange sound, or even because of the darkness: it was being alone with the dread of punishment if the missing cat was not found by morning that frightened us. When the moon was shining, I lifted my eyes skywards and pleaded with him to guide the missing cat towards me so that I could go back to bed. I was tired of the dark and I was tired of the loneliness. Most times, to my relief, it seemed that the man in the moon answered me. I would hear a rustle in the grass and a soft mew, indicating the cat's presence and the need for a lift home.

When we eventually found the animal, we brought it back to the house, where the lost cat was petted, spoiled and stroked for most of the evening, Auntie's nose practically stuck inside the cat's ear as she whispered sweet nothings into its brain. She blamed us solely for its absence and if she was still angry with us after our scolding she pushed the cat into our hair until its claws clutched at our heads, then pulled the animal away quickly, scratching us in the process.

Over the years, I spent many lonely evenings outside in the dark, scantily dressed, as a punishment for some misdemeanour or other. I tried to huddle in the darkened doorway of the barn out of the bitter wind. I became so cold at times that I had to pee myself just to feel a few seconds of warmth against my body. I didn't care about the faint odour of urine: the warmth was a welcome instant relief from the bitterness that permeated my whole body. Unfortunately, when the heat disappeared, I got colder.

Later, after I had started school, if I hadn't had time to change and was still wearing my school shorts, Auntie refused to wash them and I was forced to take them to school the next day. The smell of urine was so strong that I had to wash them in the burn at the side of the road on the way to class. If I was very lucky, I could place the shorts on the radiator beside my desk to dry them before the sport period. If not, I wore them wet and they didn't take long to dry on me. It was much better to wear wet but clean shorts than dry smelly ones.

One time, I was so miserably cold after being banished outdoors that I climbed over the fence into the field at the side of the croft where the sheep huddled in bad weather and crouched down beside them. They didn't move and the warmth from their thick fleeces soaked into my skin and made me feel better. It was good to stop shivering and get the sensation back into my face and fingers, though this comfort was short-lived. I had inadvertently vanished from Auntie's immediate vision and she thought I had run away. I think this scared her. When I heard her shouting and sensed the strength of anger directed towards me, I never again moved out of sight of the living-room window unless I was searching for a cat or the curtains were closed.

Throughout the seasons we were sent outside to carry out work for Auntie, sometimes with very little clothing on. It didn't matter on summer nights, but during the rest of the year it often became uncomfortable – painful at times – due to the severe cold. Auntie ignored us when we pleaded with her to come inside, and if we managed to sneak into our rooms when she forgot to lock the outside door she immediately pushed us back into the rain or snow or frost.

It wasn't uncommon for us to be caught outside in bad weather while we were struggling to finish a job for Auntie. If she expected it to be completed before evening, we were prevented from taking shelter inside. Even if the clouds opened and stinging rain pelted our bodies, or if the biting wind was whipping round the gable end of the croft, she didn't seem to care. We had no option but to crouch against the end wall and seek some kind of shelter from the sudden turn in the weather. If gales, blizzards or even the hottest day interfered with her plans to get a job done, she fought against it with an insanity that was beyond all reason. She was physically unaware of our distress and the effort we made to keep her happy.

The natural phenomena in the country made for some eventful evenings, especially during hot and sultry nights when the sky lit up with sheet lightning. Because of the open space, the show was spectacular.

The cats were easier to find on those nights – they practically jumped into our arms. Only when fork lightning crossed the heavens did I feel uneasy. The first time I experienced this type of lightning, I watched as it snaked through the woods, hit a chimney pot on the croft roof, bounced off the large tree at the top of the brae, arched back and missed me by inches, lifting the wool fibres on my jumper, then disappeared over a neighbouring building. I felt as if my hair was standing on end; the nerves on my skin were pulsating with fright. It lit up the whole area for a split second:

> Dark groans in its sleep and shivering silhouettes
> snake through sculptured woods
> like mythical serpents searching for prey.
> Their vapour trails hug the air, heavy in stillness.
> As dawn's birth explodes in waterfalls of Payne's grey
> like black ink on wet canvas,
> dancing chimney pots tremble with static,
> and early morning rumbles on and on.

I was very nervous for a long time after that incident and because of the fuss I always made when ordered outside in such inclement weather Auntie made a point of selecting me for the job. When I had no option but to go out in an electric storm to search for her animals, I hid in the shed at the back of the house until the worst was over. It took some time, but eventually Flogal began to ignore Auntie and approach us and I was grateful to hear the pattering of her feet as she plodded towards the shed on these frightening nights. She curled up beside me, licking my hands and knees as I crouched on the straw waiting for the storm to ease. Most times I tried to get back into the house and her mood at the time would dictate whether she relented or not.

I knew I couldn't cope with the level of emotional stress I was enduring – it was too exhausting. I needed to find a strength of will to fight the effect of her treatment. I was determined that the elements and Auntie were not going to get the better of me. She seemed to enjoy instilling a sense of fear into each one of us and fed on our discomfort in a strange and sinister way. The more we pleaded with her to be lenient, the more she chided and tormented us with her sadistic behaviour.

We soon saw a pattern emerging: Auntie never felt sorry for us or sympathised in any way when our fear of the moment became too much for us. Instead, she stood and watched as we shivered uncontrollably and our bodies shook with persistent sobbing. She seemed unable to see the discomfort she was causing or deliberately became deaf to any plea we made. No sensitive, caring adult could withstand this situation for the length of time she did and then be able to comfortably turn her back on us and walk away, leaving us standing alone to sort things out for ourselves.

During the winters when snow and frost covered the fields, it was very uncomfortable to wander about at night, straight out of bed and often barefoot. We learned to grab a few pieces of sack and tie them round our feet. We ripped the bottom out of some whole sacks, which we hid in the back shed, and pulled them over our nightclothes to keep us warm.

While I was always instantly hit by the wind's cold embrace, the beauty of the vast whiteness and the eerie stillness would fill me with awe. It was a strange world where everything seemed unusually crisp and clean, where the slightest sound travelled for miles, and where I felt I was the smallest thing on earth. As I headed towards the wood, the moon, a brilliant ice-blue, coated the path, which was hidden under scores of scumbled footprints carved in the snow by different animals. I could feel the air biting into my skin and the coldness sucking heat from my unprotected body. I knew I had to be strong. This couldn't last for ever, could it?

Once inside the wood, it felt much warmer, the trees sheltering me from the cold wind. It was very quiet and still; the thick snow cushioned any sound. No birds sang, and there was only the occasional muffled thump as drifts slid from overloaded branches to the ground below. I felt an attachment to this wood and could sympathise with the waxing and waning of its seasons. The coldness of winter became a reflection of my whole life. It seemed my time of plenty was in deep hibernation, waiting for the birth of adulthood, for the spring of youth to embrace a spirit I could not imagine.

A sadness spread around me and an overwhelming surge of hopelessness drowned the beauty of the moment. I felt terribly alone: what was I doing crouched here in the cold when I should be at home in my bed? I knew that a thrashing was waiting the minute I crept through the door. It was not my fault that I couldn't find her blooming cat.

I knew I couldn't stay outside indefinitely. It was bitingly cold. If the world around me could survive harsh weather such as this, I was going to make sure I survived in my own environment. With a heavy heart, I realised I had to go home – at least I would be warmer. I called for the cat once more and when I couldn't see it anywhere, I set off towards the croft. A few flakes of snow drifted down through the frosted air and settled like tiny feathers on the frozen ground. The moon shining through the trees bathed the night with misty luminosity. It swirled around me in a chill, damp breeze, my thin top dripping moisture as the ice melted on my warming body. The chilling mist caught my breath and caused me to shiver violently. I could still see winter-browned brambles creeping through the broken snow banks and wished they were still ripe. I was so hungry.

Often when I was wandering around, looking for lost cats at night, I would walk near the other crofts to see if I could see into the houses. Everyone looked warm and cosy; their family life looked happy, relaxed and free from stress. I stood at the top of the hill as the wind or rain whirled about me and cried, wishing that we could be part of that too. I wanted to be able to play games, read a book or laugh with my brothers and sister, just as they did, instead of being huddled together, terrified to move or talk in case Auntie yelled at us. What must it feel like, I wondered, to belong to someone, to feel wanted and never to feel afraid or hungry or alone? I knew if I knocked on any of our neighbours' doors, they would take me in and immediately sit me beside their crackling fire, but I couldn't in case Auntie found out and made me suffer for trying to make the family feel sorry for me. In contrast, to get back into my own home, the croft, I had to knock on the door repeatedly and plead with Auntie to let me in. She would eventually relent –

after a lecture – and I would go to bed for the remainder of the night. It was always with a sense of relief that I eventually pulled up the bedclothes to my chin and caught a few hours of restful sleep.

Although the croft sat on top of a small hill, the inner section was surrounded by sheds and was hidden from the rest of the farms, making it difficult to see what went on from the outside. It was easy for Auntie to treat us the way she did: there were no witnesses, and at the time very few people would believe the frantic ramblings of young children. As a result of Auntie's abrupt character and her supercilious nature, the only visitors she regularly received were the welfare officers, the butcher, the baker and the postman. She never went to the other crofts nor did she communicate with them unless she wanted something. The neighbours knew that Auntie did not treat us well but were unaware of the extent of her abuse. We were afraid to tell them the truth in case they mentioned it to her in conversation and we suffered later.

Robert sometimes sneaked down to the nearest farm and asked for food or to escape a beating. He relied entirely on their generosity and accepted everything they offered.

Over time we became acquainted with several of our neighbours. The majority were elderly ladies who worked quietly with their hens and on small vegetable plots. They were the last of the traditional crofters, dressed in nodding headscarves and woollen hats with multicoloured hand-knitted shawls draped casually over their shoulders or tied loosely round their waists. They seemed to be surrounded by rustic smells: a mixture of burnt wood, lavender balls and wet chicken feathers. They continually talked to themselves and were always very pleased to welcome visitors, especially children. I can still smell the scent of honeysuckle, which grew over their front doors, soothing and sweet. Their doors were forever open, a boiling kettle whistling on the fire, ready to make a cup of tea in an instant.

They created their own illusion of mystery; they were almost hermit-like. This became part of their attraction for me and I spent happy moments listening to their stories while watching them go about their normal daily lives, helping out when asked. Robert and I were invited into their way of life without question and were encouraged to work alongside them. We were always willing to help because a biscuit or a piece of homemade tablet was a welcome reward. Their smiles and mannerisms portrayed a true character of natural realism, a true loyalty to a way of life that was slowly disappearing from the world around them. Their trust in human nature was second to none and their stories the grandest I have ever heard.

One particular situation still makes me smile today and highlights the trust we had in those people. It also reminds me how young we actually were.

We were easily distracted when we were away from the croft and free from Auntie's distressing behaviour, so it was sometimes necessary to get our full attention by making a job more interesting. This particular day I was asked to find the eggs of one old lady's roving hens. She said her birds had been fed crushed willow-patterned plates mixed in with their normal food. This was to strengthen their shells and give them a distinctive blue-and-white design, which would be easily spotted amongst the grasses. I spent most of the afternoon searching for those special eggs but could only find the usual brown and white ones. It was a cunning plan, a light-hearted act that mixed work and play successfully. She rewarded me with a threepenny piece to spend in the village shop, where I bought a large bag full of dregs from jars that had contained boiled sweets – a sticky, sugary luxury from the 1950s.

This little lady had a welcome that was genuine and immediate; when she spoke it was as if she was taking up a conversation that had only recently been interrupted. I remember her tangled white hair, half-hidden by a knitted bonnet; how her mismatched clothing draped across her shapeless body; her tanned face, weathered like a well-cured leather, with a twinkle in her eye that sparkled in the daylight – all these things I found immediately engaging and inviting . . . so inviting that I yearned to snuggle down beside her and be her little girl.

As we grew older and were less accident prone, Auntie introduced us to the collecting, washing and grading of hens' eggs. We listened carefully and quietly as she explained the whole process to us. If we showed an interest in what she was doing, she remained quiet and in control. Most of the chickens were free-range layers, but Auntie had established, to some extent, a unique way of making sure the eggs were confined to one area. This was not always successful: as with everything else in the living world, there are always rogue players.

She described this unique process as 'deep litter' farming. I have since researched this type of hen management and can find no trace that it exists anywhere else in Scotland.

On the croft, there was a large main shed that was divided into two sections. The first was entirely reserved for feeding, with laying boxes built into the back wall. Through into the next part was an area where broodie or clochin' hens could be left in peace to do their own thing. Those hens, whose instincts for sitting on eggs are so strong that they will sit on anything, were kept in the back section, mainly for their own safety.

When any chicks hatched, they were also kept there until they were a few weeks old, at which stage they were allowed to scratch outside with the older hens.

The 'deep' part of this shed – hence the name 'deep litter' – had a small, open-air enclosed area that allowed the hens outside but kept them from escaping into the cornfields, especially during harvest time. The remainder of the flock roamed freely around the outhouses and the nearby field, making it very hard to find their eggs. It took us a long time to learn where exactly to search, and if we stood on any by mistake we were punished in the usual way. Once, after grabbing my hair and pulling me onto my knees, she made me lick the contents of a broken egg. The mixture of gritty dirt, slimy albumen and runny yolk was a disgusting vomit-inducing mess.

There seemed to be no rhyme or reason for these outbursts, but as the months wore on we began to expect them as part of our daily lives. We tried to work quickly and quietly and did our utmost to avoid any trouble, but there was always an uneasiness that my siblings and I shared: no matter how hard we tried or how helpful we were, nothing pleased Auntie. She denigrated all our efforts and only when she herself was comfortable with her own position did we receive any respite.

We were expected to stand at attention when she was speaking to us. If we began to fidget, she would scrape her nails down the wooden door and scream. This scared us and directed our full attention to what she was saying. She delighted in sneaking up behind us when we least expected it, just to whisper in our ears all the bad things we had done that day and what she was going to do to us before bedtime. She knew how to make us feel ashamed and was determined that we would not forget how 'evil' we were.

When we were being punished, we tried hard to blank out the pain, knowing that she would eventually tire and walk away. When she attacked me personally, I always felt a sort of scream inside – a silent scream, not easy to describe. It's a scream that I'm sure lies deep inside every child subjected to any form of abuse and one that is forever stifled by the inability to speak out freely – a scream that is waiting to release its power on the world and shout out to anyone who will listen. In most cases, there is no one there to care or no one who is willing to take the time to notice.

When Auntie was pulling my hair or dragging me across the floor, I tried to think of something else and the pain seemed to lessen or at least become bearable. In other words, my scalp became numb.

At first we cried out and begged with her not to hurt us, but this made things worse. We tried to catch her hands before they struck, but she grabbed our fingers and twisted them backwards, adding to the discomfort of the attack. If we struggled to move away from her, she pinned us to the wall with her body and stood on one of our feet, restricting our movements. If that didn't work, she got a tight grip of our hair and lifted our faces up, ready to slap. We learned very quickly that if we took our punishment quietly, it would end more quickly. The more we struggled, the worse she became. Sometimes if we were too subdued, she pulled us around until we asked her to stop.

She appeared to be afraid of rebellion or individual thinking. Her behaviour increased in severity if we showed any signs of objection; she would often threaten Robert and me that she would harm our younger siblings if we did not follow her rules to the letter. Within the four walls of her home, she was the confident aggressor with no one to stand against her or to tell her she was wrong.

We became so weary at the end of every day – it was an exhaustion borne from the effort of avoiding her fury. We knew we had to survive this, to anaesthetise the fear of punishment by anticipating the actual expected pain, which in turn lessened the outcome of the final beating. The more discomfort we experienced, the more determined we were to get through it.

The quiet times were few and far between. We got to know when we could speak to her and when to back away when her voice changed. Every night she listened to *The Archers* on the wireless and sometimes if she was in the right mood we were able to read one of the few books she kept on her dresser.

We tried very hard to support one another, but Auntie knew this and did all she could to separate us before she dished out any punishment. Our only option was to wait until her aggression ceased and the beating was over before going to the assistance of the punished. She was more violent in nature to the younger ones because they gave her less resistance and were not strong enough to fight back.

One day I watched her as she shook Mary, now five, by the shoulders and pushed her against the smoke-blackened grate. I saw my sister clench her teeth against the pain, her eyes filling with moisture, but she didn't make a sound. I saw her head bounce off the wall as a blow struck her ear and she slid slowly to the ground. It was the first time I heard Flogal growl at Auntie. She turned on the dog and dragged her across the floor, her nails scratching the floor as she was stuffed under the table.

By the time Auntie was finished with my sister, she was white-faced and shaking. Mary managed to stand up and run towards me; we fled to the bedroom and hid under the bed. If Auntie couldn't see us, her anger subsided quickly. She seemed to disappear into a haze of exhaustion that appeared to envelop her as soon as the child she was abusing was removed from her vision.

At the end of each frenzied attack, we could not approach her or speak to her for fear of re-igniting the outburst. She usually sat beside the fire, a faraway look in her eyes, and for a few minutes she gazed intently into the embers at one with her memories, oblivious to anything or anyone around her. At these times our movements had to be controlled and cautious; even the rhythmic rustle of crushed paper could disturb her stillness, as she fed from a packet of butternut sweets.

Every noise was kept to a minimum and, if it was at all possible, we went to our bedrooms to await her next move. If we were still standing beside her when she came back to reality, the whole thing started over again. We found that if we made her a cup of tea and put it down in front of her, she automatically reached for it when her senses returned. It was as if she had made it herself and she had not noticed that she was recovering from a blackout of some kind.

The entire day, and very often late into the night, was governed by Auntie's unpredictable moods. Our developing characters were intertwined with her decreasing levels of stability – more than once they confused the decisions we took in our daily understanding of life around us.

5

Leaving for School

As the first school holidays came to an end, we were kitted out with new clothes, ordered from the child welfare offices in Glasgow. When the parcel arrived and I was presented with a new leather schoolbag, I began to feel very excited. We would be able to escape from this place for a whole day! I loved the smell of this bag, and spent time opening and shutting the flap just to hear the metal clink of the clasp fastener. I zipped and unzipped my pencil case, rattling my pencils so much that Auntie grabbed them from me and threw them into the fire.

I had to react very quickly to save my newly acquired items – and prevent my fingers from burning. She was smacking my hand as I frantically tried to grab them. Initially, I thought she was doing this because she was afraid I might hurt myself, but she was knocking my hands towards the flame, not in the opposite direction. Why would she do that? A severe burn to my skin would require medical attention – and I knew she did not relish outside interference of any kind. Then I saw a glint in her eye; she seemed to be getting some sadistic pleasure from watching my fear. When

I became aware of what she was doing, I moved to the other side of the fireplace and, with more determination than ever, tried to save my bits and pieces.

I managed to rescue the whole case practically untouched and quickly put everything back into my bag, promptly placing it on my bedroom chair under my school uniform, well out of her sight. My fingers, although not badly burned, were sore for the next few days. I found it difficult to work properly and keep to her strict standards. The small blisters on my skin began to weep and looked quite red and inflamed. I did my best to keep them free from dirt and grime by extra washing, and made frequent requests for fresh dressings and plasters, but I sensed through my demands I was beginning to annoy her. The sharpness in her voice increased, as she rapped me on the knuckles with her stick, grabbing my hands and saying, 'I'll give you something to cry about,' callously peeling the loose skin off my blisters. The sharp, burning pain was intense and brought tears to my eyes, but she had no sympathy for me nor showed any compassion. It was as if she was unable to see the distress I was in. Mother Nature heals regardless and my skin quickly returned to its original tough pinkness.

The morning came at last for us to start our new school. After washing and dressing, we went outside to feed the animals as usual, and Robert collected fresh water from the well. There was a spring in our step, a sudden release of free energy as we carried out our chores that morning. We were full of anticipation for the coming day and our spirits were high.

I made porridge and lit the fire, while Auntie rested in bed. We were so excited to be going to school that we became rather noisy. She jumped out of bed and, without warning, grabbed our cereal bowls, emptying the contents outside, to be eaten by the geese. We were so shocked by the suddenness of her actions that it was almost funny: her frenetic movements, the clinking of her rollers, the static sparking of her nylon nightdress, the twitching of her long nose as she screeched obscenities at us, looking like something out of a child's comic book. She hobbled in and out of the house like a hen on a hot griddle, pausing to push George and Mary into the corner of the porch. She grabbed our school bags and threw them onto the slabs outside.

Robert and I could feel a snigger developing with each step she took. Our emotions were in turmoil: we were torn between a bout of laughter and deep concern for the welfare of our siblings. It took a few minutes to calm ourselves and control the giggles. It was important not to let Auntie see our interpretation of the moment in case there was the slightest chance she thought we were not taking her seriously. Most of all we were worried in case she would prevent us from going to school. It was to be our first day away from the croft in months and we didn't want to spoil it.

I felt sorry for George; he was not due to start school until the following year. And for Mary the wait would be even longer. But there was nothing we could do about it; we had to leave them. They stood and watched as we got ready. I wondered what they would do without us and what Auntie would make them do when we were not there. I was afraid for them.

Several children from the surrounding crofts came to collect us and escort us to school. They were a happy bunch and made us feel part of their group. Their noisy chatter and carefree attitude was like a breath of fresh air. They were not afraid to jump and play, and we soon joined in the games. It proved to be a long walk down a rutted, rough road, covered on both sides with broom that flowered yellow in late spring and produces black seed pods in

August, down under a railway bridge that supported the main line from Aberdeen to Inverness, and on to a crossroads, where traffic commuted to Elgin and south to Huntly. It took another 15 minutes to reach the parish school. The playground was full of friendly screams and laughter, strange accents and new faces that whirled about in frenetic circles.

Primary school was a bit strange at first. We expected to make friends quickly, but we were a curiosity. The majority of children did not understand the meaning of 'foster' and therefore we stood out as different. It drew attention to the fact that we were, in some way, not the same as them. Being children themselves, they did not have the experience to see how unhappy and neglected we were, and we never told them. It was better that way. Our Glasgow accent didn't help either and we depended on our newly made friends from the surrounding crofts to keep us company. These children supported us with friendship in the first few weeks of school and the children from the village soon accepted us as their other playmates.

School for me was the best place to be. It became my safe place, where I grew up emotionally, where I began to analyse different aspects of adult and childish behaviour and learn how to handle distressing and confusing scenarios.

I hated the sound of the bell at the end of the day: it meant home to Coxton, home to abuse and discomfort, home to a place where we were not wanted. We were always on edge, scared every time we came home in case she had discovered something we had forgotten to do before leaving the house in the morning or a task uncompleted from the night before. To protect George and Mary, we had to double-think everything. We had one story for our home life and another for outside the croft. If at any time we let slip that things were not right at home, we spent days worrying that Auntie would find out and punish us. We were never allowed to chatter freely; we were expected to stay quiet at all times, unless she asked us questions.

I was nearly always top for perfect attendance at school – even when I was unwell or under the weather, I made the effort to go. I didn't want to stay at home. Auntie would say I was pretending and accuse me of being a lazy good-for-nothing. I fared better at school, where I could sit at my desk, feel relatively relaxed and be fed something at dinnertime. I was also in receipt of much-needed attention from a caring teacher.

Robert struggled badly with dyslexia, a disorder involving difficulty in learning to read words, letters and symbols, which hampered his progress in school. The general misunderstanding of this condition did little to help Robert with his education. Auntie seemed unable to notice the struggle he had with his homework and was convinced he was deliberately refusing to do his lessons.

What disturbed me the most, and sometimes alienated me from the rest of the children, were the celebrations of Christmas and Mother's Day. I found it difficult to take part in the excited playground discussions about which presents to buy parents. They didn't understand that I had no one to send a card to nor money to buy anything. I once gave Auntie a Mother's Day card that I had made at school and she ripped it up in front of me and said, 'I'm not your mother.'

As I learned to cope with the fact that I had no parents, I began to accept that Auntie was the only mother I would ever have. Once I understood that, I was able to join in the laughter and excitement of the moment. I made the excuse that I couldn't make up my mind what I was buying and they accepted that without question.

We looked forward to playtime at school, once we understood that we were free to run around if we wanted. It took us a little time to realise this and we always kept an eye on the windows, in case someone was watching. It was very difficult not to feel guilty when we were playing; we were never able to relax fully when we were with other children. It was as if we expected Auntie to appear round every corner and give us a threatening scowl.

At home, if I lay on my bed and read I would be accused of being lazy and selfish – I was not allowed to play or have any time to myself and as a result I spent most of my playtime sitting in the shelter reading comics my friends brought me, stories about some poor ballet dancer who was brought up in an orphanage and went on to be a star! This gave me some hope for the future. I could relate to these characters who had no parents and were sad all the time. It was like looking at my life from outside my own body. In my young mind, I believed if the ballet dancer could find success and happiness, then I would too.

We didn't have the toys of the time, things like skipping ropes, hula-hoops, yo-yos and tennis balls and could only stand and watch at playtime, waiting for one of our friends to ask us to join in.

When school finished for the day, it took some time to walk home and we used this for play. We sang at the top of our voices and laughed, making fun of our guardian's strange moods and behaviour. We played a game of 'soldiers' with a plant known as plaintain that grew along the roadside. It had a long, thin stalk, with a black oval-shaped head. The idea was to hit them together until the loser lost its head. We continued to jump around until we reached the point in the road where we knew she could see us. We adjusted our clothing – if my skirt was too short, I would pull it down to its correct length, and we had to make sure our coats were fastened to the neck.

If either of us came home with torn clothes, a missing button or a dirty face and hands, we were thrown against the wall, stripped in full view of our siblings and smacked with her belt. She expected us to march home with straight backs and arms swinging. We knew she was watching us because we could see her black silhouette between the two opposing windows.

If our pencils weren't sharpened before we left school she ordered us to hand them over and broke them in half. She then accused us of not doing our lessons properly and hit us again.

We dreaded turning into the brae every afternoon, but the sight of Flogal sitting under the hedge cheered us. Her tail wagged with enthusiasm and she sat patiently until we came out to do our evening chores. She padded close beside us and looked into our eyes for approval. As long as we worked quickly and quietly, Auntie left Flogal with us. It was as if she had given up trying to keep us apart.

We never knew what was waiting for us when we came home. If Auntie's day had gone well, she left us alone to get on with the work in hand. But nothing was ever certain and we were prepared for the worst most of the time.

Our routine when we returned from school involved homework, then chores. We were locked inside to complete our homework, then we removed our uniforms and dressed for outside work, no matter what the weather was like. Everything had to be completed by eight o'clock on school days and if we behaved ourselves and finished our work without argument, we were allowed to sit down to a small tea and a quiet chat with Auntie – Auntie doing most of the speaking. If there had been any trouble at all while we were doing our chores, the instigator was punished and sent to bed without being fed. The rest of us sat at the table waiting to be accused of something else.

Sometimes George and Mary appeared distant and subdued when we came home. They were unwilling to talk about their day and appeared to be frightened to come near us. They sat quietly at the table and watched our every move, ready for any excuse to help us with the outside chores, an opportunity to escape from the oppressive atmosphere of that house. It is hard to remember just how badly treated they were and hard to imagine what they went through in our absence. Nearly every day we saw them jumping up and down above the long grasses, waving frantically, urging us to hurry home. It had been a long day for them, at the beck and call of a woman who could not sympathise or bring herself to understand the delicate needs of children. If Auntie realised they had sneaked out to greet us, she would stomp outside, grab their hair, pull them into the house and deliberately knock their heads together. When Robert and I arrived home, she threw them at us, saying, 'Here's your brother and sister. They can feed and wash you, if that's what you want.' It must have been an immense relief to see us walking up the road, to know that however small our efforts might be in the form of support and presence, just being there with them would improve their situation.

A day never passed without one of us hiding in the shed sobbing after a beating. It was the only place we could hide without Auntie watching us all the time but still be in earshot when she called us back inside. Flogal sat with us and whimpered. She licked our hands and legs until our sobs quietened. She snuggled into our arms and we smothered her with hugs. She was now our friend, our companion. She was our comfort and our solace. She was one of us.

These sheds served not only for farm use but also as a shelter when we needed it most. It wasn't unusual for Robert and me to come home from school and find George and Mary hiding in one of them, terrified to go into the house. We saw them instantly when we came up the brae because most of the buildings were in dire need of repair, with many missing a plank or two. Sometimes it was difficult to get them to come inside because Auntie had beaten them so severely; their hands and arms were often covered in bright red weals, their legs scraped and bleeding where she had dragged them across the ground. On these occasions, Auntie refused to let us over the doorstep to change our clothes and do our homework until we persuaded them to leave the security of this shed and go to their rooms.

I would hug Mary when we were alone in our room. I don't know what Robert did to comfort George in their bedroom, but Mary and I could hear George sobbing through the wall and Robert talking quietly to him. Looking back now, I believe we did our best to look after them, sometimes taking the blame for some of their small mischiefs. Mary was prone to terrible nightmares and she frequently woke up screaming, having seen Auntie's face floating in her dreams. Many times I sat up in the middle of the night singing quietly to her until she fell asleep. She always looked so small and sad, and I very seldom saw her smile.

All she ever wanted was to be loved and understood. Auntie haunted her all her life and when she tried to tell anyone about it no one believed her. Mary died suddenly aged 40, still looking for that special person who would take the time to listen to and sympathise with her. I didn't know where to turn, or how to end this nightmare.

I dreaded the school prize-giving at the end of the summer

term. It signalled an end to play: a loss of the freedom and ability to act and perform as a child. It was the beginning of the long summer holidays, the beginning of long, tormenting hours of verbal and physical abuse.

Oddly, I felt very sad that Auntie did not come to prize-giving and didn't care how we got on at school. I wanted her to feel proud of me, to clap and cheer with the rest of the parents. I wanted the glow of receiving praise for my efforts. She was part of me, whether I liked it or not. She had taken the place of my mother and was the only person I had who could take an active part in my school education, but she didn't seem to want to get involved. Her absence did not prevent me from trying to do well. I was determined to work hard and the praise I earned from the teachers encouraged me to do just that.

A year and some months had passed since we'd arrived at the croft and the thought of spending nearly eight weeks at home over the holidays filled us with dread. The daily drudgery that was our existence during that time exhausted us to the core and weighed heavily on our shoulders. Although we were very young, we were expected to muck in like grown-ups and work hard in an environment that was steeped in the ways of yesteryear. Our days were filled with gruelling physical work – there was no opportunity for our growing years to be fun and fruitful. This work was accompanied by the ever-present fear of an unforgiving woman who would not, or could not, relax her way of life. This in turn put pressure on the four of us to work to increasingly high standards. The constant threat of pain and punishment dogged our every move and haunted everything we thought or did.

Before domestic water was installed in the croft, Auntie used a basin on a metal stand to conduct her personal hygiene. Every night before going to bed, we took it in turn to fill this basin with hot soapy water, carefully draping a towel over the small wooden chair that rested at the side of the fireplace. One night, Robert was preoccupied with another task and forgot to fill her basin. Auntie retaliated with her usual level of rage at first, then something seemed to snap inside her head. She yanked the metal basin off its stand, swung it at arm's length and hit him full strength on his head. The blow was so violent that the force knocked him off balance. He staggered across the floor, clutching his ears and cradling his head, his mouth wide open, his scream silenced by the power of the assault. She turned her back and screamed at the wall, her fists pounding her rage into the faded wallpaper. Her screams turned into intermittent screeches, as she ordered him to fill it. Robert picked up the basin, his hands shaking in terror. He poured fresh water from the kettle and worked a lather into her facecloth with soap. He was terrified to go near her and desperately tried to position the basin back on the stand without getting too close to this disturbed woman. He wouldn't stop crying and this annoyed Auntie to such an extent that she pushed the soap into his mouth to try to stop him. He spat out the carbolic mess, gagging all the time as she held on to his hair with one hand and attempted to push the soap back into his mouth with the other. He squirmed like a ferret and managed to free himself from her tight grip. He ran out into the cold night air to hide in one of the sheds, dressed only in his pyjamas.

I could hear her shouting from my room while she washed. The water splashed aggressively onto the floor and when she was finished the basin was thrown against the wall. She screamed for me to clean up the mess and savagely flicked me with her towel as

I worked beneath her. I was afraid for Robert and wanted to help him. I could hear him sobbing – it was breaking my heart. Where were our parents? Why weren't they here to save us?

Auntie never seemed to remember what she was doing or whom she was doing it to, and very often the beatings or screaming stopped suddenly. It was as if a switch had been flicked and the power was lost. Her eyes would glaze over and a far-off look would replace the rage; this numbed confusion and forgetfulness left her exhausted. It seemed as if she was unaware of her immediate actions. Attempts to speak to her in the hope of calming the situation were ignored.

By the time Auntie climbed into bed that night, she had forgotten that Robert was still outside terrified to come in. I waited until I thought she was asleep and opened the outside door as quietly as I could, coaxing my brother into the relative warmth of the house.

His bedroom led from the living room, where she was lying, and it was difficult to get to it without disturbing this sleeping monster, but the desperate need for sleep and the relative comfort of our beds gave us the courage to attempt it. Creeping past her bed was strangely exciting but dangerous – our readiness to dodge a fist or whack as we tiptoed past at top speed was forever present. Even though we cringed at the thought of a sharp, stabbing pain from her stick, we could feel the excitement build as she twitched and tossed in her sleep. It was like a game of tic and tac, being ever-ready to run from the mannie. I knew that once Robert was safely in his bed and the lights were out, there was a good chance he would be all right until morning.

By now, George was five and due to begin school after the summer, but they were still babies really, just little darlings wanting love and attention, not disobedient slaves to be beaten like rag dolls whenever the need arose.

It was becoming increasingly difficult to enjoy a light-hearted moment, with Auntie hanging over us all the time, but when it did happen – for instance, when we were stumbling about searching for potatoes! – the outcome was often funnier than it should have been.

After protecting the goose eggs during the spring, our first batch of goslings hatched successfully and the job of caring for their every need began in earnest. Every morning we fed them with a special feed mix and cleaned out their enclosure, keeping a close check on their health and surviving numbers. Most afternoons we were given pieces of stale white bread soaked in water for their midday snack. We wanted to eat this bread because we were so hungry. Auntie thought by steeping each piece in dirty rainwater we would be discouraged from doing just that, but it didn't work and we ate small portions when she wasn't looking.

George loved these little birds and always sat on the cement slabs near the front door of the house to give his portion of bread. We had just finished feeding the goslings the last few crumbs one day when George let out a shrill cry and jumped suddenly to his feet. I couldn't see what was wrong at first, but then I noticed a little yellow gosling swinging from my brother's body. George's sitting position had exposed his little willie to the elements and the young goose had mistaken it for a juicy titbit. Robert and I exploded into convulsive laughter, before running after George and carefully removing the dangling bird from his stretched member. He wasn't hurt, and when freed from his predicament he burst out laughing, too.

Auntie was at the foot of the brae at the time, talking to the grocer, so we were able to enjoy the whole incident without her knowledge. She would have been unable to see the funny side, instead berating us, probably, for the possible injury to the young bird.

The goslings had a tendency to fall over on their backs when they were running and were often unable to turn themselves back onto their feet.

One afternoon, just after feeding time, as I was walking towards the house, Auntie suddenly came up behind me and grabbed hold of my arm. She slapped me across the face and pointed to a gosling lying on its back motionless at the side of the shed. She assumed it was dead and was rapping me sharply on the back with her stick. She dragged me over to the little bird, picked it up, pushed its beak into my mouth and shouted at me to blow into its mouth. I did not understand what she was asking me to do and began to gag. She then held my head forward more forcefully. I thought she was choking me! I didn't realise she wanted me to save it.

At the end of the day, it would have been one less goose for the butcher and she was determined not to run at a loss, if at all possible. It was obvious that she didn't want to put the gosling's beak into her own mouth, so mine was the only alternative.

The bird recovered quickly and the thought of the gosling's disgusting beak in my mouth was wiped from my mind with the immediate relief that punishment this time would not be forthcoming.

The croft house extended lengthwise and apart from the living quarters, a barn and a stable were built within the croft structure. This barn contained a variety of logs for the fire, farm implements of all descriptions and a wooden horse for sawing sticks. Our hand–eye coordination as nine- and eight-year-old children had not developed to the point where we were able to work successfully, which made the tasks Auntie laid out for us extremely difficult.

At first our hands became seriously blistered as we struggled to understand the push-and-pull movement required to successfully work the heavy two-handled saw. We learned very quickly to keep our hands away from the serrated blade after sustaining several deep cuts as we worked. By the time we had finished our first load, our hands were covered in pieces of old hessian sackcloth to stop the blood from falling onto the wood. Auntie refused to treat our wounds and accused us of being weaklings, which meant we had to work out a treatment for ourselves.

At the end of each day's work, we wiped the blade with oil to prevent rust forming on the teeth. It was difficult to apply without scraping our hands on the sharp steel, but we got better with practice.

Some logs were faster than others to cut and we got to know the types of sticks to take home from the wood that would make our job easier. Well-matured and dried pieces fell away from the saw blade quite easily and those were the type we targeted the most.

At first, we worked at a leisurely pace, but soon speed became the essence of praise or scrutiny, the wooden horse being an ideal instrument for measured punishment. Auntie could administer blow after blow without any chance of a child escaping. Once she caught hold of our hair, she would drag us to the solid wooden structure, where our legs were jammed between the outer and inner frames, trapping us completely. She then bent us over the struts, thrashing with a belt until her energy was spent.

Robert was the first to be punished in this way. I remember just being afraid. The funny thing was that we felt sorry for whoever was being punished, but were glad when it wasn't us. It is probably hard for an outsider to understand, but it was a sense of survival that made us react this way.

When Auntie's mood turned sour, nothing stopped her in her tracks. Sometimes we hid in this barn when she was throwing things about. Again, as long as she didn't see us, we were relatively safe. We rarely had more than a few seconds' warning when one of her unstable moments arose. The degree of misunderstanding towards our immaturity was shocking and distressed us greatly.

One incident in particular haunted me for many years. It was just before the Easter holidays of 1958. George had been at school since the previous summer. He was becoming a real big brother to Mary and was continually telling her how difficult school would be for her when her turn came in the autumn. One morning Mary and George's discussion became quite heated and they began to quarrel quietly. Auntie, still in her bed, ordered them outside. Within minutes of getting dressed, she had dragged them both into the barn and locked them inside. Lying in a corner was a big barrel of tar used to creosote the sheds and a large bag of goose feathers, a sure temptation for any young mind. When lunchtime came, I heard Auntie go outside to bring them in for something to eat. Suddenly, there was an almighty scream.

I ran out just in time to see Mary, covered in tar and feathers, being dragged from the barn. The attack on her was so vicious that she was unable to keep her feet on the ground. Auntie was yelling at them both, shaking them violently. She shouted at Robert and me to clean up the barn floor or be punished, too. There was plenty of sawdust lying about, so we swept it onto the tarry mess. The congealed lumps were then scooped into a bucket to be used for another job.

George and Mary had become so bored, being locked away for such a long time, that they had decided to pass the hours by playing a game of cowboys and Indians, not realising that the mixture of tar and feathers they had found in their search for amusement would be difficult to remove once the game was over. I thought Mary looked really funny – it would have been nice for Auntie to see the amusing side, but she didn't and both children were severely punished.

They were both dragged along the ground, their knees scraping along the loose stones, their hair twisted and pulled like some torn rag. Each child was bombarded with a mouthful of abuse, which turned the air blue around them. They disappeared into the house and the door was locked. We listened to their screams and cries, helpless to protect them. Once Mary was cleaned up and ordered outside, she disappeared round the back of the shed and came back clutching a bunch of wild flowers, a handful of buttercups mixed with pink and white daisies bound with tufts of grasses. A peace offering to a lady lost in her own world of turbulence.

'Sorry, Auntie,' she whispered, handing them over, but before we could blink the precious bouquet flew from Mary's hand, scattered by the force of Auntie's stick hitting them. The look of hurt in Mary's eyes said it all. When Auntie disappeared into the house, her straight leg scattering the small stones in her rush to be gone, we helped Mary pick up the fragments of petals and grasses and placed them inside the barn on the window ledge.

George was still crying after his beating, but we managed to persuade him to come into the barn with us in the hope that it would help him forget the pain and rejection he had just experienced. We wanted him to feel better, but sometimes it was very hard to make them forget. The punishment inflicted on our siblings was so harsh and so brutal that the psychological hurt lasted much longer than the actual pain. The rejection of any loving response to their small mischievous pranks and a lack of any intimate patience bore into those two little children and robbed them of any understanding of adult ways and values; it destroyed any hope they had of a normal, mature relationship in the future.

After supper that evening, Mary and I went into the field and dug up a young sapling. We scraped damp dirt into a battered bucket and planted the small twig between two stones to give it support from the weather. After several months of watering and weeding, the pale green leaves grew darker and the spindly twig grew more branches and spread into a small bush. Several months later it produced a small cluster of lavender flowers that opened almost shyly, producing a gentle fragrance. I saw Mary smile as she gently fondled the flower and held it to her nose. It grew into a fine bush, which we planted in the field behind the shed, where it flowered for our remaining years on the croft.

The barn was full of old farm-working implements from a bygone age, all rusted with neglect. Every surface was cluttered with a miscellany of objects collected over decades of families, broken, rusty handmade tools, the evidence of thrifty generations of farming folk. Proof of a former busy croft, with horsepower the main feature, lay across the wooden beams or dressed the dirty, whitewashed walls in a quiet array of bizarre-looking equipment. Lidless handmade boxes scattered in an untidy fashion spilled their contents of chains, hooks and unusual-shaped objects onto the cement floor. Kittens hid among the cut logs, with beetles and creepy-crawlies of all kinds, and a haunting chill hung in its silence.

Leaving for School

The door scraped into yesterday,
a musty darkness poured from its gaping mouth.
I gasped as airborne staleness stirred
the sleeping shadows like alien shape-shifters,
and farm tools clattered in the sudden draught.
Lugged sacks bulged like overstuffed pigeon crops.
Feral bats creaked time with splintered oak beams,
and rust-coated chains hung through torn hessian.
Daylight blinked at me through spider-crusted windows,
suddenly I was the intruder, I scuttled out into fresh puddles,
leaving the ghosts to slumber in their coffin of shadows.

Auntie assumed from the word go that we should be fully continent and in complete control of our bodily functions, but Mary and George were still under five and were prone to accidents, especially when shouted and screamed at. This verbal abuse would stop suddenly and the child responsible for the wet pants was dragged unceremoniously across the ground, slapped across the face and hustled out of his or her wet clothes, whereupon the bare bottom was soundly smacked. Sometimes Mary found it difficult to stop peeing on demand and this made Auntie scream louder.

If I was within reach, Mary was pushed towards me and I was ordered to make her stop. She was always shaking and sobbing, and all I could do was hold her tight until things settled down. I washed her pants in the rain barrel, and if we were allowed into the house, I helped her into a clean pair. Most times, however, Mary had to wander about until bedtime without underwear, her bare bottom frequently on the receiving end of Auntie's sharp stick.

Auntie didn't care for this childishness. She viewed our

behaviour as a weakness, one she could not understand or control. She was unable to soothe our uncertainties or change what she classed as deficient. Our immaturity scared her to such an extent that she was physically unable to deal with our daily needs.

By the late 1950s, George began to have problems with his breathing. The stress levels that Auntie created by insisting that he behaved more like an adult than the little boy of six that he was eventually resulted in asthma. Every time he had an attack, she beat him until he managed to get his breathing under control. She screamed at the top of her voice as he crouched on the ground, struggling for breath, then ordered him to stand to attention. When he couldn't, she hit him with a belt, trying to stop what she classed as a tantrum.

We were forced to stand and watch him struggling. At first we tried to protect him, but this made her angrier. She threatened and shouted at us to stop him wheezing. We did not understand his ailment nor what was happening to him, so just tried to calm him, which seemed to stress him all the more. We felt helpless and ever so sorry for him.

Auntie got in a panic – she pushed us around, grabbing our hair and our clothes. She didn't seem to be able to cope with the crisis. I didn't know it then, but she later told me she was a trained fever nurse, so she should have known how to handle George and make sure he was given the correct medication for his condition. This training seemed to have hardened her outlook on life, so instead of comforting George, she took his behaviour to be a rebellion of some sort and treated it thus. He was so afraid of her and the punishment to come that he would get his breathing under control.

Many times when I came home from school I found Mary hiding under the bed, shaking and crying, and when I managed to coax her out I noticed that her ears were bleeding. She was too frightened to tell me what had happened, but I noticed that the coarse sweeping brush was always lying around in the hall when Mary was confined to her room. I thought this very strange because the brush was for outside use and was normally kept in the barn. I came home early one afternoon and caught Auntie prodding savagely at something under the bed. To my horror, it was Mary.

She was trapped hard against the back wall, with very little room to move. She couldn't crawl out for fear of a beating and, every time she tried, the broom handle pushed her back. Auntie had worked herself into a frenzy and didn't hear me come into the bedroom. Mary was sobbing uncontrollably and I shouted at Auntie to leave her alone, but she did not hear me.

I took hold of the brush handle and refused to let go. She began to punch me on the arms and try to prise my fingers open to release the firm grip I had on the broom handle, but she couldn't get near me – I was equally determined not to back down. Instead, she grabbed hold of the bristle end and swung me round, pulling me through the door and out of the house still hanging on to the broom handle. She pulled and pushed me in all directions and when she realised she wasn't getting anywhere she shoved me into the beech hedging, where I lay until she disappeared inside. I held on to what was her instrument of abuse for several minutes and felt a certain sense of triumph. I revelled in my small victory, but also remembered that I had to go back inside quickly in case she had decided to take her defeat badly and punish Mary further.

It did feel good to win for a change and, with each step we took towards breaking her control of us through extreme aggression, our confidence grew.

* * *

I don't know if Auntie sometimes felt guilty about the way she treated Mary because in her quiet times she spoke about her differently, calling her the pretty one, praising her openly to the child officer or showering her with praise when she took her out to buy something from the baker's van. One day an old dressing table appeared in our bedroom for Mary to keep her clothes in. I was not allowed to use it; in fact, once I was caught looking in the mirror and she pushed my nose against the glass, squashing my face until it hurt. She told me that I didn't need to see my face, as it wasn't pretty enough. I didn't need a dressing table to try to improve my looks. She continued to say that Mary needed this mirror for herself, to develop a self-confidence in her self-awareness, and I wasn't to distract her by looking in her mirror. If I needed to see my face or brush my hair, the reflection from the window was enough.

The best part of my day was always early morning before our guardian woke. It was a brief, quiet moment when I could lie peacefully, the calm before the storm. I would watch daylight flicker at these times like butterfly wings on the ceiling or the leaves blowing gently in the wind, their shadows casting a reflection into the room. I listened to the rain tapping on the window, counting down the seconds to disruption and confusion. I heard the frost crack on the glass, the swish and thud of snow as it slid from the roof, and the early birdsong that signalled the emergence of spring.

Mary lay asleep beside me. I could see the muscles around her eyes tightening and her closed lids twitching at whatever monster was trapped within her head. I wanted to wake her, to calm her torment, to ease the troubled contortions of such a beautiful and innocent face, but I knew I would only wake her to a reality she was terrified to face. I snuggled down beside her and cried for us both. When she looked peaceful and at rest, I longed for the moment to never end: her little white face, free from tears and confusion; her small fingers, tucked under her chin. A quiet peace existed for a few precious moments, bathing her whole body.

The slightest movement within the house disturbed her sleep and her first reaction to this noise was one of wide-eyed fear until she realised I was still beside her. We always hugged in the morning before getting out of bed, then we washed and dressed quickly before Auntie began shouting for her breakfast. Our new day had begun, nothing would change, and before bedtime came round again Mary's tear-stained face and nervous look would return to haunt us all.

We were terrified to speak to anyone about our life on the croft. We didn't know who our friends were or if all adults were of the same nature as our guardian. We were afraid that we would be chastised for speaking out against her and afraid that whatever happened we would still have to stay with her. We knew our parents didn't want us and were unaware of any living relative. We also knew that any attempts on our behalf to end this nightmare would be dealt with behind closed doors, resulting in severe, relentless punishment. No one would hear us or be able to protect us.

When I heard my brothers or sister crying, I felt guilty and asked myself many times what kind of big sister was I, that I couldn't help them. I often fell asleep at night feeling helpless and inadequate.

After one extremely harsh thrashing, Robert managed to squeeze out of the door before she locked it and ran, crying, down to a neighbouring croft. She didn't follow him and the rest of us were locked in our rooms. We could hear her bustling about and rustling at some papers. She was swearing and calling Robert from heaven to hell. Some time later, word came from the croft that the RSPCC had been called in and would she bring the other children down. At last, after nearly three years, I was convinced that we would be removed from this place and this woman, but I was very wrong. I watched her face as we walked down the road. She was very quiet and I could see she was slightly disturbed. Her whole body jumped and shook as she stumped down the hill, her breath hissing past a half-smoked cigarette, the unrolled ringlets of hair where curlers were hurriedly disengaged from her head bouncing and twisting from the act of walking. I sensed she was trying to calm down, to defend herself at any cost.

We had to face these people: we wanted to ask them to help us, to take us back to the home in Dunoon where we were happy. We stood beside Auntie and listened to what they had to say. They asked questions about school, about our friends, our health and if we went to Sunday school. We were not allowed to speak unless it was to answer yes or no. They asked Auntie about reports they had received from some neighbours and she told them, rather convincingly, that there was no substance to them. They had misunderstood her training methods and believed the words of a little boy who wanted attention. Auntie told them that we had misbehaved more than usual that morning and we deserved to be punished, nothing more, nothing less.

She followed by saying that it was important to our development that we learn right from wrong. She went on to say that she had bought something nice for our tea as a reward for saying sorry. She knew how to handle her household and felt she should not have to explain her methods. As far as she was concerned her ways were working and the children would agree with her – which, unfortunately, we did, because we had no choice.

She convinced the visitors that we were being silly children and all that was really wrong was that we were missing our parents. They believed her and ignored our whimperings. They also dismissed the neighbour's comments, saying they had overreacted to a young boy's hysterical complaints.

Once they were satisfied that everything, as far as they could see, was under control, they left, leaving us to bear the brunt of the whole affair. We walked behind Auntie up the rough road to the house, listening to her incoherent mutterings. She forced Robert to walk in front, prodding him roughly with her stick until we reached the croft. He was bundled into his bedroom and whacked until we heard him crying and pleading with her to stop. We put our fingers in our ears to try to dull the noise, but it didn't help. I took George through to our bedroom, and Mary and I sat with him on the bed and stayed quiet. When darkness fell, I took George through to his bedroom, where Robert was already asleep with exhaustion, his pillow soaked with tears. Auntie was sitting at the fireside reading a paper. She didn't look up as I passed.

'Goodnight, Auntie,' I said, but she took no notice.

The neighbours never interfered in the same way again. It was very difficult for them to help us because Auntie did not like us going to other crofts. For as long as we lived at Coxton, we were inside only two of the other crofts. If we had to take a message to one of our neighbours, we were not allowed to stay and had to come home immediately. It was as if she was frightened that we would say something against her.

One of the crofts in particular was a temporary place of refuge when things were really bad and we were able to sneak down for a biscuit. Children of all ages appeared to come from every corner of that house. It was a proper functioning family that seemed to work well together, every child's need attended to without question. The house was always full of laughter and the sweet smell of home cooking oozed from the warm kitchen, no matter what time of day we arrived. We mostly went there at weekends and were automatically invited to sit with the family to watch a black-and-white television broadcasting some of the favourite programmes of that era, for example *Dixon of Dock Green*, *Z Cars* or, the most exciting of all to me, *Emergency – Ward 10.* Robert and I were fascinated by them all. If we stayed too long, Auntie came prancing down the hill and marched us home. The neighbours tried to tell her that we were not doing any harm and to leave the bairns alone, but this made her angry. She didn't argue with them, but the look in her eyes made it clear that it was time for us to come home. She prodded and pushed us all the way to the croft.

There were times when we gave her the impression that we had been asked to work on this neighbour's croft in order to get away from the house. It seemed to satisfy her for a while, until we came home and she taunted us by saying that she didn't believe we were working and was convinced we were sitting around doing nothing. She was right! But we never owned up to this and she was none the wiser. We needed the company of these people; we desperately needed their care and compassion. Love soaked everyone who entered into this family and we needed as much as we could get.

Whenever representatives of the authorities visited the croft, Auntie never failed to pull the wool over their eyes; however, in the notes I have there are questions raised about the way she told the same story over and over again, about how well liked we were in the community, and how happy we were.

Her attitude and the way her strange moods perceived us dictated the handling of our daily lives and we were learning very quickly that there were certain things we had to keep quiet about. If she thought we were lying or had spoken out of turn, we were dragged to the kitchen sink, where our mouths were washed out with carbolic soap. The strong taste churned our stomachs. We weren't able to eat anything at meal times because of the soap that was embedded in our teeth, giving everything a disgusting flavour. We were subsequently given the uneaten food for the next meal, unheated and practically inedible.

I remember one afternoon I noticed she was baking some gingerbread. As usual, I thought it was for her and tried not to let the sweet smell of cooking upset me too much. Robert and I had just finished sawing some sticks for the fire when she asked if we would like a piece of cake, as she felt that we had worked hard that day. We couldn't believe our luck and accepted an unusually large slice. One bite told me immediately that something was wrong – it tasted of soap. I told Auntie and she blew up, accusing me of making a fool of her. When she asked Robert, who would eat anything, for his opinion, he agreed with me. This made her so angry. She stood beside us and watched as we chewed into this dark sponge with little dots of something yellow scattered throughout it. She would not let us go until we had eaten every bit. We weren't sick, but the unpleasantness lingered for the rest of the afternoon. I don't know to this day whether she mistook a bar of yellow soap for a slab of margarine as a genuine mistake and didn't want to admit to it, but the rest of the gingerbread disappeared and the whole incident was forgotten by the time we came in for our frugal supper.

It was very hard sometimes to figure out why Auntie reacted the way she did, especially when things didn't go her way. Her hysterical response to chaos, which exists in every family where young children are struggling to understand the rights and wrongs of life, resulted in pain and confusion. Where a child's curiosity is normally patiently understood with a degree of compassion and that child is gently nursed through its formative years, at Coxton for us it meant rejection and it meant neglect.

6

My Hut in the Woods

Auntie had a particular dislike of the male species. It was as if she felt she had something to prove to them. From an early age, she treated Robert and George dreadfully, grabbing their private parts in an aggressive and inhumane manner by twisting and pulling with a force that brought them to their knees, crying in agony and unable to move. They were forced to strip in front of her and she appeared to revel in their discomfort. She had a habit of throwing them outside naked, forcing them to stand to attention until she was satisfied that they were reduced to a quivering mass of masculinity. This type of abuse continued for many years until the boys grew big enough to protect themselves. When she began to lose control over them, she reverted to other methods and locked them in their bedroom for days without food and water.

It is probably difficult to understand why they didn't break their way out and defy her, but conditioning is a bad thing and prevents any logical reaction. And where would they go anyway, once they had escaped? No one was going to believe them. While our neighbours could take an interest in us and try to help us where they could, they were not going to get into trouble for interfering. We would always end up back at Auntie's anyway – there was nowhere else to go.

Auntie knew how far to go with any discipline she administered before the consequences might get her into trouble. The time limit of their confinement was three days at the most, then the door was unlocked and the boys were either thrashed or pushed outside.

One afternoon she unlocked the door as usual, but before she could confront my brothers the grocer's van came up the brae. Without time to relock the door, she went outside to greet the grocer in her 'what a nice person I am' guise. While she was in the van, the boys, almost fainting for want of food, sneaked into the living room and unlatched the food cupboard, where she stored her homemade jams. They were so hungry they tore off the paper covers and scooped out handfuls with their fingers. They were so engrossed in feeding themselves that when they heard the van's engine start up they just bolted for their bedroom, leaving the cupboard door unlatched. The slightly opened door revealed a number of massacred jars. Without a word, she went into their bedroom and dragged them both into the living room. She produced a soft, new loaf that she had just bought from the van and told the boys to cut it into slices and spread it thickly with homemade jam. She thought she could punish them by giving them too much to eat to make them feel sick, but the opposite happened. They were so hungry that they gulped down every morsel, remembering to repeat the words: 'We can't eat any more, Auntie. We feel sick.'

We learned very quickly how to respond to some punishments, especially those that would, in the end, be advantageous to our survival. In these cases, the more we pleaded with her to stop, the more she continued, to our benefit. She was unaware of what we were doing and how we were able to manipulate her methods to suit our needs.

Her inexperience and ignorance in the care of young children was obvious and we took advantage of every opportunity. She seemed to feed on our discomfort and thrived in strength and confidence as she watched us squirm and fumble. This time she was in her glory; she stood firm and watched the boys devour every piece of bread, wanting them to be sick, and became impatient when they weren't. She whacked them with a stick and prodded their stomachs until she got tired and left. When I came into the house, everything was quiet and the boys were recovering in their room. They smiled at me and said they weren't hungry any more, that the beating was worth that at least. Their door was left unlocked and the crisis was over for the time being.

We were so hungry all the time that we tried every method we could think of to get food. During a lunch break from senior school, I went into a fruiterer in the high street to buy a bag of pears. I said it was for my mother who was in hospital, but I had lost my money. I promised I would come back the next day with the right amount. This kind lady filled the bag and without hesitation handed it to me. She said that she didn't want any payment and wished my mother well. I left the shop feeling guilty because I knew that I could never pay back her kindness. I was very surprised and relieved that she had believed me. I took the bag of fruit home, hid it under my bed and Mary and I ate it after the lights went out that evening. Although we thoroughly enjoyed every piece, I realised it was a form of stealing and I never did it again.

Our meals were very small, consisting of a cheese triangle or a boiled egg on toast, or often tattie soup made with the water used to boil potatoes the day before, with not a trace of any vegetables or seasoning. A slice of loaf spread with Stork margarine dipped in sugar was one of the regular meals we ate. Maybe, if we were very lucky, or she was expecting a visitor at mealtimes, a thin water-pastry apple pie would appear. At the weekend, she boiled beef and gave us the fat that was wrapped round the meat to help keep it together while cooking. She told us that it was good for us and that it would give us strong bones. We mixed it into our mashed potatoes to help us swallow the disgusting greasy mess. Flogal sat under the table at mealtimes, hoping for a quick titbit – pieces of fat became her biggest treat. When Auntie wasn't looking, we gently slid small pieces onto our laps and the dog dutifully ate them. Sometimes we could hear her gulping down these chunks of fat, but Auntie never seemed to notice.

We watched with envy as our foster mother cut the meat into edible slices and chewed it in front of us. I don't know if she did this deliberately or she genuinely thought the fat of the meat was good for us.

When I think back to the food we were forced to eat, I distinctly remember jugged hare served as watered-down soup. I don't know where the unfortunate animal came from, I only hope it wasn't something the cat brought home from the woods. I can still see it hanging from one of the rafters in the shed. It was still alive and blood was dripping from its neck. I didn't realise it then, but it was our supper. A disgusting smell rose from our plates; the grey-brown colour resembled curdled dishwater. No matter how loud she shouted or screamed, we wouldn't eat the mess of our own accord.

She became so irate that she forced the stinking slush into our mouths by holding our noses, one at a time, until we couldn't breathe and had to open them. We were all physically sick. I don't think she expected us to react so violently and threw us outside. The taste was obnoxious. In fact, we thought she had poisoned us.

We tried to get inside for a drink of water, but the door was locked, so we dived for the rain barrel and drank until the taste disappeared. The sick feeling, mostly psychological, stayed with us for the rest of the day.

As on many occasions, that night we went to bed hungry and unloved.

Over the years, our foster mother seemed to flit about endlessly, her eyes devoid of any emotion, a wild look that we all learned to dread. No matter where she moved around the croft, inside or out, she seemed to dwell inside a bubble that we all tried very hard not to burst. A fear of her fiery outbursts kept us from becoming too involved with her emotionally. She seemed to have lost all knowledge of what was right and wrong. Her emotional outbursts made no sense to us at all. We treated the brief and rare periods of affection we were shown with great suspicion, as we realised they were very temporary.

I do believe she was lonely and had been most of her life. I also think that this was one of the main factors in her application to foster children. Approaching her sixtieth year, she felt she was no longer able to work and maintain the croft by herself. I think she assumed that, being young children, she would be able to train us to run it for her. But it didn't work out as she had expected. Having no experience with children of any age, she failed to recognise the importance of natural development and play. Her frustration at us played a large part in the awakening of her unstable mind. Any information and advice she might need relating to our welfare was not immediately available and a cry for help would not have been instantly recognised. She was in a difficult position. She had taken on a tremendous responsibility, thinking she could cope alone with four city children, a task that few people would have been willing to undertake.

Sometimes there were moments when Auntie was quiet – almost kind – but these times were very rare and because they were always preceded by a severe emotional outburst she was often unapproachable. She wanted to be in total control of her world and she knew that the only obstacles in her way were us, but she needed us. She had grown into her environment, becoming part of the stones and mortar, and appeared to strangers from the outside as a kind, cheerful but eccentric old lady who had given up her life to care for four unwanted children. Her attitude could change instantly and she could present herself as the perfect foster mother. But when she was alone with us she grew thorns, sharp as blades.

To the neighbouring crofters, our guardian's behaviour had always been bizarre, but because they had never seen her severely angry it was difficult for them to understand what she was really like. They knew we were being mistreated but were not aware of the severity of the situation.

Often on a clear, frosty night, they heard her shouting at us but didn't know what to do to help. In the '50s and '60s, no one was very keen to meddle in someone else's family life and the policy of the time concerning my siblings and me was 'at least you were all kept together'. I don't know how often I heard those words over the years, when I tried to tell someone about our situation. It used to make me feel angry. I know everyone meant well and I understand now how difficult it must have been to stand by and do nothing to help. It was equally hard for me to see that the neighbours were right: it would have been much more difficult for us to cope psychologically as a family if we had been separated.

About three-quarters of a mile away, there was a fairly substantial wood consisting of pine trees and silver birch, where we spent many long days, especially during our school holidays, clearing the area of dead and fallen trees and branches. Once we had collected the wood into a pile ready to take home, we played with Flogal, who by this time would follow us into the wood. We chased her round the trees, her tail tucked in between her legs as she scampered in and out of the undergrowth until we were out of breath. We continued with play until we thought Auntie would expect us home, then gathered our wood pile and dragged it back to the croft. We would then cut them into logs and stack them in the barn for firewood. These woods, with their sharp odours of root and nettles, steaming with damp after a heavy rainfall and bathed in rich brown pine needles in autumn, became our playground, our safe haven, a world Auntie never entered. It was a place where we always felt comfortable and, most importantly, where we could be ourselves; a place where I could sit under cover and listen to the rain's soft patter as it fell on the millions of pine needles carpeting the forest floor, a soothing sanctuary of restfulness. For me, it was a mysterious ground that breathed magic into the air.

A small mountain burn, turned orange by copious deposits of iron ore, ran past the entrance to the wood and along its whole length. This water provided another source of enjoyment, with its rippling stones and gushing pools, and seemed to reflect our moods. If we were out in the dark near the wood's edge, we could hear the water's voice lamenting in the night along with our tears, or if I was lying in the grass, hiding from Auntie, the burn seemed to whisper a comfort as it travelled to the river and freedom.

Every summer, during the hottest days, we took off our shoes and socks and cooled our feet before trailing our sticks and the pieces of dead wood home. I was so desperate for affection that every time I went to the wood for firewood, I scratched my own legs, making them bleed in the hope I received sympathy, a kind word or a cuddle. None ever materialised, and I was left standing with sore, bloody legs and ordered to wash myself clean. I often hid behind the sheds and cried for my parents, wishing they would come and take us away from here. After a time I gave up any hope of seeing them again and just cried with unhappiness. I so wanted someone to hug, I hugged any animal that would let me.

Not far from the burn sat the remains of an old shepherd's cottage. Its overall appearance showed signs of domestic antiquity. Weather and the passage of time had eroded the walls considerably, but the essence of place remained strong and alive. We spent short breaks there, among the loose boulders and invading grasses, among yesterday's ghosts – voices from the past whispering in the wind.

We managed to time our play between collecting wood and checking fences for holes and broken posts. The old ruin hid the entrance to the wood from the croft and we learned to time our activities to work around Auntie's expectations. I often sat inside this old cottage, which was open to the sky, and tried to imagine the family that might have lived there. Did the shepherd have any children and did he love them? It was a very romantic thought, but not realistic. I could not in any shape or form imagine how hard life must have been in the early days of the twentieth century. But

I longed for a home of my own, where I was loved, where I was permitted personal things, where everything I did mattered and had some meaning, and this little house allowed me to dream.

By the age of ten, I yearned for some place to sit quietly, a place where I could be me, where Auntie could not find me. I used the time allocated to collecting firewood to my advantage by building a substantial hut – my hut – from bent branches draped over a large upturned root near a small stream that led deep into the wood. It was the perfect place, situated under a clearing in the middle of a pine cluster that was floored with moss-covered stones and brown pine needles. The branches laced across overhead, almost shutting out the sky: underneath was a dim gallery of honeycomb light where small sparkling sequins of sunlight danced through the branches and settled on the soft ground. There was a calmed stillness – only the persistent trickle of the stream heading for the burn at the entrance, and high up in a curl of breeze the occasional rustle of leaves from several mature silver birch, broke the silence. This was my place of refuge. Even Robert, my closest brother, was unaware of its existence.

I collected broken branches to form the main structure and lined the base and sides with old torn hessian sacks. A small battered set of drawers found on a rubbish dump became my treasured piece of furniture. Those drawers were filled with a variety of objects – rope for skipping, comics I had collected from friends at school, old writing jotters for drawing and writing poetry. I loved reading and writing poems, but every time Auntie came across one she destroyed it. She treated art in any form with disgust. I wanted her to read them and say they were good, but each time she accused me of being unworthy of her praise and wasting her time with my nonsense. I needed to write and release my feelings somehow and I found that if I wrote them down and read them out loud in the privacy of my own space, I could help retain my sanity and release any bad thoughts I had about Auntie and the people who were responsible for sending us to this croft.

Painting pictures with words helped me hide from reality and kept my emotions stable. I loved the power of words, the way they could capture a moment in time and keep it alive for eternity, the way I could tell the world how I felt without fear of being accused of telling lies or inventing stories. It was a great relief to unburden my problems in this matrix. At the same time, it was an emotionally invigorating exercise. It allowed me to see and understand life on a different level and finally store these thoughts on paper, where they remained, harmless but not forgotten.

I don't know how many poems were written during those years, but they were left behind to rot in the hut in the woods. Pens, pencils, bashed tin cans that I used for boiling eggs and vegetables, most importantly a box of matches to make a little fire for cooking – they were all sneaked out to the woods with me. I learned very quickly to look after this fire and watered it down before I went home.

Gooseberries grew profusely at the edge of the wood, along the side of the burn where I got my water for cooking, thickly fringed with nettles and bramble bushes. These berries were best eaten when turning red or you risked getting a sore stomach. Sometimes when the clover was in flower I boiled the berries and flowers together, sweetening the overall taste. I knew the flowers were not poisonous, as I used to put them in my mouth to sip the delicate flavour. When faced with lack of nourishment, a person will try anything to satisfy that hunger, no matter how gruesome or unappetising it may seem – except cat food.

I remembered once reading somewhere that you could eat hedgehogs, but that once killed the animal had to be wrapped in mud before baking it on top of a fire. When cooked, the baked mud was peeled off, taking the hedgehog's spikes with it, leaving the flesh intact for eating. Not so! I sourced my poor wee hedgehog, and closed my eyes and drowned him in the burn, then I built a small fire, coated him in mud and threw him onto the flames. After a short time, when I thought he was cooked, I fished him out with a stick, only to be faced with an exploded mess. I had forgotten the most important thing – to gut and clean him. I tried to sample the grey meat because I felt guilty about killing the animal, but the look of it made me feel sick. I quickly scored this off my future menu and gave the little hedgehog a proper burial. For days, I returned to the little pile of leaves and earth and put daisies and buttercups all around it.

I was always on the lookout for something interesting to cook with the ingredients around me. One day I noticed a recipe for nettle soup in an old country magazine that one of the old ladies had given to me. As these plants grew profusely among the wild grasses that I walked through every day, I decided to try and make this promising dish. I did not have any herbs or seasoning to add flavour, however, nor an onion to give some sweetness, but I managed to pick fresh, bright-green nettle tips as detailed in the recipe. I washed them in the burn and boiled them in my tin can until they were soft and palatable. I offered some to Flogal in a small tin – she sniffed at them, sat over them and peed! Was she trying to tell me something? I tried my plateful anyway. It wasn't too bad, rather tasteless, a bit like wet lettuce soaked in lemon juice, but I felt no ill effects. I guess the main thing in its favour was its warmth on a cold day.

I could only ever spend short periods of time in my hut in the woods for fear of being missed, but I think I couldn't have survived without those precious moments of independence and sanctuary. It was my pine-smelling wonderland, a place where I felt free, where birdsong permanently filled the air. The attraction of mystery was all around me and I could lose myself in these distractions and dream of a better life and a brighter future.

One day while I was boiling some eggs, I heard a noise outside my hut. I immediately thought Auntie had followed me. I instantly became very afraid. I crept out, expecting to be bombarded by abuse or hit by a stick, only to find an old gentleman standing alone and looking anxious. He stepped back from the hut, not sure who was inside. I remained unsure of him for some time and avoided contact as much as possible, but as we became more familiar with one another, we began to converse, gingerly at first. He spoke with what seemed to be a foreign accent. Soon I realised he was the hermit Auntie spoke about and this wood was his home. I hadn't believed he existed; I thought Auntie had invented this person to keep our stay in the wood to a minimum. But it wasn't fiction, he was standing beside me, looking exactly as she had described.

Most of his days were spent making wood sculptures. I don't know if he sold any, but he gave me a present one day of a wooden mouse, beautifully carved and polished. He played what I thought at the time was a scruffy, battered guitar with only four strings, but I realise now it was a ukulele. He had a quiet, deep singing voice, which was very pleasant to listen to. I let him read some of my poems and he put a few of them to music, which pleased me immensely. This dear gentleman was the first person to encourage me to write more and I will always be grateful to him.

When he began to trust me more, he told me stories of his previous life. He had been taken prisoner during the Second World War and brought to Scotland. His family had been killed during the war, so when he was released with the other prisoners, he decided to stay here and take a chance in a place where everyone had been kind to him. He felt there was nothing left for him to go home to. He had wandered round the country, doing odd jobs for food, and had always managed to find sleeping areas among the many woods and forests dotted around the country. He kept clear of heavily populated areas and tried not to cause any aggravation, so no one ever challenged him and he was nearly always left alone.

By the time he reached our wood, the years had caught up with him and he was no longer able to wander long distances. He was harmless and never bothered anyone. He had built his shelter further into the wood, though I never saw it. I don't know where he got his food from, but on rare occasions I found a little present of biscuits or a piece of fruit tucked in to the flap of my hut. I knew he never went inside: every time I went home with my collection of sticks, I made sure I placed a small pile of stones just inside the structure to alert me to any intruders, and they were never disturbed or moved.

We sat on fallen trees and chatted for short periods during the summer months of 1959, then one day he was gone and I never saw him again. The wood became very quiet after that. I missed the security of this old man, though I believed he was around somewhere, even though I did not see him when I visited my hut.

Several months passed without further incident, then one day as I was preparing another bundle of twigs to take back to the croft, I thought I heard voices at the back of the wood and went to investigate. A small crowd of people were stood arguing beside a multicoloured wagon. It appeared to be made of dark wood and looked as if it might be pulled by a horse, but I couldn't see any animals. A small fire was burning and hot fat from what looked like rabbits crackled onto the flames, as the carcass roasted on a spit. Several raggedy children were playing with pieces of stick, and dogs were lolling about in the heat of the fire. Although I was curious, I was reluctant to hang around in case they noticed me. They were strangers in my environment and I was afraid of them.

The following week, I was back working among the fallen trees when a woman and some children came up and spoke to me. She was very friendly and offered me some sandwiches. I hesitated at first when I realised that she was one of the gypsies I had seen, but the food looked so appetising and I was so hungry. I sat down at the side of the burn and ate my fill. I got on quite well with this family for the short time they were there. Apparently, though, they had been playing rather loud music in the late hours, disturbing the crofters and their animals, and the police had been called in to move them along. Since they were camped at the far side of the wood, our building and the crofts beside us had not been affected. I never heard or saw them again and I, for one, was very disappointed at their departure.

Frenetic fiddles screech the dance, twisting, turning.
Cartwheels of lace-tipped reds and greens, weightless, distorted.
Their bursts of acrobatic, balletic silhouetted heads,
breathing wood smoke and brandy-soaked roasting rabbits.
Hot twigs snap and crackle, spit burning tangles into oblivion,

as the opiate night sways the dying swans
through their light fantastic until the last spark turns to ashes.
Tired candlewicks, black and curled, swing the edge of darkness
where donkey shadows wax and wane the blue mist
that whispers down in silence
beside the sleeping gypsies, who died at dawn.

7

Flogal

In time, Auntie's dog Flogal became my constant companion. She followed me everywhere, listening to everything I said, revelling in the attention she received in the process. When I was locked in the back shed, she squeezed underneath the door and sat beside me. She listened patiently to my problems and appeared to sympathise with my fears. She seemed to know when I was scared and whimpered when I cried. I hugged her neck and discussed my future plans with her and knew she was pleased when her tail wagged with enthusiasm.

Throughout the seasons Flogal was by my side, watching everything I did. Her nose pushed into everything I worked on and her boundless energy made me smile. She spent precious moments in my hut, quietly and patiently listening to my poetry and looking at me with mournful eyes as I attempted to sing her a multitude of popular songs of the day. Many times we cried together, her head nuzzled into my lap. Every time I looked up, her tail wagged and she lifted her eyes to look at me, as if she was saying, 'You'll be all right, as long as I am with you.' When I started to smile, she perked up and things were all right again.

On rare occasions when Auntie was in one of her strange quiet moods, we escaped into the fields and hid in the tall grasses. We lay in our nest watching the sheep graze lazily along the brow of the hill, inhaled the smell of wild grasses and followed the butterflies as they flitted from one stem to another. We became aware of the tiniest insects drifting in the breeze, the rustle of every blade of grass and the movements of the clouds above. Flogal made me laugh, as she tried to flick the butterflies with her tongue as they passed her face. If one landed on her nose, she tried unsuccessfully to knock it off by sneezing. We lay there for hours, it seemed, watching clouds change shape from castles to dragons to ships and elephants, her cold nose resting under my chin. Dandelion seeds floated past in the autumn air and hundreds of our wishes blew away in the wind. They were our lucky fairies, our hopes and desires for a better future for all of us.

Time stands peacefully still,
Submitting ideas as dreamers at will
Build visionary castles of copious desire,
Creating images built to inspire.
Allowing romantic ideas to take flight,
To laze in the warmth of utopian night.
Deliciously free from normal routine,
Sublimely sedated, calmly serene.
Designer of beauty, ambitiously spread,
Quixotic visions dreamily read.
Extreme fabrication engages the trance,

Flogal

Hypnotic conduction performing the dance
To faraway places encrusted with gold
Where fairy-tale characters never grow old.
Lost in the daydreamer's fantasy world
Star-gazers bask in wonders unfurled.
Encased in a blanket of fanciful rhyme,
Lost in the dreamer's perception of time.

Stinging nettles rubbed against my bare legs and arms, going unnoticed in the quiet moments spent among wild, coarse grasses that flirted in the wind. I picked dandelions and squeezed out the white sap from the stem, plaited wild grasses and rushes, and hatched a £20 plan to save us all. In my naivety, I thought I could divide this money into four and rent a small house for myself and my brothers and sister. I decided £5 each would be enough to start a small cottage industry making dandelion cream to cure spots, forming baskets, trays, hats and furniture from our plaited grasses, all with a price tag of £20. I felt I would be able to recover our initial investment very quickly by selling all our goods and we would never have to want for anything again. I could look after everyone and my £20 plan would work perfectly. The impossibility of this idea, never mind the legal aspects, did not come into it. It seemed so simple. The only problem I could see was how to get £20 in the first place. My plan, with all my enthusiasm, soon faded into the distance, along with the dandelion seeds floating in the wind.

Although those times spent flitting around in dreamland with my best friend were very short, I absorbed them all and stole every chance to repeat them.

Flogal lived and worked with me on that croft for five years until one day I noticed a lump on her hind leg. I did not realise how serious it was; I thought she had just knocked it against something hard. Day after day, I watched her lump get worse and couldn't understand why it wasn't getting better. I rubbed her leg to try and stop the swelling and checked every day in case the skin had broken and it had become infected.

Flogal didn't seem to let it bother her and I was beginning to accept that maybe she was getting old and this lump was just part of the ageing process. It wasn't until Auntie sliced it with a sharp knife that I feared the worst. It was very unusual for her to treat her animals in this fashion and this frightened me. I became very angry and upset – I had had to hold Flogal down while she used the knife. I couldn't stop shouting at her and continually tried to push the hand holding the knife away from my friend. When I realised that no matter what I did or said she was going to do it anyway, I let go. The thought of Flogal lying there, with her trusting eyes, was difficult to accept and the sooner I let Auntie do this dreadful deed, the sooner I could comfort her and help her recover. Deep down I knew Auntie thought she was doing the right thing, even though it was outwith my understanding.

She grabbed my arm, trying to quieten me, and threw me against the shed wall, pulling my hair. When she became tired of hitting me, and was finished with Flogal, she pushed us both into the shed and locked the door. I sat and hugged my dog, while she licked her wound clean. I stroked her glossy black head, speaking softly to her all the time, trying not to listen to her whimpers. It took quite a while for the bleeding to stop. Not long after that, Flogal became very unwell. I would feed her before I went to school and again at night before bed. I laid her in our shed, where we had spent so much time consoling each other, and kept her warm with straw and sacks. I made sure she was clean and watered, and as the days wore on I pleaded with Auntie to get someone to help her. Flogal became so weak that I had to feed her water from my cupped hands and let it drip slowly into her mouth. Then one day I arrived home from school to find she was gone. I had lost my best friend, my companion and my helper.

You came with me quietly to the hole in the ground
where we drank together. I held your collar as you
gently lapped from the well. The cast iron buckets clinked
as I lowered them in, catching the clear fluid.
It rushed in like a dam bursting its banks.
You licked the spill and your tongue stuck
to the cold metal. Your tail wagged pleasure
and your eyes burst with loyal affection.
Over the long years we must have walked miles
to that old well, and it seemed only fitting
that when your time came,
I would take you back one more time.
Your ghost came with me quietly
to the hole in the ground,
and I laid your memory to rest
beside the spring water.

After some months, a pedigree orange-and-white miniature Shetland collie dog arrived to join the family. She was cute and Auntie named her Morag. We were never allowed to handle her unless it was necessary and she became our foster mother's new pet. In fact, we came to hate this little dog, who barked at and nipped us every chance she got. During the night when we were asleep, Auntie brought this dog through to our beds and encouraged her to nip our ears or our chins until we woke up and climbed out of bed, sometimes to brush our shoes or to make her a cup of tea . . . and this tea was very rarely to her liking.

Every time I handed her a cup, I knew something would be wrong. Was it hot enough or did I put in enough sugar? If she really wasn't pleased, she would empty the cup into the sink and ask for another. Sometimes if she was very agitated, she threw the cup at me – I had to be prepared to catch it in case it broke, which would make her anger explode. If the cup hit the dog, woe betide me.

Morag was allowed to stand on the table and eat her food in front of us. Every time we moved, she growled. This amused Auntie to the point where she laughed out loud. She treated this dog like a figure of royalty, and sat and spoke to her all day, showering treats of all kinds in her direction. It wasn't the dog's fault, but for the first time in our lives we wanted to cause harm to one of her animals. But we didn't.

Summer was the time of year when the child welfare officer came to check that all was well with us and that our minds and bodies were in good health. Over time we became aware that this visit was looming, as our foster mother's moods changed dramatically, from aggression and dislike to relative calm, with a false sense of compassion. Our work was reduced to a minimum and just before they arrived we were told to play outside. Sadly, by then we had forgotten how. Instead we stood in a small group and watched the visitors come up the brae and into the house. We were left outside for the whole visit and did not know what Auntie said to them. Did she tell them that we were difficult children? Or did she pretend that everything was all right? If we had been punished before they arrived and looked upset, she told them that our pet duck had died, or we'd lost a kitten, or that we had been a little bit naughty that morning.

It didn't seem to matter to the visitors that we looked unhappy or that we were clutching one another when they arrived. In fact, we tried to look as sad as possible, but no matter what we did or said they always believed Auntie's explanations.

When Robert and I were older we did try to tell them how we felt, but Auntie's response to this was to coax the younger ones to hug her, then say that Robert and I were getting too big to want a cuddle from their Auntie. She knew that during our on-coming teenage years rebellion and discontentment would become normal behaviour for us. If at any time there were signs of the visitors disbelieving her stories, she proceeded to tell them that she had been unwell and was just getting back on her feet again. This sympathy tactic always worked. She had a tale ready to cover any eventuality and no questions were ever thrown in our direction. It wasn't long before the visits changed to the beginning of the year, when we were at school, and our progress report was compiled from Auntie's account and the headmaster's records. This resulted in a false monitoring of events, which I presume was always to her advantage.

Mary was often absent from school and although this was recorded in her notes, nothing was done about it. She rebelled at school, often hitting other pupils in her frustration. She had become more insular and aggressive, her loneliness overwhelming. Any time Auntie was approached, she insisted that Mary was a poorly child, mentally as well as physically, and everyone believed her. Reports from the school were sent to Auntie and swept aside. The school never queried the reason for Mary's disruptive behaviour and took it for granted that it was due to her supposed mental disability. This was her desperate cry for help and it went unnoticed.

In her second year at primary, Mary came home with lice in her hair. She must have got it from school, but I got the blame. Auntie called me through to the living room and asked me to comb Mary's hair. It was not long before I noticed that she had white flakes of some sort stuck to the side of her head. I told Auntie about it, because I thought she had forgotten to wash the soap out of my little sister's hair when she had shampooed it earlier. She turned round quickly and pushed me onto the stool beside the sink, grabbing both my ears. I could feel my eyes begin to water as she twisted them and frantically asked what I had done wrong. She began shouting at me and scolded me for giving my sister lice. I knew my head was clean and she was passing her guilt on to me, but I knew I couldn't tell her that. While she pulled and tugged at my hair, I tried to control my sobs by looking at the patterns on the handmade rugs at my feet. I held on to the side of the chair as she pulled me and the stool across the room with tremendous force, letting go suddenly, causing me to fall over the sofa. I let go of the stool and ran for the outside door – but as usual it was locked.

She grabbed my hair again. My head was swimming – little dots swirled in front of my eyes as I was twisted back and forth like a rag doll. I collapsed on the floor gasping, my whole world suddenly filled with painful distractions, lightness flickering in the back of my head. I closed my eyes, trying to black out the sensation, my head pulsating like a kettle drum. I felt my body being pulled along the wooden floor, over the doorstep of the now open door and along the cold cement flagstones. She just dumped me on the stony ground outside.

The sobs came in spasms, as I tried to control the urge to cry. I glanced at her face as she walked away: it was twisted into a grotesque caricature, a hideous mixture of contempt and anger. What had I done that was so bad? What made her hate me so much? Was she jealous of my youth, or did she resent my presence in her life?

Minutes later she reappeared and ordered me back to the sink. She slapped me across the back of the head, then handed me a fine-toothed comb and a bottle of oil, instructing me to comb Mary's hair until it was clean. It took some time to do this, and by the time I had finished Auntie had calmed down and was sitting at the fireside pushing the glowing embers with her iron poker, occasionally stirring the coals in the grate.

While things were quiet, I took Mary through to our bedroom, washed her hair in the basin and covered it with a towel. She was quite upset and we sat and talked until suppertime.

Auntie had no idea what was happening to us. She couldn't get close to us emotionally, so she didn't notice immediately when something was wrong with us or we were unwell. When she did, she dismissed it and left us to deal with the problem ourselves. We tried anything we could think of to help ourselves get better – we washed our own sores and let them heal naturally; we let tummy bugs run their course; we lay under the trees in the orchard when we felt dizzy and slept for short periods during the day – but some things we couldn't fix by ourselves. While the four of us comforted one another, we very often infected our siblings in the process, though we always recovered within a few days. Auntie never really came near us when we were ill except to give us enough food to keep us above starvation level.

I was in agony most of my school years with sore feet. I couldn't walk squarely on the soles because of painful pads on the balls of both feet. Every time I stood on a stone, the sharpness of the pain brought tears to my eyes. I was forced to walk on the sides of my feet to avoid any discomfort.

I asked Auntie if she could help me and look at them, but she refused, so I did my best to deal with this condition for the rest of my childhood until I was able to personally get it treated. A few seconds with a scalpel and the offending corns were removed. It was such a relief to walk normally and not look as if I had flat feet.

Our health was seldom checked, apart from the school nurse's inspections. Any problems we had were never seen to or corrected – Auntie made sure we kept them to ourselves. The doctor responsible for our care was therefore unaware of our health issues and had no reason to suspect we were unwell.

Each season of the year brought a different kind of abuse, especially in terms of the physical hardships of the various jobs we had to do. School holidays were very busy, the long summer days often being too short to complete all the tasks we were given. Even in winter, if we were unwell with colds or flu, we couldn't escape the many outside chores Auntie had planned in our daily schedule.

The croft had to be maintained throughout the year and we were her unpaid workers. All children brought up on a croft or holding (smaller than a croft) have to help with the extra chores that this kind of life dictates, but an understanding of what a child is capable of achieving is usually uppermost in the parent's mind. Auntie was constantly surprised at how little we achieved, and became very impatient and angry with us. One of the many sad things about our childhood is that if she had treated us differently we would have responded in a more favourable manner by helping her to run a successful household and keep her croft running smoothly. Auntie just did not know how to encourage us or how to bring out the best in us.

Some jobs were more enjoyable than others and one of my least favourite was preparing the many outhouses surrounding the main building for the winter months. Each one had to be creosoted and repaired before the bad weather came. It was tedious, tiring and took all day. Stirring the thick, black liquid and brushing it onto the sheds made my wrists ache, but we had to keep going until every one of the sheds was coated.

To help the time pass, we sometimes chatted, as all children are inclined to do when faced with a long, unexciting job. We could see this angered Auntie – she wanted this job to be finished quickly and had no time for our idle conversation. She would pace up and down in front of us, sucking the cigarette that always dangled from the corner of her mouth, her metal rollers clinking together as her pace quickened. She seemed to see us as wilful, disobedient children who deserved all that she could inflict upon us.

Robert, by now ten years old, with a head of blonde curls, was quick-tempered and very protective towards me. He was growing taller and was nearly the same height as Auntie. Although she remained the ultimate controller in his life, he very often tried hard to fight against her unreasonable rules. Because of our ages, Robert and I were very close, as were George and Mary. We supported each other when our lives became unbearable, and so when Auntie targeted me without reason this particular day, throwing tar at me for working too slowly, Robert reacted instantly, and quite violently.

Robert moved like lightning. He picked up the tin with the tar and threw it back at her. It covered her clothes and ran down her legs into her slippers. She then picked up an axe that was lying against the inside of the shed and swung it towards him. I could see him shaking with anger. He wanted to hurt her, he wanted to kill her. She was threatening him, pushing him too far, and he reacted instinctively without any thought of the consequences. He knew that he was going to be severely punished and didn't care any more. He grabbed the axe mid-swing and swung it back, missing her by inches. I saw him shaking as he realised how close he had come to hurting Auntie. He knew what was coming. He knew he had to prepare himself for a severe beating. He looked at Auntie's face and watched it turn pure white as she ordered him into the barn. He was beaten with a rough stick, which scraped the surface of his skin, making it raw and bloody. He was then locked up and denied food and toilet for the remainder of the day. I was made to finish the job and sent to bed without supper.

It is difficult to imagine the fear and stress involved in our day-to-day life at the croft. I still find it difficult to understand why we did not run away. Of course, over the years Robert did and was repeatedly taken back by the police. There was no one to help and nowhere to go.

We were all watched like hawks after this kind of incident in case we tried to sneak some food out to the unfortunate child. When I asked him later how he'd managed to get to the toilet, he just said, 'I peed over her logs.' We sniggered at the thought of Auntie handling the urine-soaked chunks of wood and then eating her shortbread biscuits without washing her hands.

Another task we feared each year was sweeping the chimneys. The ladder used was far too long and had to be positioned some distance from the rooftop, making our climb to the top extra long. It was wooden, very old and rather rickety; the rungs were slack and creaked as we gingerly stepped on them. Auntie stood underneath this ladder and whacked at the rungs as one of us crept the entire length to the chimney. She grabbed the sides and shook them until we pleaded with her to stop. In extreme cases, she knocked us off and left us hanging on to one of the rungs. The drop to the ground was not excessive but was scary nevertheless. Climbing back down was often more nerve-racking, as we had to avoid Auntie's stick. She moved it behind us constantly, so we couldn't see where it was, sniggering to herself. We could hear her and would have kicked her as we descended had we had the courage.

Her sadistic streak emerged more and more as time went by. Sometimes it felt as if she was experimenting with us. She refused to help if we got stuck or found a task too difficult, instead playing on our anxiety and fear.

One year, as we were tidying up the living room after cleaning the chimney, Auntie lashed out at us, shouting about the black soot on the floor and how slow we were in cleaning up the mess. She accused us of being careless, and most of the day was spent scrubbing floors and washing down walls. She watched us as we struggled, and if we didn't work quickly enough she screamed and rubbed soot into our faces and mouths until we choked and gagged. After one particularly cruel episode towards Robert, as Auntie turned away, Robert pretended to play the banjo like the black and white minstrels we watched on the neighbour's television. He never failed to make me laugh and I will always be grateful to him.

We tried to cope with the emotional and physical abuse she continually vented on us by trying to make light of each incident, though it was impossible to do this until she got tired and moved away. Our youngest siblings were never able to see it this way or understand our way of coping; they retreated into themselves mentally, making their life in adulthood an endless and desperate struggle.

Good days arrived with the rain, as our outside work came to a relative standstill. Only necessary tasks, such as feeding the animals, continued. When that was finished, we were locked in our rooms and allowed out only for toilet and mealtimes. There was nothing to do but sit on the bed; sometimes we had no enthusiasm to invent. Rosebud, the doll I got from the children's home – the doll I loved so much – sat and stared at us from the mantelpiece, still wearing her blue knitted hat. Her playing days were over and only at bedtime, once the lights were out, was I able to lift her down, give her a hug and cover her up with one of my vests to keep her warm. In the morning, she was replaced faithfully on the dark mantelpiece and left to gather dust. As long as I could see her and talk to her when I felt lonely, I felt reasonably comfortable. She sat there staring into space for the whole ten years. I was never allowed to spend time with her or given a pram to keep her in. I left her behind the day I walked away from the croft and I never saw her again.

When we were locked in our bedroom during bad weather, Mary and I stood together at the window and watched the rain stream down the small panes. We traced the water down the glass with our fingers to see which line reached the bottom first. It made us laugh when both streams combined and no one won. There was nothing to do or play with. Books were at a minimum, so word games and stories became the answer. As long as we were quiet, Auntie left us alone. Sometimes we heard her shuffling about in the boys' room, throwing things about. We just hoped she wouldn't come through to us.

Outside our window, we watched a monkey puzzle tree as it bent like an old man in the wind. Its dark silhouette twisted and swayed violently and we danced quietly, imitating the erratic movements of the branches. I was intrigued by the appearance and elegance of ballet dancers, and tried but failed miserably to move like them. We pirouetted round the room in time to the tree's movement, but always ended up giggling at the other's pathetic attempt. I could hold my hands in a reasonable position, but no matter how hard Mary tried to do the same, all she succeeded in creating was a good impression of a pair of claws. She was so funny when we were alone together and I miss her still. Somehow we could relate to this tree, for we too were in a part of the country we didn't belong to. Like this tree, we were struggling to escape the unnatural convulsions of a strange environment and alien behaviour we could not understand.

Strong winds and heavy rain were regular features of this part of the country and, as the croft sat on a small hill, it was open to the elements. I rose one morning after an unusually gusty night and, once dressed, made my way round to the henhouse to feed the poultry. I collected whatever eggs I could find. Just as I was about to step into the front area, a small corner section of the roof partly collapsed behind me. It wasn't very heavy, but I didn't want it to fall down, as the chickens would escape and I would be in trouble again, so I stood, holding up the corrugated iron panel for some time, listening to the rain splatter like bullets on the metal roof, the loose end banging in the wind against the beams with a melancholy sound. It was not until the baker's van arrived that I received any help. He brought across two washing poles and we used them to support the roof, allowing me to get out.

He took our guardian's biscuits into the house and told her what had just happened. She must have been a little embarrassed to admit that she had not come out to see why I was taking longer than normal to do my work. The baker asked if I was all right before he left. I missed school that day. I had been careless – she blamed me entirely for the destruction of the henhouse.

She grabbed my collar and took me to the shed to fetch a selection of tools, then stood over me while I attempted to repair it. I was not able to do so, so she pushed me onto the gravel, stood on my hands and dragged me across the ground. My knees scraped on the loose stones, skinning them badly. I was left to stand in the rain until one of the crofters came round to fix the roof and only then was I allowed inside. I spent the rest of the day in my bedroom, picking small stones from under the skin on my knees.

The baker's weekly delivery consisted of shortbread rounds for our foster mother. She hid them in the back cupboard near the fireplace and we were not allowed to touch anything in there. I used to wonder what these biscuits tasted like. After weeks plucking up the courage, I eventually succumbed to temptation. I waited for her to go outside, then looked in the forbidden cupboard. I saw that a packet was already opened and helped myself to one round, eating it quickly, keeping an eye on the window for signs of her return. Once I'd tasted the biscuits, I couldn't resist trying again another day – this time I took two, stuffed them into the top of my navy knickers and sneaked out to the shed, where I savoured every morsel. I made sure I only did this on an odd occasion, so as not to be found out.

Finding food was extremely hard at times and we often went hungry. Any person passing by the house was a potential source of nourishment and we discovered that if we were polite and friendly, there was always the chance of a biscuit or sweetie.

The postman came every morning with mail and any small item that had been ordered from the village shop. He rode a large red and black bicycle, with a basket at the front, which held a sack full of letters, and a bracket at the back, which carried any parcels. In his top pocket was a bag of sugar boilings, which he sometimes shared with us. He was a lifeline to many elderly crofters and was the first to notice when anyone became sick or needed help.

During the school holidays, Robert and I often waited at the top of the road to get a lift on his handlebars down to the croft, but Auntie did not approve and eventually spoke to him. After that it never happened again and we lost touch with our friendly mailman.

He came up one weekend with his own children so they could meet us, but we were not allowed to speak to them. Following his visit, we spent several unpleasant days ducking every time she passed – it was our fault the mailman had felt sympathy for us, and we were punished with her stick or her hand. Auntie did not need any outside involvement in our lives.

8

Autumn Colours

We became good friends with the son of an important member of the parish through Sunday school and, because of his prominent status, we were permitted to go on cycle runs with him to Lossiemouth via the back roads, away from the main traffic. It was much-needed respite from our life on the croft. With good weather, and the company of a very polite and happy boy, we were able to appreciate a few hours of laughter and play. Our friend seemed to enjoy his time with us and even the discomfort of riding our old, rickety bikes did not spoil these trips. They were a boost to our well-being and lifted our spirits; in fact, we enjoyed them so much that even the inevitable harassment from Auntie could not spoil the lift they gave us. She often punished us by pushing us off our bicycles when we arrived back at the croft, and if her mood was exceptionally foul she would remove the chains.

We confided in this young boy, telling him about our foster mother and the way she treated us. We didn't feel threatened by him because he was in our age group and speaking to him honestly seemed to help psychologically. He lived some distance from the croft, which also helped to put us at ease, as we felt quite confident that our secret was safe with him. He was a breath of fresh air in our unpleasant existence.

In the Glasgow City Council records, there is mention of a letter of concern from the boy's parents, stating that in their opinion Auntie was not a suitable candidate to care for four young children. However, in a follow-up statement from the authorities it was stated that they had received a letter in return from Auntie to say that the oldest child – myself – on reaching her teenage years was being a bit rebellious and was refusing to help in the home. It was suggested that I might have been using some families to get sympathy as a result and was somehow taking advantage of this particular family's attentions. The report said I would grow out of this behaviour and that it was nothing to get unduly concerned about. This was never followed up.

Many people wanted to help us and, for a long time, it was difficult to understand why no one else reported the abuse. By the friendly way they treated us, it was obvious our neighbours realised, to a certain extent, that things were not quite right: we were very undernourished and extremely pale in colour. I assume they put it down to the fact that we were missing our parents and that was enough to quell any doubts they might have had, or perhaps they just didn't know how or where to start. In the 1950s, it was not easy to question things, and there was no system in place encouraging anyone to speak on our behalf.

It was always good to return to school after the long summer holidays – to get away from the household routine and discipline that dogged our waking hours. I couldn't wait to see my friends. At playtime, we talked freely about everything from the latest girls' comics to the newest game in the shops. Like so many children of the '50s, we were rarely given anything new and we all accepted this. Most working families did not have the extra money or the resources to compete, as they do today, for the possession of material things. We were grateful for everything we got and we didn't miss what we didn't have. But still, it was liberating being able to talk about these kinds of things beyond our realm of experience without being told to be quiet – a nice change for us. At least for part of the day, we were allowed to be children. It was better when George and Mary joined us and we didn't have to worry so much about them, but as always the first term of school passed so quickly, and before we knew it the October holidays had come round once again.

During these weeks of holiday, work began in earnest to prepare for the coming harvest and to make the croft ready for the winter months. The two orchards were bursting with fruit, although we saw very little of it: apples and berries of all description were picked, washed and sorted by us, then put into punnets for delivery to the shop in the village. We had to take extra care not to let any juice land on our faces – our fingers would be smacked sharply with whatever Auntie was holding as she accused us of eating the berries! All fruit unsuitable for selling was boiled and made into jams or hung in muslin bags to drip, making the perfect jellies when the juice was re-boiled with sugar. Jars were filled, dressed and sold to regular customers. I became adept at hiding a couple of jars under the large table in the milk house, then shared them with Mary after we'd gone to bed. I don't know if Robert and George did the same; it was easy enough for me to sneak some into our bedroom, but I knew if I gave some to the boys they would have to walk past Auntie with their jars and the possibility of getting caught would spoil it for us all. It was too risky, and I felt sorry for them because of it.

I much preferred the October holidays, as there was more to do outwith the confines of the croft, away from Auntie's unpredictable behaviour. There were even more opportunities to escape her venomous attacks when we were invited to work on other crofts and farms around the local area. Once Auntie's permission was granted, we joined the neighbours for berry-picking or to take part in the potato harvest. The tractor and farm cart picked us up around 5 a.m., along with the other workers from the neighbouring farms. It was extremely hard work because the fields had to be picked clean in case of an early frost, otherwise the potatoes would rot and be unsuitable even for the animals.

At the end of the morning session, following the tractor and digger up and down the open drills, picking up potatoes and chasing any mice we saw, the farmer's wife arrived with large enamel kettles filled with hot milky tea, bags of sausage rolls, biscuits and scones, all home baked. Then at the end of the fortnight, we were invited up to the big farm, where wooden tables and benches were set out to feed the whole squad. Broth, stovies, carrots, turnips and trifles were on the menu: a thank-you for all our hard work. The sun was usually setting as the trailers, full of happy, singing but tired workers, returned us home. Some sense of achievement belied our sore backs – our dry throats from talking and laughing too much were part of the exercise.

The money we earned was handed over to our foster mother, then we were sent outside to do our usual work before bed. We never received any pocket money from what we had earned, however the two things we did benefit from were the copious amount of food we consumed and the friendly, enjoyable interaction we had with all those lovely people.

Although we worked very hard during those days, Auntie never praised us and always made us feel bad for having left her alone. When we came back, she often pretended she was ill and made us do everything for her. She confused us with her behaviour, staggering across the floor as if she was light-headed and going to faint. I didn't know if any of it was true – if there was a possibility that she was not faking it: it was not obvious to me at the time. I would hate to think that she had been unwell and we hadn't noticed.

On days like this, after working hard in the fields, then looking after her on our return, I couldn't understand what it was she wanted from us. If we worked well and earned some money for her, we were wrong for leaving her alone, but if we refused to go to any of these things we were punished for being disobedient. We couldn't win whatever we did.

I remember one time refusing to go berry-picking. I can't remember why I didn't go. But she locked me in the shed with a bundle of darning and a pile of shoes to clean. I regretted the decision to stay at home. I was not given any food, though I managed to sneak into the house when the postman called in the afternoon. While she escorted him down the brae on his departure, I took the opportunity to grab a few slices of bread.

From that day onwards, I took every chance I got to work away from the croft. At least I was fed and watered and more able to live to fight another day.

In the early days of our stay at the croft, binders were still used to cut and bind the corn, which was then placed in stacks to dry. I remember working for one of the neighbouring crofts, helping with this job one year, and sitting during our break, soft hay filling our hair with chaff and our noses with dust that smelled of summer, looking at the sheaves of grain neatly stacked all over the field and thinking how marvellous Mother Nature was in structure to be able to hold a complete summer's yield of crushed grasses, cut wild flowers and a harvest of ripe crop in just one of those small neat parcels.

Later, the threshing of the corn was done by a combine harvester that travelled round the crofts separating the ears from the stalks. Although this method was much quicker, the grain had to be completely dry before work began, as any moisture in the grain generated a heat that when stored caused serious mould problems, unlike the days of the slower binders, when the corn could be cut dry or damp without any lasting damage.

When the fields were cleared, we raked the chaff and leftover stalks into lines to dry. This was bagged for winter feed and bedding for the animals. Geese were allowed onto the stubble fields once the crops were harvested. They gleaned the grain and added manure at the same time.

The first thing I noticed when the harvest was over was an overwhelming silence, a peace that said a job well done.

During these active weeks, we were well cared for. There is nothing that tastes as nice or feels as good as drinking mugs of tea and eating scones that have been baked on an open griddle, while sitting with friendly country folk on a pile of freshly mown hay. It is a time of hard work, where everyone pulls together to share the day's labour and to appreciate one another's role in the order of things. I watched the menfolk work non-stop until dusk, with short breaks for nourishment, their happy, rosy-cheeked women by their sides, supporting everything they did. I could see, even in my youth, how proud they were of one another's achievements.

He walked the twilight of Scots pine bathed in moon's stigmata.
Grey smoke snaked perimeter edges, rolled between silvered moonbeams
and danced with cloud shadows into the darkening night.
An eerie quiet hung in the air and he drank the stillness.
Farm machines etched the sky, their steel skeletons a macabre
outline of crusted chaff and black grease, held the night's hush.
Their silver nimbus haunting a spent harvest, a field of
nakedness that bared an undergarment of straw and stubble.
His croft basking in soft moonlight,
a flour dusted kitchen, her whitened nails from stretched dough that fed a hundred workers.
He could see his wife in her foetal bed, exhausted, yet content,
waiting for the sun to rise and ignite her sleeping chaos,
a chaos under her control. He glanced up at the Harvest Moon,
its full belly reflecting the end of a good season.
Bursting with pride, he followed the blue pathway home.

As the day slipped into early evening, the spicy smell of summer changed into a cool freshness. A faint smoky haze of white butterflies filled the air like sugarplum fairies and a patina of white dust coated our clothes. We dusted ourselves down well before trudging up the hill to a home where children were expected to behave like adults at all times, constantly struggling and forever looking for a few words of praise or a hint of affection where none came. We could always see Auntie watching from the top of the hill during the day and we did our best to ignore her. We knew she wanted us back to the croft immediately the harvest work was finished, but the farmer's wife would not let us go until we ate our snacks. Auntie once tried to stop this by saying that we had to come home and do our own work, but the crofters told her that we had worked very hard and, like everyone else, deserved their thanks. They also stated that they would be offended if she went ahead and forced the issue. I think she realised that it would be unwise to contest this. Even though we had been elsewhere all day, she managed to hoard work for us to do before we were allowed to retire for the night.

But for these magical days out of the croft, during the drawn-out weeks of October holidays it became increasingly difficult to avoid contact with Auntie's ever-swinging stick and hissing tongue, permanently clicking and sucking on a twisted cigarette. It was important for our sanity to find places where we could hide from her scrutinising gaze, though we had found to our cost that it was a bad idea for all of us to hide in the same place at the same time. Soon, each of us found his or her lonely haven.

Nearly every hideaway was discovered eventually and destroyed, and relief became harder and harder to achieve. The simplest places were the safest, and I found mine among the bushes and steep banks under the beech hedge at the foot of the brae. Auntie couldn't see me from the house window and I was outwith the immediate confines of the croft. I could relax for short periods in the dappled shade, where insects buzzed and darted and strange rustlings could be heard beneath every plant and clump of grass. I made daisy chains and dandelion pendants; I played with odd-shaped stones under which worms and grubs lived out their lives in the safe, comfortable darkness until I let sunlight flood their world. I watched them frantically scurry for shelter and gently replaced the stone on top of them. I marvelled at their small world of activity, a complete natural universe. I lay back under the hedge to watch the birds soaring among the clouds and wished I could fly with them; I watched the fields in their seasonal glory change from snow-covered mounds and dusty autumn golds to summer greens and spring blossoms of daffodils and crocuses. But I always stayed within shouting distance of the croft, ready to stand to attention if I was discovered, armed with the believable excuse of searching for hens' eggs.

The beech hedge surrounding the croft turned a rich copper in autumn. It grew to a great height – approximately ten feet, if not more – and we were given the responsibility of cutting it once a year. The tall ladder we used for sweeping the chimney came out again, though this time we got plenty of support by resting it against the thick branches. Hand-held shears cut slowly and by the end of the day our hands were sore and covered in blisters. The hedge was in full view of the neighbours, so Auntie put on a brilliant show of feeding us well and pretending to show concern if anyone passed by.

Although it was hard, relentless work, Robert and I did have fun doing this job and the day passed quickly. Generally, we were doing a good job and this pleased Auntie.

As long as we remembered to speak as little as possible, her mood remained stable and an unusual calm came over her. If it could be like this all the time, I used to think, life on this croft would be more enjoyable. I felt sorry that she didn't seem to realise this. I knew that if she was able to tolerate us more and accept us for the children we were, we would be only too willing to work with her and help her in anything she asked us to do. But it was a compromise she could not undertake or understand.

By the end of the summer, the leaves on the hedge were very dry and dusty, and sometimes we found it difficult to breathe. For George, though, it could be treacherous. One year he took an asthma attack from inhaling too much dust from the crumbling leaves. As he wheezed more and more, Auntie grabbed him under the arm and tried to march him up to the house. We could see he could hardly walk upright as his breathing got worse, but she pushed and pulled his small body up the brae, thumping his back to make him walk properly. He was panting so much he was unable to speak to her and this seemed to infuriate her even more. She was convinced he was pretending because he did not want to work. When they got inside, she beat him with her belt.

Robert and I followed them up to the house, not because we would be able to stop her but because we wanted to help George by being there. She didn't see us, as she was focused on what she was doing to our brother. We waited outside and listened to her screaming, ready to run down the brae and commence work before she noticed that we had stopped without being told to. George eventually managed to calm himself down through fear, as her anger increased. He was then locked in his room until he was in control of his breathing again.

Before evening came, I was handed a large scythe with a solid wood handle and told to cut down the thistles that had grown in

Robert, me, Mary and George:
taken for the child welfare records, circa 1957.

At primary school, 1958–9. I'm in the front row, far right.

The school as it is today – closed. For us, it was a haven from the brutality at the croft.

Me with Rory O'More the cat, and Mary patting Flogal.

Our safe place: the railway bridge as it is today.

A recent view from the croft towards the railway bridge.

The elderly lady whose hens laid 'willow-patterned' eggs, standing to the left.

The shepherd, our friend, to the left.

The storyteller with his grandchildren, rather than the ramshackle bike he used to trundle home on dark nights.

The croft as it is today

Front view

A small room inside the croft – the tiny windows made the interior so dark and dingy.

The sink with one cold-water tap – we had been living at the croft for three years before this was installed.

The croft from the brae.

The front and only
door to the croft.

The barn door,
where punishment
was often administered.

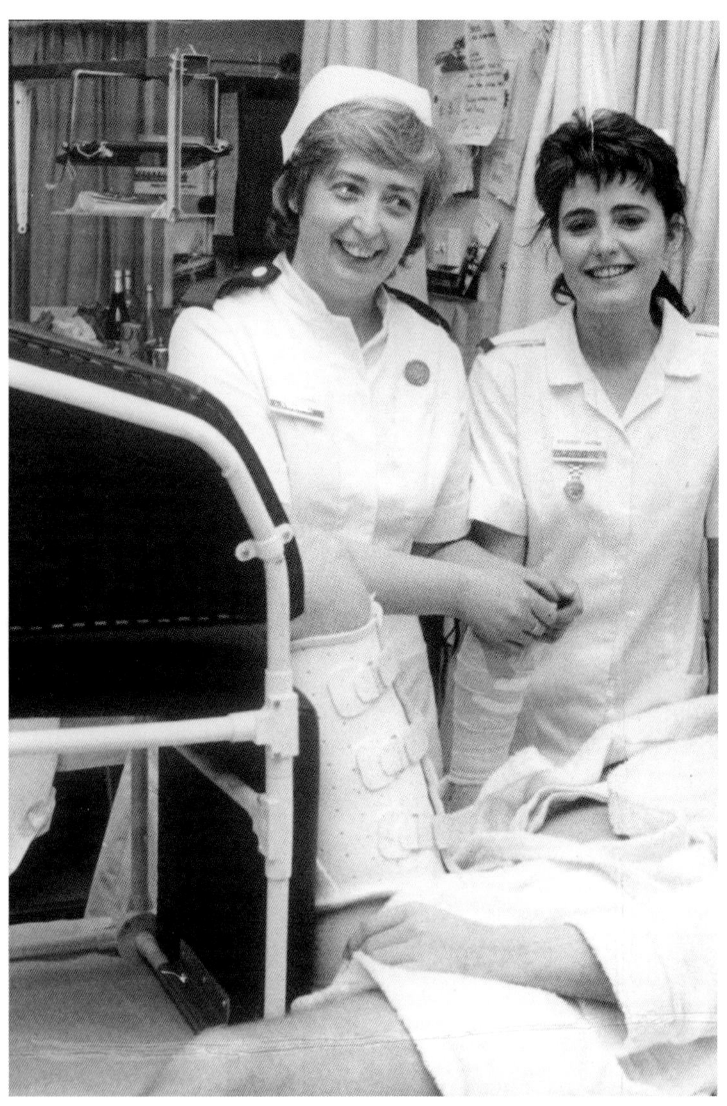

With a colleague in 1986, 20 years after leaving the croft.

the large field where the cows fed. This job was done twice a year, in late spring and late autumn, to prevent the cows from chewing the sharp spikes on the plant. These caused their mouths to swell and, as a result, they were unable to feed sufficiently to maintain their health.

The scythe was very heavy and the blade was extremely sharp and long, but I knew Auntie would be watching from the window, so I could not put it down until the field was cleared. It was very hot and tiring work, but I wasn't allowed to stop for a drink of water or even a toilet break. I was still working when Robert finished his own work and he took over and gave me a rest. Between us we got the job done to her satisfaction.

The cut thistles then had to be raked up and were added to the pile of leaves and branches cut from the hedge earlier in the day. This substantial heap was ready for our yearly bonfire. When the sky began to darken, the fire was lit. There was a time limit on bonfires, so the flames had to be dampened and out by late evening.

We stood and watched the red glow spread through the leaves, fascinated by the changing appearance as the fire collapsed into heaps of glowing dice. We inhaled the sharp and spicy smell that came from the acrid resin of some of the branches.

Robert and I waited until the embers died down and then dampened the whole area around the bonfire with pails of water collected from the well, leaving a black charcoal mess.

This was one of our busiest days, but at least it came to an end with very little harassment from Auntie. We were exhausted, but were fed without a row and allowed to go to bed at a reasonable hour.

As the season progressed and the crops ripened, every living creature could feel a change in the air. The fields transformed from pea-green to rich yellow and orange. Among the trees, birds gathered for the journey south, and the hustle and bustle of unbounded energy sent every man and animal into the throes of activity, each preparing his tasks to survive the forthcoming winter.

Take time to walk through woods
in late August, early September
when orange and lemon moods
turn winds and reddening skies
into a season of pungent foods.
Savour the sweetness as autumn tones
skim across snake-like streams
where greys simmer among gravelled stones,
and every footstep beats the long grasses
iced in pastry cases of pine cones.
Peel back ferns and squeeze the zest
of ripe blackberries, let the juice drip
through your lips and sip from Nature's best.
Roll browned hazelnuts in your hand,
crack the shell and taste a year's harvest.
Wander into fields stripped bare,
feel the crisp, chaffed underfoot
crunch your way over autumn's fare.
Back through woods alive with birds,
their feathers rustling a changing air.
Turn the leaf carpet with your feet
and watch the hot sun baste it dry.
Allow time to rest on a shady seat.
Sample the quietness, serve it to memory
and enjoy at last, a summer's fruitful retreat.

Auntie had a disconnected relationship with the local church and its minister. She never attended services or took part in any of the activities. As far as I am aware, it was through the minister that she acquired the references and information to foster children, and her association with him eventually resulted in our attendance at Sunday School. The church was situated near our primary school and we managed to get there quite safely by ourselves. Our first visit proved to be a welcoming experience and this encouraged us to return on a regular basis. It was an excuse to be away from the croft and Auntie was happy to accept it. She was not overly religious and mostly kept her beliefs to herself, but Grace was said before all meals and Sunday was recognised as the Sabbath and work and noise on the croft was kept to a minimum, as was the case in most homes in that era.

Church soon became a place where my siblings and I could feel a sense of security and peace. In particular, our involvement with Sunday School boosted our confidence. It became a haven for us all – somewhere we felt safe, a place of undisturbed peace where no one treated you badly, where everyone saw you as a special child and unselfishly invited you to take part in the many celebrations throughout the year.

Along with Christmas and the summer picnic, Harvest Thanksgiving was one of the busiest times in the parish calendar. It was the time of year I loved best, the time for gathering in the crops and bringing the community together to celebrate the end of a productive year. It was a time of plenty and goodwill to all. The church was filled with produce of every kind, set out in a magnificent display, from nearly every croft or holding in the vicinity.

The colours of autumn – rich gold, copper and the deep browns and beiges of crisp, freshly baked breads, mixed with an orange harvest sun – bathed the church's interior. An intense feeling of warmth and security filled the inside of the building. Often, when the church emptied of people, I stood alone, absorbing this sensation. I walked down the aisle, feeling much as if I were in a cathedral: there was the same stillness, the same sense of space in the high ceiling and the same feeling of wonderment.

I remember one year in particular it was nearly midday and the shafts of light streaming down through the stained-glass windows were almost vertical. This light gave everything a nimbus of gold mist. It was overwhelming and brought home the reality of life on the croft and the complete absence of maternal affection we had to endure. Occasions like this brought tears to my eyes, instilling within me a deep longing to be someone's little girl. I was ten years old, but I still wanted to be that little girl; I still had that longing to be loved and understood, to be the child I was and the child I should have been. The whole interior of the church that day felt like a warm cocoon where harm and discord were not invited and I inhaled it deeply.

I watched the sun kiss the wooden chancel
and creep across the regimented pews
devouring the darkness before it.
I shivered slightly and focused
on the fresh flower displays,
a living corner of light and Holy care,
their perfume spraying summer into the chilling air.
The longer I stood inhaling this peaceful building,
the more I realised how small I was in the order of things.
Yet to be here, standing among the Harvest yield

and the humbleness of it all, sent a power so extreme,
that all breath and life seemed to vanish,
baptised into the essence of this place.
This House of God, this very special place.

All members of the Bible class, of which I was one, were allowed to help arrange the display. Although it was a small parish, donations were plentiful and at the end of the service, parcels containing a variety of goods were distributed to the elderly and those who needed it most. A basket, filled to the brim, was delivered to our house, but we very rarely got any benefit from its contents. Sometimes we managed to whip out a packet of something when Auntie wasn't looking, but that was the extent of our reward.

Our involvement with the church meant we had the opportunity to escape Auntie's grasp and enjoy time playing with other children our own ages. She didn't like it when we were asked to go anywhere that she couldn't keep an eye on us – she became nervous at the thought. But in the end, she had no option but to allow us to take part.

In the last week of the summer break, we looked forward to the Sunday School picnic. Every year we met at the church to board a hired bus destined for the seaside. The other children piled onto the sands, their chatter and excitement electric – we watched them jump about and when we saw that they didn't get into trouble we did the same.

Mary and George always sat close together, but they were smiling and that was good. Being able to play within a group of happy children and tolerant adults who showed nothing but care and affection towards us was overwhelming and extremely comforting. After taking part in organised games, each child was given a paper bag full of sandwiches, one cake and a drink of juice. Ice cream was served at the end of the day before we boarded the bus for home.

Every time we arrived back from the outing, Auntie was waiting with a sullen face, tapping her stick against the table leg. She didn't want to hear anything about our day. Our bubbles of excitement burst immediately as we entered the house. She made us feel guilty for going and insisted she had been unwell while we were out having fun.

The mental abuse continued all evening and very often we were locked in our rooms until bedtime. We were not fed again that day, as the food we received at the picnic was, she said, enough.

It was hard to understand why she acted in such a manner, especially when we had done nothing wrong. We wanted her to be happy for us, but she said nothing. It was as if she was envious of our good times.

Christmas in this church was also a special time for us. Everyone surrounded us with love. We felt happy there, where we were welcomed openly. We could join in and feel the happiness that surrounded every family at this time of year. There was a small amount of tasteful decoration and a large tree decorated with homemade bits and pieces crafted by the Sunday School children to brighten up one corner, and the carols were sung with enthusiasm. We were always sad when the Christmas service came to an end: we had to return home to a place where happiness and goodwill did not exist.

9

Darkening Nights

Very little excitement came our way during our long stay on the croft, but when the unexpected did happen we made sure that every precious minute of it was savoured and mentally devoured. Amusement, after all, was a rare commodity in our lives and we grasped every opportunity to enjoy a moment of fun.

The summer of 1958 had been warm and sultry. A water ban for all gardens had just been lifted and Mary was starting school in the autumn. Just as we were going to bed, there was a heavy rumbling deep within the chimney breast. At first we thought a bird had flown in and become stuck in the narrow space, but Auntie got flustered, asking if we had put anything unusual onto the fire. We had no idea what she was talking about and our vacant looks and negative responses fuelled her agitation. She jumped to her feet, grabbed her stick from the back of the door and ordered everyone outside. The stick whacked our thin-pyjama-clad bodies and bounced off our bare heels as we jumped across the threshold. She screamed impatiently, pushing everyone out into the warm evening. We couldn't understand why she was behaving this way until we looked skywards in the direction of a hissing, spurting sound. The chimney pot was glowing and a fountain of sparks shot into the night sky.

We watched spellbound as tiny bright flickers of light danced like fireflies in the wind, falling onto the corrugated iron, where they bounced frenetically against the metal roof, disappearing again into the darkness. We were hypnotised as the firework show flared then died down within the space of several minutes; we inhaled the burning smell of hot soot, secretly wishing that the croft would burn down with Auntie inside.

Suddenly, there was a huge crackle and a dull thud from the chimney. We all jumped, including Auntie. A glowing mass spread into millions of red specks, spilling across the rooftop and down to the gutter's edge. The bird's nest teetered there for several seconds, then disappeared into red dust. We clung together, hoping we wouldn't get the blame for this incident, watching Auntie's expression closely for signs of irritation. But she stood quietly, her stick tapping rhythmically on the cement flagstone, and waited until the glow from the chimney pot slowly disappeared into the night. Once everything had calmed down, we were ushered back inside to set about cleaning the grate of burning hot ashes.

As usual, *we* were to blame. Somehow, without her knowledge, we had set the chimney alight and caused the sooty mess that coated the immediate vicinity of the fireplace. We tried to calm the situation by saying sorry for everything, hoping the frenzy would die down, but it was difficult to know quite how to react when she was shouting at us. She could not see through the film of hate that coated her mind and the torment that seeped through her veins. She fidgeted from one foot to the other, rapping the metal grid where we worked, missing our fingers by inches. Once the hot, sooty mess was cleared away and the dark-grey stains splattering our pyjamas cleaned with a wet cloth, we were allowed to go to bed.

Along with the occasions that we were allowed away from the croft to help the neighbours with their harvest work, there were times when Auntie seemed willing for us to take part in outside activities. Her motivation, as always, was her need for praise. She wanted to be complimented on her ability as a foster mother and, on a practical level, required favourable details to put into her yearly report for the welfare officer.

When I was ten, I decided I wanted to take part in the fancy dress competition that was held at the Autumn Fete. To my surprise, Auntie consented, even suggesting that she would make me a costume. I had visions of becoming a beautiful princess, a ballet dancer or Cinderella, but on the day Auntie appeared with an old woollen shawl, a tattered brown curtain (which I wore as a skirt) and a well-worn basket, or creel, filled with cardboard cut-out shapes of fish. The basket was tied to my back with a leather strap. I was horrified, and disappointed. I did not want to go to the fair dressed as a Buckie fishwife! Like a typical young girl, I wanted to look attractive. I felt the costume was degrading and that everyone would laugh at me. I naively thought she was trying to belittle me in front of my friends, underhandedly reminding me of the substandard background I came from. I was never able to achieve her high standards and I felt she was mocking me.

If only she had explained and shared her ideas with me, I would have understood what she was doing and not felt so bad or hated her for it. She became very annoyed at my disappointment, insisting I either go to the fete in her costume or spend the night in the barn. She had spent a long time making the outfit, she said, and was determined to drag me there if necessary. I reluctantly tottered my way to the show, expecting everyone to snigger behind my back, but to my shock and her later amusement I won first prize.

When I came home with my winning certificate, she pulled the costume from me and prodded me forcibly with the basket, scraping the jagged edges across my bare shoulders. She shook me violently, threw me into the corner and stood on my sock-covered toes. Her face was contorted, an image of contempt. She was basking in her success, enjoying every minute. I listened as she continually reminded me of my stupidity, of my immaturity, adding that I would never amount to anything special and to get rid of any fancy ideas or notions I had for the future. She told me that her experiences in life had made her a good judge of character and because I had none to boast about I would find growing up difficult. After all, I was a foster child from the slums of Glasgow. I should always remember my place in society.

She pranced about, waving the outfit in front of me, threatening to make me wear it when school re-opened in a few days unless I did what I was told without question.

Robert and I were held responsible for the actions of our younger siblings. We tried very hard to keep them under control and keep them safe, but I yearned to be able to play with them instead and not have to be aware of everything we said or did. It was so hard to see them sitting in a corner or huddled at the side of the barn out of the wind, trying to keep out of Auntie's way. They often looked so confused and very uncertain of what they were expected to do, while trying to keep out of trouble at the same time. Sometimes Robert and I could hear Auntie shouting and screaming at the younger ones, but we couldn't get in to help them because she had locked the door to keep us out. Other times she would call us in and push us all into one corner, lashing out sporadically as she rattled the door to get our attention. If there was a sudden lull in her crazy behaviour, we all dashed for the front door before she had time to lock it. We could hear her leg scraping across the floor, but we didn't look round – we kept running.

Every muscle in our bodies seemed to tremble with a mixture of fear and amusement if Robert muttered something funny under his breath. This made her scream and shriek like a banshee. But those remarks helped us all to cope. He would shout: 'You've forgotten your broomstick – don't bother looking for it, we've chopped it up for firewood. Now you can't fly! You can't catch us any more!' Or 'If you twist your knickers any further, you'll blow up like a balloon when you fart!' Robert kept us laughing, even though we knew she would beat us later and starve us for the remainder of the day.

We fared better as a result of some circumstances, but they were few and far between. As Mary and George reached the age of six and seven, they became more independent. They began to realise that Auntie could not and did not want to give them love and affection unless she had an ulterior motive. Like Robert and me, they began to grab every light-hearted moment that arose and make the best of it. Those times proved that we could work with Auntie and have a reason for understanding her, albeit to her benefit in the end.

At Halloween, the evening was always relatively calm compared with the normally stressed atmosphere in the croft. Our guardian almost seemed happy as she dressed us in a mixture of rags and crêpe paper. She flitted around on tenterhooks as our excitement increased, her controlled agitation always threatening to burst forth any second. She knew this exercise was important if she wanted the neighbours to think she was encouraging us to take part in certain festivities. She also knew that guising would result in a favourable return. We always arrived home with a basketful of eatable produce with which she could top up her personal food cupboard. Her report to the child authorities would contain a detailed account of the evening and add substance to her so-called 'good' record.

I could see her struggling to maintain a friendly disposition to keep us in the right frame of mind for visiting the neighbouring crofts. She knew that tearful children would give cause for concern and thwart her plans for free food. We wanted to give her a hug – we liked her this way, naively thinking she was being genuine – but when we moved towards her she roughly pushed us out into the night, reminding us to recite our poems and sing our songs properly.

On these nights, she seemed unusually at ease, probably because she knew the crofters, being aware of our home situation, would be kind and generous. She was right, of course. Various items, ranging from biscuits to tins of meat, were placed willingly into our baskets, with extra goodies for us to eat on the move. The crofters played along, making us laugh by pretending to guess who was hiding under our masks, and we believed that they really didn't know. When we arrived home and gave Auntie the basket, we were given a small tea and sent to bed without any sign of trouble or aggression. She looked pleased with our evening's work. Those nights we went to bed reasonably happy and reasonably fed.

Thinking back to these meaningful times, when we could genuinely feel something other than fear, brought back memories of distributing poppies round our area to help fill the collection tin for Remembrance Sunday. For me, this was one of the saddest things I became involved in through the community. By now, I was reaching my teens and, more and more, I felt the pressure of not being wanted. Maybe it was because of the lack of love and affection in my home life that it affected me so much; maybe it was because I was getting older and was becoming more aware of the bigger picture, life beyond the croft. I sometimes felt disconnected from the world around me and getting involved in a project that required a lot of thinking and sensitivity made me realise that this world that I thought was a cruel place for me had also been cruel to many people.

It was the local minister who asked Auntie if I would like to help and she could do nothing really other than agree that it would be good for me. It allowed me to learn a little more about world history and past events, they felt. She also knew that it would help to improve her reputation as a good mother. Personally, it made me feel important and did bring home to me the reality of war and of the soldiers who died to give us all the freedom we have today. All in all, it was an exercise that took me away from the croft and I welcomed it with open arms.

As I wandered round the crofts in the dark, I tried to imagine what the soldiers, many very young, had had to go through. If I looked up at the sky, I could see images in the clouds of Highlanders swinging their kilts as they ran into battle. I could in some way identify with these young men and sympathise with what they had gone through: while they had fought for their country and their families, I, in my own way, was fighting for my life and my sanity. I could, to some extent, feel their fear and anxiety as each day took its toll. I could sense the heaviness in their movements and the sadness that surrounded them at every turn.

I cried for the evil of war, I cried at the injustice of life, I cried as I recited war poems out loud to the darkness around me and I cried for the battle I had lost when my parents deserted me. By the time I reached the last house, I was in need of friendly company. I knew exactly where to go, a place where I would find a kindly soul with a patient heart. As soon as she opened the door, the note of sympathy in her voice welcomed me. It was as if she understood what I and my siblings were going through. There was always a scone at the ready.

I remember her wood-burning stove covered in drying clothes, the smell of soap and the sensation of fresh, damp air filling her house. Her sight was failing badly and she wore spectacles with extra-thick lenses to help her see. A solid wire guard surrounded the hot fire to protect her from severe burns. Nothing fazed her: she chopped sticks with an axe and went for long walks, often taking a wrong turn. Nothing was too much for this lovely old lady and she showed ultimate patience when dealing with inquisitive children.

I soaked-in all the praise I received from wonderful people just like her in the community and revelled in their kindness. I found it hard to understand why our foster mother was so different from them. She lived the same country life, with the same ups and downs as everyone else, but she lacked the warm, friendly, tolerant nature found in all these dear people. She lacked the sympathetic approach needed to survive in this harsh environment.

During this time, I thought more often of my father and how much I missed him. He was forever lost to me and I cried again for this loss. I knew within my heart I would never see him again. I would never sit beside him at the table or listen to his tales of ghost ships or battle cruisers fighting their way across the Atlantic, or laugh when he put his Royal Navy hat on my head, covering my eyes and ears in the process. What had gone wrong, why did he not want me any more? I had given up on my mother. I couldn't understand why she had deserted us and had given up trying. Why had she dismissed us completely? I knew within myself that if I ever became a mother I would die before I hurt my children and the world would have to end before I deserted them. I was determined to put my heart and soul into a future, if I had one, to make a success of anything I did, and I was even more determined that Auntie would not prevent me from doing so. The more positive I became, the more strength I seemed to muster.

I managed to stretch my poppy-distributing over two evenings, in the process collecting a nice hoard of home bakes to hide at the foot of the brae, which I would share with my siblings under the bridge on the way to school the next day.

It was one of our safe places, under this bridge. Auntie couldn't see us and we could sit in shadow, sheltered from the weather, eating everything we'd managed to save or acquire from other sources. Sometimes it was a small morsel, other times a mini feast. We consoled one another, laughed at silly jokes and wished for a fairy godmother to transport us to a happy place while we sat here. We yelled at the world and screamed as a steam train passed overhead, chasing the clouds of steam to the other side. We cried for our parents and the hopelessness we faced every day. This bridge was our refuge. It was where we prepared ourselves for the journey home and the fate that awaited us. It was like being in a mother's womb, cocooned from harm and safe from outside pressure. We wanted to stay there, but we couldn't.

* * *

Many instances served to highlight Auntie's instability and another at about this time serves to illustrate the harsh environment around us. It was Mary's seventh birthday and Auntie had given us bread and butter covered in sugar for our supper. We whispered 'Happy birthday' to her over the kitchen table. It was late summer and very mild. The evening sun had slid beneath the horizon and dusk was falling. Auntie ordered us outside after we'd finished eating and told us to stand in line. She placed a white cloth on our heads and told us she was going to do an experiment.

She said someone had told her that bats were attracted to white material. She said she had an interest in bat behaviour and we would be taking part in this exercise. She was animated, demonstrating the flight patterns of these little creatures by swooping and circular hand gestures. She told us about bats that sucked the blood from animals and children, clicking her tongue as she watched us squirm at the very thought of it. Then she warned us to keep still unless we wanted to be bitten. It made little sense to us and I have never understood the reason why Auntie did this. She had nothing to gain, except the thrill she seemed to get from witnessing the fear we experienced as something touched our heads and tugged at the cloth. She stood behind us, her breath spurting in short gasps as she flitted about from child to child, tormenting, touching, hissing. We were afraid to move.

Sometimes the pressure became too much for Mary and she screamed and shuddered as Auntie announced, 'Here they come again.' I remember her desperately clinging to my arm, staring at the ground, as Auntie tried to drag her from me. She raised her head now and again to get her balance, taking care to avoid eye contact with this screeching woman. Of all the punishments Auntie could inflict on Mary, being locked out and the dark were her greatest fears. I saw her glance into the darkening night, into the endless silence that would haunt the fields and surround her. I could almost see, with great effort and remarkable control, a deliberate change in her behaviour, to pacify Auntie and to suit the moment. I watched as she reached out to me, hesitated, gained a strength of confidence unusual for Mary, then slowly and quietly calmed down, allowing Auntie to drag her away from me. She stood alone quietly, shivering and waiting.

I felt emotionally naked: I couldn't help her any more. Once we were separated, our foster mother kept Mary at a distance. If my sister moved in any direction, Auntie whacked her with a stick and screamed into her face. I felt so sorry for her. Although I never saw those bats, either because they flew too fast for my eyes to spot in the fading light or they didn't exist in the first place, I could picture them, silent, threatening, weaving their swooping patterns over and around us. By the time this exercise was over, Mary was a nervous wreck and Auntie was in some kind of dream-like trance. She drained all she could from that little girl and left us all mentally exhausted. Outside in the dark, we comforted and supported one another. School was due to start after the summer break and we couldn't wait. At least Mary and George would be safer there, away from Auntie's clutches.

Every year, as the nights darkened and winter drew near, the work on the croft increased. Animals and buildings had to be prepared for a long hard spell of cold, extra wood needed to be dragged home and cut into logs for firewood, and any broken planks on the sheds had to be repaired, or, if the holes were small, patched with hessian sacks soaked in tar.

Most of our extra work was done in the fading light of a winter's evening and when the outside jobs were completed we were given tasks of a different nature. Some were very interesting, but the majority were things Auntie did not want to do herself.

Covering most of the floorboards were handmade rugs consisting of old crêpe stockings and pieces of cloth cut into long strips. Old potato sacks were stretched onto a wooden frame and these strips of material were crocheted into the sack backing with a large metal hook. This built up into a thick tapestry of multicoloured designs and was very warm and comfortable to sit on, especially when the evenings dragged into early mornings and we had nothing to do but sit and watch the frost bite into the small panes of glass, carving incredible patterns of ice crystals across the cold window, every design different and every one an artist's masterpiece.

Unlike it is for children of today, new socks were rarely available. When holes appeared, they were darned over a mushroom-shaped wooden implement. I enjoyed doing this; it was fascinating to watch the hole disappear gradually, each strand of wool weaving new life into the torn sock. As long as I worked diligently and without complaint, Auntie remained content. If I became distracted or my progress slowed for any reason, she became impatient with me. I was surprised on one occasion when she grabbed the metal hook I was holding and viciously stabbed the back of my hand with the blunt end, making me promise to fully concentrate on the work in hand.

On winter evenings when everything was covered in snow, the monotony of trying to look busy was relieved by necessary outside work. It was an immense relief to escape from the cramped atmosphere of the croft and the unpredictable nature of Auntie. We had been five years at Coxton and had by now acclimatised to the extremes of country weather. Even so, the beauty of a clear winter night brought a freshness that did not exist inside the croft. The night cracked in the silence, as we stepped into the cold air. Streams of stars spread across the rich navy sky, and through the woods blue-white lights sparkled from small windows dotted round the countryside. The coldness stuck to our nostrils and stung our wet lips. Icicles hung from the corrugated iron roof and dripped endlessly onto packed snow. A strange quietness hung over the croft. Every little noise was heard for miles.

The most distinguishable sound came from the sheep shuffling about as they huddled together to keep warm. Part of our job was to encourage them to change position regularly and prevent them from sticking to the ice-coated ground. They had a tendency to shelter near the outbuildings, away from the strong biting winds and blizzard conditions that could last all night, and it wasn't unusual to come out in the early morning and find an old sheep frozen to the spot. During the night, strong winds buffeted the snow-laden bushes, causing the branches to snap and break on top of any sheep that was sheltering nearby. The sheep didn't move until we physically lifted the twigs; they didn't seem to have the sense to free themselves and the weaker ones did not survive.

By the time our evening work was finished, our hands and faces stung and throbbed with ice-coldness. We longed for a warm drink or a heat by the fire, anything that would get the circulation back into our fingers and ease the pain that pulsated through our limbs. Sometimes, if we were very lucky, I was allowed to boil a kettle and make tea, but most nights we received nothing.

Our clothes were soaking wet and stuck to our bodies like glue. We were frightened to ask Auntie for a towel in case she responded with a shout or a scream, and we didn't want to upset her. I think she just didn't notice we were wet and it didn't cross her mind that the younger ones might have needed her help.

Once in our bedrooms, we used blankets from the bed to dry ourselves, then crawled under the covers to seek warmth, hoping that Auntie would not come for us in the middle of the night.

Occasionally, our evenings were spent listening to the wireless, which was tuned in to programmes we couldn't understand. We were not allowed to converse with one another unless it related to schoolwork. Robert would sit quietly in the corner until bedtime, his eyes grave and his expression serious, very often without supper, his bottom throbbing from a prior beating. The two youngest ones were found either huddled together on a cold mat or standing shivering in a corner, frightened to move or talk for fear that Auntie would lash out at them. Her stick was always at the ready to strike a disobedient child, her good foot poised for contact with a tiny leg if it happened to get in her way.

Mary and George wanted nothing more than to escape to their beds and hide under the covers, where they felt safe. They needed this rest to strengthen their minds and bodies for the horrors of the next day. Sometimes I felt brave enough to suggest that they would be better in bed and offered to take Mary through to her room. This, in turn, drew Auntie's attention to George and he too was allowed to leave the living room. I could see the relief in their eyes as they got up to leave. It was the only thing I could do to get them away from the stressful atmosphere of that room.

Some nights Auntie was so lost in her own chaotic thoughts that she ignored everything I said. Time lost its meaning and no one got to bed early. We had no choice but to wait quietly and patiently until she decided it was lights out, then we were finally able to retire.

Before electricity was installed in the house, paraffin was

collected from the village or brought to the croft by a van to fill the tilly lamps. On winter evenings, the room was bathed in a bone-whiteness from these lamps, coating our faces in a pallid glow – a ghostly look – with dark shadows etching deep into our skin. A plunger on the base was pressed in like a bicycle pump at regular intervals to maintain the pressure of the glow. If we forgot to take turns, Auntie yelled and thumped the table, making everyone jump with fright. The corners of the room were always in shadow; an orange flicker darted from the lit fireplace, causing these shadows to pulsate in every direction, creating fragmented images across the table where we sat. It was the nearest we could get to the fire, though Auntie's body seemed to consume any heat before it had a chance to reach us, with the result we always felt cold. When she left the room to go outside to the toilet, I often grabbed the poker and moved the embers around to free the trapped flames within. She caught me on one occasion and hit me with the red-hot end. My hands nipped for days. That was her job – I was told I must not touch the fire in case I put it out. She said there was a certain way to stoke a fire to keep it burning and I lacked the necessary experience. And I believed her.

By the time I reached my teens, Auntie was 64 and seemed slightly more approachable. When I caught her in a reasonably quiet mood, I found that I was able to ask about her past. This engaged her in a conversation that lasted most of the evening and resulted in a less stressful atmosphere, allowing the nights to pass without serious incident. She talked about her sweetheart who had been drowned at sea when his merchant ship was sunk by the Germans during the First World War, of visiting London and dressing in the modern clothes of the 1930s. She showed me photographs of a happy, attractive woman, who in no way reflected the person sitting beside me. She spoke of her time as a nurse in the fever hospital in Carlisle; the bicycle accident at the end of the Second World War that had injured her right leg and the surgery she received at the time that caused the paralysis of the knee joint.

The accident ended her career in nursing and forced her into the mundane job of housekeeper and eventual owner of her employer's croft. I began to realise that her past had affected her badly and scarred her mentally for life. After listening to every detail and hearing the emotion in her voice, I wanted to understand her ways, her moods. I wanted to please her. But she did not let me close enough.

As long as I sat beside her on the floor and stroked her straight leg, she remained calm. The monotonous scraping of flesh on crêpe stocking filled the room and, for a short moment, the sharpness in her voice melted into a comfortable drone. I could tell that she had many regrets by the manner in which she told her story. The haunting look in her eyes and the trembling of her fingers said it all, as did her occasional laboured sighs, as she stopped to flick her ash into the fireplace.

Fostering us was a desperate attempt to bring her life into focus, to settle her mind in the company of young children and, by doing so, inadvertently accept her past and heal the mental wounds that disturbed her waking hours, but she had forgotten the most important part. She needed to be able first and foremost to understand those immature minds, to respond favourably and sympathetically to their needs as children, and be able in herself to cope with any rejection they might show at the beginning of their stay. After all, she was the adult with years of experience behind her.

Always, after these intimate chats, nothing would change. The next morning she would continue to abuse us whenever she needed to feel superior and her violent outbursts frequently bordered on profane insanity.

From our very first winter at the croft, it was the job of Robert and me to go into the fields in the mornings before school and break the ice or clear the snow from the sheep's feeding troughs and fill them up with a mixture of warm, wet oats and hard pellets. There was an old ram named Johnny who waited for me each morning and when I turned my back to fill the feeding trays, he used to butt me with his hard nose. Every time he knocked me over, he sniffed into my ear, pawed at the ground and walked away with what seemed like a look of disgust. He never hurt me, but it was difficult to finish the job when he was in that kind of mood. It was practically impossible to keep at bay the icy wind and blinding snow that stung my eyes and chilled my fingers while watching out for Johnny's antics. I eventually asked the shepherd to make a smaller trough, just for the ram. This enabled me to feed him first and it worked perfectly. On the odd occasion, Johnny strutted his authority, letting me know that this was his territory. He was 'King of the Field' and he knew it!

Once the animals were fed, cut logs were brought into the house to light the fire and newspapers were rolled into rings to act as firelighters. Auntie lay in her warm bed all the while, shouting orders, impatiently waiting for me to make the porridge and get the younger ones ready for school. She ate her breakfast and pretended to fall asleep again until everyone was ready to leave the house.

We wanted someone to look after us for a change, to wake us up in the morning with a friendly 'Good morning' and help us with whatever jobs we had to do. For once, it would have been nice to get up to a steaming bowl of porridge and a warm crackling fire lit by a friendly and trusting parent. But Robert and I worked well together and once all the outside jobs were completed, we turned our attention to the younger ones: while he concentrated on helping George, I gave all my attention to Mary.

For the first three years at the croft, Robert's main responsibility in the morning was to collect water from the well. It was situated below ground level, so it never froze solid and just a few taps with a stone broke the icy surface. After that a cold water tap and sink were installed in the main house, making it slightly easier for us all.

There was so much work to do in the morning that we were often late for school. Sometimes if Auntie was in a vindictive frame of mind, she would not let us into the house to change into our school clothes. She knew lessons had started but appeared to enjoy our discomfort. By the time we reached school on those mornings, the early session was well under way and we were scared to go into the class and face our playmates and inquisitive teacher. Each time, we were scolded and given extra homework – homework that Auntie did not allow time for. We wanted to explain, to tell her that it was not our fault, but we knew she would not believe us.

Sometimes the stress of being late was so intense we couldn't face the repeated embarrassment of standing in the middle of the classroom and thinking up a believable reason why we had not arrived on time. We wanted to tell the truth, but knew we couldn't. Instead we walked about the countryside, often hungry and cold, until we saw the other children going home at the end of the day. If it had been exceptionally cold or wet, we sneaked into the lunch hall for dinner and joined the afternoon session, hoping the teacher would accept our weak explanation of sickness without a note.

Very little was ever said about our irregular attendance and usually the school day passed without incident; however, one day, in my final year at primary, the teacher asked me to stay behind after morning lessons and asked if I was having any problems at home and if she could help. I plucked up enough courage to confide in her, trying to explain what life was like on the croft. She listened patiently and sympathetically, then allowed me to finish my story and go for lunch. I don't know if she believed me, but as far as I know she never reported anything to a higher authority. My story must have been mentioned in the teachers' coffee room because it suddenly became easier for us to sneak into class without confrontation or threat of extra homework.

Winter made our daily tasks more difficult and added to the burden that was life at Coxton. The intense cold was hardest to bear: it permeated through our bodies and numbed our senses. The absence of heat in our bedrooms prevented our clothes and footwear from drying out completely, so they were soaked in a perpetual dampness throughout the season. We seemed to shiver continuously and sought shelter in sheds, under hedges or against any available wall.

As the years went by, the lack of warmth and undernourishment took a toll on our health, resulting in a continuous stream of viruses and runny noses until the first relief of spring gave us a chance to recover from the severe weather.

On icy mornings before the milkman delivered bottles to the croft, we took it in turn to cycle or walk to the main farm. By the time we got home, ice crystals had formed throughout the milk. Auntie would give us a short, sharp lecture about taking too long, then the churn was placed in a warm basin of water to thaw. This churn held enough to keep Auntie going while we were at school, where free milk was given to all pupils on a daily basis. In the evening, if we were lucky, the remainder of the churn was watered down for a drink at suppertime.

When the fields were covered in snow, the chickens, geese and ducks were not allowed to wander away from the croft, and every morning and night they had to be fed and watered. At the weekends, the shed doors were opened wide and we were given full responsibility for their safekeeping. We kept a close eye on their progress and made every effort to keep them within the confines of their sheds. It was especially difficult to find the white geese against the snow-filled fields if any of them escaped unnoticed. The whiteness was blinding and hurt our eyes, as we frantically searched for movement in the snow. We knew we had to find them before darkness fell, otherwise Auntie would keep us outside until the birds were returned safely; we also knew that we would be punished for letting them out in the first place.

The white vista was immense and seemed to go on forever, broken only by small patches of trodden snow at the shed openings and a shining sludge of brown earth dotted round the hens' enclosure, where chickens scratched like fury, pecking at every tasty morsel they could find. They were the jesters of winter, the jitterbugs of time and the trusting flibbertigibbets of all living things. They lived within a cacophony of sounds: thawing ice as it crashed to the ground, incessant scraping and snorting as animals searched for food, constantly dripping water as it splashed into the rain barrel and the disturbing sobs of neglected children hiding among dilapidated sheds seeking refuge from the cruel world around them. In a world where silence can be deafening, the variety of noises filtering through the air became somehow comforting: it was a lifeline to sanity and reminded us that all living things, including us, had to survive the harshest of environments.

We soon learned that geese are excellent guard dogs. They alerted us to the arrival of all strangers, and to Auntie they served as an alarm bell. She had the extraordinary ability to impress any person who came for a short visit. She could distract them with a fabricated story, with deliberate intent to deceive, or concoct a misleading mirage of lies, an illusory account of life on the croft with her foster children, and send visitors away with an image of unselfish devotion. The geese were her security, keeping intrusion into her territory to a minimum and helping her control the intrusion to suit her own purpose.

The birds flapped their wings at anyone they didn't recognise or anyone with the audacity to turn their backs and run! They charged, hissing and squawking, in a display that terrified everyone who came near the house. Over time, we learned to live with those birds, learned to understand their strange idiosyncrasies and treated them with respect.

George, the gander, was a powerful presence. He guarded his partner, Jenny, with fervour. It was a passionate enthusiasm that bonded the two birds for life. One day while she was sitting on eggs, I attempted to enter their enclosure to fill their food dish. After a few episodes of hissing and feet-slapping, he reluctantly allowed the empty bowl to be filled, but as I moved back towards the entrance I was cornered against the fence, unable to move any further. I stepped slowly sideways towards the gate, he followed, neck outstretched ready to attack. I was still very unsure and afraid of him, and that fear caused me to react instinctively. I could feel my pulse racing as I reached out with both hands, grabbed hold of his neck and swung him off his feet, throwing him away from the gate. He landed on his feet with a dull thud, a fluster of feathers, a few squawks and a shake of his head. While he recovered from the sudden shock, I rushed through the gate. I spoke to him over the fence to make sure he was unharmed. From that day onwards, he kept his distance, always giving me a wide berth, and as long as I respected his territory he tolerated me.

Winter was the season when these birds required extra care. The geese were heavy birds and had a tendency to slide dangerously on the ice-covered paths. When they were out of their enclosure, it was imperative to keep them moving. If they decided to rest on the ground for any length of time, their webbed feet stuck to the spot and warm water had to be trickled round where they stood to release them.

Winter activities revolved round the animals, keeping them fed and watered – their welfare was paramount. Our need for warmth, comfort and nourishment didn't seem to matter to Auntie. I tried to tell her that we were cold and hungry; I tried to ask her why she was so unreasonable, why she treated us the way she did. But I got nothing in return.

When I began to show signs of teenage rebellion, I spent most of my time standing outside, whether it was in the pouring rain to cool me off or out in the snow to sharpen my mind. Those times I would sneak into the henhouse, trying very hard not to disturb the birds. I knew if the hens became too restless Auntie would know I was in their shed and drag me back outside to stand to attention. I relaxed as the warmth seeped into my body, giving instant relief from the cold shrieking wind or the sharp sting of driving hailstones. I cuddled down amongst the straw and listened for the click of the house door, which meant I was expected to be back outside, standing where she had left me. I was determined to keep secret my place of shelter. It was to be one that I would use over and over again.

When the croft was snowbound, snowdrifts covered the windows in a blue, eerie whiteness. It felt as if we were sealed inside a cocoon, or under the sea looking out through thick, cold foam. It was like being inside an igloo. The bone-whiteness reflected into the croft and shone much-needed brightness into the hallway. This whiteness stretched over the roof and completely enveloped the building. The front door, our only means of entry and exit, had to be cleared every morning before breakfast. When severe weather was forecast over the wireless, we had to dig our way through massive folds of snow with a spade that sat inside, against the grandfather clock. On these mornings, Auntie was unusually lenient and patient. I assume she thought we would work harder to clear the eight-foot snowdrifts if she left us alone – that way her animals would be fed more quickly. But clearing large amounts of snow is very difficult: where do you start?

I remember George and Mary, being the smallest, rushing into the drift, pushing themselves forward by tunnelling with their hands. Robert and I smiled at each other because they looked like little moles scurrying to dig the biggest hole. The snow was soft and fluffy, so was easily manoeuvred. We stamped with our feet to flatten a path into the middle. The drifts sloped away from the house and got easier to clear as we moved forward. Path after path was cleared and the exercise kept us warm. By the time we had finished, the whole place looked like a complicated maze of white mounds, the way finally cleared to feed the animals and get to the barn for firewood. The snow was piled to such a great height that Auntie could not see us from the house window, so we were able to fit in a few moments of quiet play in between our jobs.

That day it took a long time to finish everything and by the end of the morning we were famished. We went inside looking for food but, as usual, I had to make porridge for everyone. Auntie was still in bed waiting for her 'servants' to feed her.

10

Towards Christmas

During the school holidays and term breaks, the days seemed to go on for ever. Endless chores were completed and more invented to keep us occupied. We were never finished for the day: there was no relaxation and no play. When Auntie ran out of ideas, we were locked in our rooms with nothing to do and only allowed out again if she had thought up something for us to do or to accept punishment for some crime.

Auntie always found different ways to demean us – initially it was through violence and fear, then she started to use verbal abuse. She seemed to enjoy telling us that we came from the slums of Glasgow and were good-for-nothings. She never tired of saying that we should be grateful that she had taken us in, that no one had wanted us, which was probably true but it was the last thing we wanted to hear at that time.

I was determined to prove her wrong and did my best to act in what I thought was a 'ladylike' manner, always trying to show consideration and sensitivity to everyone I met. I concentrated on good manners and respect always for the other person. At times my behaviour annoyed Auntie, to the extent that she found it necessary to mock me. Her mimicry and comments intended to insult and hurt. She was determined to undermine any progress I made towards development of mind and feeling. She addressed me as 'Lady Muck' or 'Miss Prim and Proper', imitating me in a calculated and controlled way. She once forced me outside to march up and down the path with a white glove on one hand, waving to her as I passed. She found this highly amusing. If I stopped without being told to, she pushed my arm above my head and smacked my elbow with a stick, her face so close to mine that thick spittle, her clots of malice, stuck to my eyelashes. Her eyes looked as if they might pop out from their sockets and her cigarette danced sporadically between her lips.

While I was parading up and down, I suddenly realised she was following close behind me; I could hear her bad leg scraping along the ground, small stones and hens' dirt spraying the back of my legs, her rasping breath blowing against my neck. Without warning, she grabbed my hands and inspected my nails. She nipped and squeezed them with the tips of her fingers, twisting and pulling them, asking why I was using a white pencil to paint the inside of my nails. I didn't know what she was talking about.

The volume of her voice increased and I felt my stomach tighten. She let go of one hand and I knew to duck, as a slap or a fistful of knuckles pressing into my cheek was about to come. I knew she wanted me to admit to using a pencil and prove that I was the disobedient and flighty child she thought I was, but I couldn't because I wasn't. It wasn't my fault that my nails were unusually white and I took great pride in keeping them neat and tidy. I had never seen the type of pencil she was talking about and, after a few minutes of sharp pain, she let go. She then bent down and scooped a handful of mud from the wet ground and proceeded to squeeze the dirt under my fingernails. I was horrified. I felt sick and dirty.

I tried to make sense of what she was doing as she waved my hands in the air. I knew I had done nothing to deserve this, but I knew I couldn't stop her. I pleaded with her, but she ignored me. I tried to forget the pain and had no option but to let her drag me round the sheds until she tired.

I wanted to think about something else, to blank out the hurt, hoping it would end soon. My mind raced back several years to an incident at the children's home when I was seven. It was the first and last time I was given the strap at school, for throwing a stone in the playground. I was playing with friends when I noticed a boy following me around. No matter where I went, he was behind me at every turn. I became so exasperated I picked up the first stone I could find and threatened to hit him if he didn't leave me alone, but he persisted. I ran into the girls' toilet, knowing he couldn't logically follow me inside, but he did. I was so shocked and incensed that I instinctively threw the stone and accidentally hit him on the face.

Before I knew what was happening, a teacher had rushed in and pulled me into the classroom, where I was told to hold out my hand and was smacked sharply with the belt. I hadn't meant to be bad at the age of seven, and I hadn't meant to be bad now. I had acted impulsively then and accepted I had to be punished for it, but now I was confused. I was beginning to think it didn't matter what I did, it was going to be seen as bad anyway.

My hands were hurting, just like they had been after the strap several years ago. I couldn't wait till she released her hold; I couldn't wait to run from this mad person. She pushed me against the wall and released her grip, and I ran round the side of the house and scrubbed my hands in the rain bucket. It crossed my mind that I might spend the rest of my life obsessed with cleaning my nails, never managing however much I washed. But I was being silly and overreacting – I was being a neurotic little child. The nightmare scenario passed in a flash of dismissal and, shivering incessantly with cold and pent-up emotion, I concentrated on removing the muddy mess from my nails. When I returned to the front of the house, Auntie was gone and the moment was over.

We tried very hard to avoid punishment when possible, but somehow it found us. Extreme physical and mental discomfort was something we all had to endure. The mental journey of adjusting to our new environment was proving to be a long one and Auntie was becoming impatient with our slow progress. Our time was spent continually looking for a way to escape punishment and finding a situation that might lessen the stress this inevitably caused.

There were times when I was literally suffering from mental exhaustion. Over years, I listened to the same taunts, day after day: I was good for nothing; everything I did was inadequate; that I would turn out like my mother, an irresponsible adult who not only couldn't look after herself but also failed miserably as a mother and a wife. Everything I tried to do was condemned, or scorned, or destroyed in front of me.

I desperately needed to retain some self-respect and hang on to my self-esteem. I think that is why Auntie did her best to staunch my 'Miss Prim and Proper' attitude; at times I think she felt I was taking over and was succeeding in the fight of mental gymnastics. I often found it easier to pretend I was someone else and became lost in my imagination; it was better to assume a make-believe character rather than accept what I was: a foster child with very little hope of a great future. In my hut in the woods, I was an explorer; with my books of poetry, I fled into a world of illusion and possibility: my dog Flogal listened faithfully to my fantasy adventures and the many attempts I made to build my self-confidence to a level that I could handle, keeping in mind the necessity to retain a sensible outlook well within the boundaries of normality.

As the years progressed and each season presented different difficulties to solve and more opportunities for us to improve our daily routine, we became adept at working along with nature and taking advantage of Auntie and her methods. Winter provided several occasions to make the moment work in our favour, especially when the weather was bad. School, for instance, was difficult to reach after a heavy snowfall, but we always made a concerted effort to get there, despite the cold wind and deep snow. If word came from the headmaster via the neighbours that school was cancelled due to bad weather, we conveniently forgot to pass this message to Auntie and went anyway. A morning spent under the bridge or just walking in the snow was better than being locked in our bedrooms for most of the day.

Sometimes en route to school the snow was so deep that the only visible features on the landscape were several inches of fence posts, sticking up like black dots above the drifts. This gave us a rough idea where the road was. The snow was blindingly white, with a hard crisp surface, and took our weight nicely. We managed to walk quite a distance before we plunged to our waists into hidden ditches or dips in the fields. It evolved into a game, as we manoeuvred ourselves past every obstacle, laughing all the way to school. It didn't matter if we arrived late on days like that because we had a good excuse, and if by midday the wind had risen, bringing more snow to fill up the roads, and the headmaster decided that 'long distance' pupils should head for home, off we set into gale-force winds and horizontally drifting snow.

One specific day, Robert and I struggled for several yards, finding the way forward very difficult. We were tired and eventually sat down at the side of the road. After several minutes huddled together, a neighbour with his tractor stopped to check if we were all right. He seemed concerned and said we must keep moving or the cold would numb our bodies. He told us to walk behind him and follow his wheel tracks. The powdery snow sprayed up from the churning wheels like foam from an angry sea and the snow crystals seemed to hang in the air, sparkling in the single light from the driver's cab. By the time we reached the crossroads, we looked like two tiny snowmen.

We followed the tractor past the railway bridge, where the farmer had to take the other road. He told us to hold on to the fence posts until we caught sight of home. We arrived at the croft, shivering but safe. Auntie did not notice we were cold; she did not care. She was snug as a bug in her little house, everything done for her by four little children who struggled day and night to please her, who coped with heat, rain, wind and snow to work her croft and who wanted, more than anything, to be loved and cared for by her.

Her indifference and callous attitude to the conditions we found ourselves in was clear one day when the headmaster, who had received a storm warning, decided, as usual, to send his pupils home early. Before we had gone any distance, the sky darkened and a snowstorm burst from everywhere. Icy winds turned the air into sleet, making us shiver involuntarily into our coats. The snow battered against our heads, our noses and chins stung with cold, and visibility turned to zero. It wasn't long before we had lost our way and could go no further. We noticed the dark outline of a shed or outbuilding and decided to shelter behind it. We huddled into the lee of the dyke at the side of this building, the frosted stone striking a chill through the clothes we were wearing. It was so cold – the icy wind bit into our cheeks, forcing us to crouch closer together in an effort to stay warm.

After a time, I don't know how long, we began to feel quite sleepy and actually much warmer. Little did we know what a dangerous situation we were in. Hours seemed to pass and it was getting dark. We were scared and knew that we should try to reach home, but we did not know in which direction to walk. I was getting desperate and very concerned for my brothers and sister, and was on the point of coaxing them out into the cold when I felt someone tug at my sleeve and lift me up. We were put into a tractor bogey and covered in sacks. The man had been out chopping some firewood when he heard little Mary crying. He recognised us and took us home.

I am sure this man saved our lives. The majority of houses in those days didn't have telephones, especially in outlying districts. A red phone box was the main source of telecommunication, and schools were therefore not able to let parents know to expect their children home early. Auntie was pacing up and down as we walked in and this time I think she was relieved to see us. We were glad to be home, but very apprehensive. We knew we would be in trouble again for drawing attention to ourselves and taking an outsider home. In that moment, we wanted to be spoiled, to be reassured and comforted.

We put our wet schoolbags into the hall and went into the living room, hoping for a hot drink. Auntie was standing in front of the sink, pointing to the front door. We were home safe and no one cared, nothing would ever change.

Quietly and obediently, we went back outside to do our evening chores without any warming nourishment, dry clothes or sympathy. We went hungry to bed that night, still shivering. It took us a long time to feel warm again, physically and mentally.

We could do nothing about our wet clothes, which were still damp when we put them on again in the morning. My rubber boots remained wet and mouldy for most of the winter; towards spring, when rains and warming winds made the snow wet and slushy, I developed severe chilblains. The itch was intense and came with a hot burning pain that woke me up in the middle of the night. The more I rubbed, the sorer it got. I was refused sensible help and chastised for causing a fuss. Auntie would douse my feet, first in cold water, then hot. The pain was excruciating. She held them for several seconds in the heat, refusing to notice my struggle. By the time she was finished, tears were streaming down my face. I couldn't sob out loud; I couldn't show ungratefulness. The heat intensified the itch and I was so desperate to soothe the irritation that I tried everything from butter to toothpaste. I found the answer in a tin of Gibbs toothpaste – the relief was outstanding and the discomfort eased dramatically. I was glad when the snow disappeared and once again I could wear normal footwear.

Our shoes often remained damp all weekend and on a Friday evening had to be polished for school on Monday morning. No matter how much polish was added to the wet leather, a dull shine was all we could achieve. This made Auntie very angry, and usually during Sunday night, just as we were drifting off to sleep, we were dragged out of bed to shine those shoes again with her little Shetland sheepdog yapping and nipping at our bare heels.

The dull weather and dark nights reflected Auntie's moods and during the winter months she seemed to be more down than usual. Her tolerance decreased even further and she was unwilling to go outside even to the toilet. She had a pail that was kept by the sofa and the boys were forced to empty this pail several times a day. Her insistence was relentless: she gave the excuse that she had been sick and wasn't able to empty it herself.

The weeks leading up to the festive season were miserable and depressing. Auntie continued to be restless and shouted at the slightest thing. We could do nothing right; in fact, she even seemed pleased when she found a reason to hurt us. She called us liars and threw anything she could find in our direction; she pranced around, flicking her stick and striking our legs; she hissed and called us buggers of hell. She did not like us and we knew it.

Every time we passed her flaying body, we had to give it a wide berth, for if we were caught it was extremely difficult to get away. She hung on to us, twisting our hair, our fingers or our skin. She dragged us over the floor and out into the cold and left us lying in a heap. We pleaded with her to stop, but this made her worse. Speaking to her was the only thing we could do in the hope she would eventually hear us and let go. Sometimes it worked and the pain ended, but most times she released her hold when she herself had had enough.

As Christmas drew near, it was time to round up the geese and ducks that we had looked after since they'd hatched. It was the most unpleasant of all our tasks. All those lovely birds, most of whom we had given names, were caught and killed by us for the butcher. He was due to come the week before Christmas Eve to take the prepared birds away and the pressure on us to make this deadline was immense. It was difficult working under these conditions as Auntie flustered around us, shouting and screaming orders. Her feelings for those birds had changed from concern to hate and very often she threw them at us. It didn't seem to matter how she handled them any more, as they had come to the end of their usefulness.

Hens and ducks are fairly easy to handle once you know how, but geese are heavy and awkward. So it was nearly impossible for us to break a goose's neck – our hands were just not strong enough. The only successful way was to place a stick across the neck of the bird, stand on each end of the stick and pull as hard as we could until the bone snapped. It was the cruellest thing she ever forced me to do and I cried until I was finished. Auntie stood with a stick as well, but hers was used for whacking our legs if we refused to do the job. She would egg us on by threatening us with a beating. It was normal practice in crofts for hand-reared birds to be killed in this manner during the festive period, but with so many of us under ten years of age we were not ready mentally for this adult exercise.

One night leading up to the celebrations, I was out hunting for a lost cat. The fields were covered in thick snow and the stars shone like diamonds in the navy sky. I had asked Auntie the day before if I could go to the carol practice in the village. I felt I was old enough at 11 to look after myself, but I was not allowed. I could hear them singing. It was beautiful. The music and the visual imagery of a peaceful world made me feel very sad and I longed to be part of it. The melody filtered through the trees and quivered in the slightest breeze. Whenever I recognised a tune, I sang as loud as I could. The carols opened my mind and stole every bad thought and memory. The music temporarily freed me from anxiety and lulled me into a world of euphoria. It seemed to be the most natural way, apart from my poetry, of free expression and emotional control. I didn't think anyone could hear me, but on reflection, if I could hear the singers from nearly two miles away, the neighbouring crofts could hear me, too. I was in my own little world, where I felt nothing could harm me. Although I was alone, the calmness was overwhelming and made me cry. I wanted a hug, but no one was there.

Every Christmas Eve, I got the job of preparing the goose that either Robert or I had killed earlier in the week. It was cleaned, stuffed with oatmeal and onions, and covered in dripping, ready for the oven the next day. Robert topped and tailed the sprouts, scraped the carrots and peeled the potatoes, and then we both made the fruit jelly. I have no idea where all that food went because our helpings were so small. Our plates were filled mainly with vegetables and one slice of white meat. If we didn't eat everything, we didn't get the jelly.

The first few Christmas mornings stockings were at the foot of our beds and we had to write to our child welfare officer in Glasgow to tell him what we ate and the presents we received. But it was not long before this stopped altogether.

Christmas was not a happy time. We got presents from other people, but I don't remember what happened to them. The more we got, the more she made us feel that we were not entitled to them. She called them rubbish and several were broken or discarded by her. There was never a relaxed, family atmosphere in that house and because of Auntie's behaviour we were afraid to be happy. Her stare was hypnotic and our eyes never left her face when she was talking to us. Her whole demeanour made me feel terribly insecure and self-conscious. It was as if she was monitoring every movement and anticipating our next reaction. We continually tiptoed round her volatile persona, avoiding igniting the slightest spark that might trigger her fragile frustrations.

Every time she detected a hint of light-heartedness in our behaviour, she quickly dampened down our spirits by hitting us or ordering us into a corner. Once in that corner, she trapped us with a piece of furniture and proceeded to lash out. We couldn't move and had to wait until her fit of anger was over, then we were released. We desperately wanted her to like us, and sometimes we could see her trying, but she was never able to quite get there. I felt sorry for her sometimes and tried to speak to her, but she would not react to friendly talk. The only way I could successfully communicate with her was on an educational level. Whether it was a news update, a flash from her past or a subject at school that I thought might interest her, these subjects often saved the day and gave us all a rest.

We wanted to be good, wanted to receive praise, yearned for a little kindness and understanding, but we didn't know how to go about it. We tried everything from being extra nice and helpful to keeping our rooms tidy and our clothes as clean as possible. Nothing worked.

One year Robert and I received sweetie money during our Christmas holidays for a small job we did for a neighbour. We thought we would buy Auntie a present, hoping that we could stay in her good books for a while. We went to the village shop and the assistant gave us a small box of perfumed hearts to put into Auntie's chest of drawers. When she opened the parcel, the look of horror on her face frightened us and we backed away against the wall, wondering what we had done wrong this time. She wrongfully assumed we had bought soap and became very angry, accusing us of suggesting that she needed a wash.

She went to the sink, filled the kettle and once the water was hot enough, poured some into a basin. Robert at ten was nearly as tall as Auntie, and she had to push him to the ground before she could grab his hair. She pulled us across the room, ordered us to strip and wash with the pretty coloured hearts. We scrubbed diligently, trying to work up a lather, until they finally gave up the ghost and broke into tiny pieces. Muttering continuously, she tipped the basin of lukewarm water over us and pushed us onto our knees to dry the floor. She flicked the towel across our necks as we worked and told us not to buy such rubbish again. She said we should have given her the money to help with the household bills.

We were so hurt and sad that our attempts to befriend her had failed. We swore there and then that it would be the first and last time we bought her anything. Life with this woman was difficult and soul destroying.

This episode urged us to branch out into our surroundings and search for any doors that could open to us behind which we might gain support and learn to interact with the older generation. We needed to understand how other families worked and grew together. It made us sad at times when we watched other children play with their parents and grandparents that we were not protected from harm in the same way. It made us appreciate the little time we had in the company of these people and we listened to everything they said.

One of my favourite ancients was a friendly old man who often walked home with me on dark nights, trundling his ramshackle bike, which squeaked and rattled as the wheels bounced from one hole to the next. His storytelling was second to none: I was fascinated and entranced with tales of honey bees, mad bulls, flying ships and a moon filled with cream cheese. The latter was the best of all and so believable. I was heading towards my teens, with an imagination open to new information, ready to believe in a world of fiction and fantasy.

Each month this man placed a hooked pole round the sharp edges of the moon to pull it down. It took five hundred pounds of cheese to fill her to the brim, he said, and when I asked him why, he proceeded with great enthusiasm to explain that every morning when the sun rose, she ate the cheese for breakfast and if he did not fill the moon regularly, she would lose energy and never be able to shine again. To this day, the moon arouses a feeling of intense emotion in me and when I'm in a reflective mood and feel the need to remember, I only have to glance up to the heavens, especially on the night of a full moon, to realise just how lucky I am.

In later years, when I was working as a nurse in a hospital, I often stood outside after a day's work to gaze up at the moon. By then, I was aware of life's uncertainties, but remembering how this small silver ball smiled down at me in the troubled years of my childhood helped me to cope and gave me comfort. The moon kept me company all those years, as I found myself walking the fields alone instead of cuddled down in a warm cosy bed or while listening to my favourite old man, probably open-mouthed, eyes fixed on his wise, weather-beaten face, enchanted and thrilled by the telling of those fantastic tales, as he patiently walked beside me.

I remember dark country roads,
hollow footsteps pacing time
under the railway bridge.
Grass-lined pathways

melting into oblivion,
that outer-edged nostalgia.
My sole memory of schoolbags,
homework heavy, slapping gaberdine.
Me, and the darkness as one.
On the skyline,
black feathered woods
swayed with menace in the breeze.
A sheep's cough warped the silence
and rushing water from hidden burns
gurgled for breath.
A rustle in the long grass
tolled a rodent's death knell.
In the distance
square yellow beacons
danced a ghostly jig
under skirts of corrugated iron
that shone in the moonlight.
They were my lighthouse
in a stormy sea of blackness.
They were my passage home.
Me, and the darkness as one.

Country roads are exceptionally dark in winter, but this darkness was somehow peaceful, free from the pressure and abuse that followed us everywhere inside the croft. I felt that I could hide in it, and although I was never afraid, walking home without the company of my elderly neighbour often became unsettling, especially when the moon was hidden behind thick cloud and shadows flickered erratically round the countryside. Familiar sounds without visual stimulation became distorted and alien, my vivid imagination creating macabre, frightening images that seemed to follow me home. A sheep's rasping cough could mimic, almost perfectly, the sound of a man coughing and spluttering.

One night, a rough cough burst forth from behind the fence, catching me unawares, and because I couldn't see anything I mistook a sheep for a man hiding in the grass. I took off like a bolt of lightning and ran for the cover of the croft, panting with fear, my imagination burning like an inferno, my head throbbing like a steam engine. Once I reached the security of the brae, I stopped to catch my breath. It took a few minutes to realise how stupid I'd been and, with a sigh of relief, I tried to stifle the fit of nervous laughter that was raking my body. I went inside to tell Auntie what I thought was a funny story, but she turned her back on me, told me not to be silly and ordered me to my room. It was very hard to share a light-hearted moment with her, and I felt this was one we could both have been able to enjoy.

I was very aware, by then, that living on a croft involved hard, demanding work. The majority of children with this kind of upbringing were encouraged to thrive within a caring and safe environment that gave them confidence and formed their strong characters, but we were missing the most important element of all: the love and interaction of a devoted parent. There was a severe absence of humour and a lack of togetherness, which the children and their parents who lived roundabout us had. Like all children, they were punished when they misbehaved, but they were never, to my knowledge, made to feel that they were unwanted or unloved.

If Auntie could just have seen us as children, the same way other grown-ups could, with a lot to learn, and not as young adults who didn't want to know anything, she might have been able to get closer to us. But we were her aliens – a nightmare she was trying desperately to control and she hated us for it.

Robert used to say that we would pay her back one day for all the torture she had dished out. He said that before we left the croft we would throw her into the cold well and cover it with a lid, so she would never be able to do the same to anyone again. He didn't care if she spent the rest of her life shivering in that hole and, at the time, neither did I. Bravado was our means of survival, often accompanied by the anticipation of success.

11

The Shepherd

We had very few visitors to the croft, but one in particular came on a weekly basis. Our guardian rented out part of her arable land to a shepherd whose farm was some distance from the croft and her fields were used as extra grazing for his animals. This served two purposes: bringing in extra income and keeping the grass growth under control.

The shepherd, by now our friend, checked his flock once a week and trained his dogs for field use. He never came into the house, but often asked Auntie if we could help him. We followed him about the fields, but he never asked us to do anything that would place us in any danger or would be too much effort for us.

In contrast, Auntie often sent us out to disentangle his sheep from barbed wire in bad weather or in autumn from the rambling bramble bushes that grew profusely along the edge of the burn. Trying to grab the wire or spiky bush from around a trapped sheep often resulted in scratches to our arms and legs. The animal struggled furiously, desperate to free itself from the wire, its long, thick winter coat catching on the barbs and dragging our hands and legs into the fence. When we eventually returned home, our abrasions were not washed or dressed. Instead we found ourselves, once again, in trouble for being careless, in trouble for not handling the wire correctly and for the gory mess we presented. She told us that we were responsible for the welfare of these animals and we naively believed her.

She was jealous of the friendship we had with this shepherd and resented our willingness to work in the field when he was around, so she introduced an element of fear to the relationship, saying that we might lose his attention and friendship if we let his sheep perish in the cold or get injured in some way. I now know that this kind man would not have abandoned us and would have been horrified had he known that we had been forced out in such bad weather to help his sheep with Auntie's threats hanging over us. He was good to his flock and when we were in the fields with him, he did everything he could to keep us safe from harm.

During lambing, he worked with an assistant and sometimes asked us to hold the sheep's head to prevent the animal standing up during the birth process. These lambs arrived into the world hot and steaming, a small membrane covering their tiny bodies that the mother instinctively licked clean. We could not handle the newborn lambs until they were accepted by the ewe and if we were very lucky we were given a bottle to kick-start the feeding of the smaller ones.

Occasionally during clipping time, after a long day spent in the field, we helped the shepherd collect the heavy fleeces, which he piled into his van. He was a kind and patient man with a bright, rosy complexion. I followed him everywhere like a dog, and although I must have been in his way many times, he never complained. We got to know when he was really busy and kept out of his way.

He was concerned for our welfare and continually asked if we were all right. We found it difficult to tell him what was happening on the croft and how Auntie treated us. At that time, we found it practically impossible to trust any adult totally. We were afraid in case they spoke to Auntie, afraid that she would react violently towards us and punish us severely because of it. We did not want to lose this valuable friendship.

The shepherd was a welcome relief from the pressures around us; he was the only person we could depend on for friendly praise and encouragement. He never forgot to bring us sweets, which we ate as we followed him about the fields. We couldn't take them home or keep them in our pockets because if Auntie found them we were denied supper. Other times when we were outside doing washing or other chores, he might surreptitiously throw us a chocolate bar, which we quickly broke into pieces and stuffed into our mouths, practically swallowing the rich, creamy nectar before it had time to melt. I knew he wanted to help and he did all he could. I believe he would have found our mistreatment difficult to prove and was probably afraid that he might make things more unpleasant for us in the long run if he interfered.

By the time I was in my teens, I was naturally becoming more and more curious about the world beyond the croft. Auntie disapproved of anything she didn't understand and was very uncomfortable with the modern way of life, so trying to experience new things required a little ingenuity and a lot of risk. She was confused by change and unable to accept anything unfamiliar. This ranged from fashion and food to the way she saw the world in general.

One Saturday, Auntie sent Robert and me into town to get some item she couldn't buy in the village. I can't remember what it was, but I recall we had four pence change. I convinced Robert to spend the leftover money on a bag of chips – a stupid thing to do.

We had heard from children at school that chips were extremely tasty, but our foster mother always refused to cook potatoes this way and we knew there was no chance in the near future that she would change her mind. We decided to risk it and wandered into the first chip shop we saw. We were given a large portion of chips. The fat oozed through the newsprint onto our fingers. The newspaper poke was hot and steaming and rustled furiously as we thrust our eager fingers into the bag, grabbing handfuls and stuffing them into our mouths. I looked at Robert – his eyes were wide with pleasure as he swallowed with a ferocious hunger. We felt warm and full by the time we reached the station to catch the bus out to the croft.

Then it dawned on us that if Auntie found out what we had spent her change on, we would be severely chastised. I suggested we tell her that I had bought a chocolate biscuit and shared it. I knew this would be more acceptable and the final outcome would be less severe.

When I got home I explained what had happened and, although I could see she was angry, for once she didn't lash out. I was relieved but uneasy because I had lied to her. I set the table for tea and, just as I thought she was going to dish up the food, she asked me again what I had done with the change. She told me to describe the biscuit, its size and shape, and to say from which shop I had bought it. She wanted exact details and was making me feel very uncomfortable.

I knew my earlier impulse was about to get me into severe trouble. Lies and deception, for Auntie, were two of the worst sins imaginable.

I looked at Robert for support, but he refused to look back at me. He sat with his eyes staring down at the floor. I reluctantly repeated my story, digging my grave deeper and deeper, frantically gesticulating the size and shape of this biscuit and trying to remember what I had said previously, hoping that my brother hadn't given her all the facts.

Her face suddenly went white. She rose from the table, grabbed my hair with both hands and pulled me from my seat. I felt my feet leave the ground as she swung me against the wall, splitting my nose. Blood poured everywhere. She threw me into a corner until supper was over, then pulled me to the sink, where she forced me to peel several potatoes, cut them into slices and put them into a hot fatty pan. She stood over me as they cooked.

Once they were brown and crispy, she slid them onto a plate and ordered me to eat them all. She thought she was teaching me a lesson, but like the incident with the boys the year before, with the bread and jam, I thoroughly enjoyed my punishment. It was the most delicious meal I had tasted in a long while. The more I pretended I didn't want it, the more she forced me to eat the chips. For once, I was having a good time. I was the best actress in the whole world!

This time I did not feel sorry for my brother: he had let me down. I did not want to share the food with anyone.

This act alone brought home to me the reality of how the decisions we make determine the consequences of our actions. It was an important lesson about how we conduct our relationships with those we come across.

About this time, I was becoming more aware of my appearance. I envied my playmates, as they experimented with make-up – I was forbidden to touch Auntie's powder or handle her beauty products. She lectured me on flighty behaviour, reminding me of my mother's failures and how she was now waving a tambourine in the Salvation Army. I remained curious, however, and watched my friends as they became experts in the art of body beautification. One day while dusting the furniture, I noticed a lipstick lying on the dresser. I couldn't resist the urge to touch it, to feel it, to use it. I pulled off the top and was faced with a thick, bright-red stick of wonder. I set to and attempted rather clumsily to apply it to my pouting lips. It felt smooth and warm and slid easily across my mouth. I was so engrossed in what I was doing that it took me a few minutes to realise that I could hear Auntie's leg dragging against the loose stones outside. She was coming inside. I panicked and tried to wipe my mouth clean. I did not have a mirror to check my appearance, but ultimately thought I had been successful. I quickly put the top back on the lipstick and returned to my work, as if nothing was wrong. I was convinced that she wouldn't notice.

She stopped and looked at me with a strange expression on her face. She asked what I'd been doing and innocently I said working. She was outraged. She reacted instantly, calling me a slut and a whore. She covered me in the bright-red lipstick and threw me outside. She grabbed the duster from my hand and ordered me to go up to the croft at the top of the hill and ask the crofter's wife if she could spare some cotton wool. She was determined to embarrass me, to cause the greatest amount of discomfort she could think of and prove to me that I was not worth the ground I stood on.

The lady who greeted me was very sympathetic and told me that young girls experimented with make-up all the time and this made me feel much better. She gently cleaned my face, gave me a biscuit and sent me home. I made sure I ate this biscuit before

Auntie saw it and remembered to look as if I had been given a small talking-to. This seemed to satisfy her to a certain extent and the matter was allowed to rest for the time being.

Facing this kind of humiliation and abuse day in, day out wore us down over time and all of us at some point contemplated running away. Robert tried several times, in fact, but on every occasion his attempts were quashed. While I tried to believe that eventually I would grow up and somewhere out there I would find the happiness that I had missed at the croft, my siblings saw their captivity differently. Their actions were more desperate and spontaneous than mine.

Every time they escaped, the police brought them back. The authorities dismissed every excuse they gave for running away immediately after hearing our foster mother's account of the whole affair. In a very controlled manner and with a touch of false sentiment, she managed to convince the police that she was innocent of all charges. She thanked them politely and informed them that she was having to cope by herself with four troublesome foster children. As we were now teenagers, she insisted, we were rebelling against her.

She convinced them that she was in control of her household and was able to handle the situation. She presented a pretence of so-called relief, with a few crocodile tears – just enough to be noticed in the dim light of evening.

Her story dwelt on the safe return of the children and she hugged them in front of the police, a sign of affection for their eyes only. No one noticed that it was a one-sided hug and that the runaway child was silently crying for help. She had sole control over us and, with no one to check her methods, she could do whatever she liked.

The nearest I came to escaping life on the croft was after I dropped a large bowl of eggs, which I had just washed ready for grading. I watched Auntie's face change into a grotesque mask of hate. I didn't hesitate: I turned quickly and managed to squeeze past her and out of the door before she had time to lock it. I panicked, and for the first time ever flight became a desperate need – I had to get as far away from this house as possible.

My heart pounded in my chest. The beating of my running feet seemed to mimic the mechanical sound of my heartbeat. I ran as fast as I could across the field to the wood. Then I crossed the fields and headed for the main road into the village. Could I manage to get a lift to Glasgow and find my parents? I naively thought that if I managed to find them and tell them how we were being treated, they would come and rescue us. I didn't know how far away it was and I didn't know if I was even going in the right direction.

I began to thumb a lift, hoping someone would stop and pick me up. A car pulled over shortly after and the driver asked me if I was going into the village, but when I told him I was going further south, he looked at me suspiciously, made an excuse and drove on. I wanted to run away, but I didn't know where I was going or how to get there. The more I thought about my situation, the more I realised that I couldn't leave my siblings behind to feel the consequences of my selfish actions. I had to go back, say I was sorry and take whatever punishment she dished out. I had no choice.

But this desperate need to escape stayed with me. Every time I went to the village I wanted to just keep walking, to get as far away from Coxton as I could. I didn't know what lay beyond this village or where the roads would lead me – but I knew that if I didn't come home, the police would find me and take me home to a beating. So I just didn't try.

One day when I was walking to the shop, a man I knew by sight only stopped and asked me if I wanted a lift. I asked him if he was going near Glasgow because I wanted to see my parents, and he nodded and said he would do his best. We drove through the village heading south, as promised, but he turned into a side road and stopped the car. He began to talk to me in a strange manner and, I don't know why, but I began to feel uneasy and moved closer to the car door. He began to ask me things I didn't understand and tried to kiss me. He reached over and, as a tractor pulled up behind us, he tried to grab me. Startled, he immediately pulled himself together and drove away. He took me back to the village and dumped me there. He didn't speak or give any explanation for his behaviour.

I wanted to tell Auntie when I got home and be comforted by her, but she made it impossible. She made no attempt to listen, merely pushing me roughly against the door. I went through to my bedroom, sat on the bed and cried.

A week later, this same man stopped to pick me up again, but I refused to climb into his car. He became aggressive and threatened to tell Auntie what I was doing – that I was looking for lifts from men – and I believed him. I was so scared that I reluctantly climbed in beside him. When the car reached the crossroads where I would have normally got off the bus, the police were stopping all the vehicles because there had been an accident and they were looking for witnesses. When the car stopped, I took the opportunity and got out as quickly as possible.

I didn't see him again for several weeks. On this occasion, though he once again stopped to pick me up, I categorically refused, ignoring his threats and taunts. When I told him that I had spoken to my foster mother, he drove off, never to be seen again.

Again, I wanted to tell Auntie. I desperately needed to unburden myself, to let her know how I was feeling. She could have reassured me, told me that I wasn't bad, and helped me to understand why this man had acted this way. I asked myself, was it because I was a foster child? Did he know that I would be scared to tell someone in case I was accused of telling lies and consequently punished?

At this point, I felt the child in me was lost for ever and the trust I had in the kind men I knew around me wavered for a short time. I was amongst kind country folk who had a great respect for all living things and treated all children with hearts of gold, but at this time my faith in human goodness faltered. At the root of the problem – the black spot in our lives – was Auntie, for her heart was made of stone.

All our dirty clothes were cleaned in a wooden tub outside as the sink in the living room was too small. This tub was filled with soapy water and we scrubbed the clothes with a brush against the washboard. Once clean they were fed through a mangle. The water that squelched out of the clothes and into a wooden tray was later used to water the rhubarb and gooseberry bushes. The soapy concentrate helped to keep the plants pest-free. A washing line stretched from the goose shed to the wood storage shelter and poles were used to keep the clothes from hitting the ground. If we did not work quickly enough, or were a little bit too noisy, she grabbed the scrubbing brush from us and rubbed it roughly against our arms and legs until we were crying. She rubbed the cleaned clothes across the ground and threw them back into the tub to be re-washed.

Water and children go very well together: they are a superb matrix for play, a magic toy that we couldn't damage or get into trouble for destroying. But even that small pleasure was spoiled for us. We tried very hard to introduce a fun element into everything we did, but each time she could see we were trying to enjoy ourselves she would push us around and made the job more difficult for us to do, giving her an excuse to dish out fresh punishment or add to our workload.

We never received any pocket money for the chores we helped with in the house and, although to us this was not important initially, it meant we often felt let down and unable to participate in sweetie-shop visits with the neighbouring children. Auntie was paid monthly for looking after us and brought money home in a brown envelope that she kept on the windowsill in the living room next to her settee bed.

As Robert got braver with age, he took small amounts for himself, being careful that she had paid a few household bills first and, in this way, she never seemed to miss any. He shared the sweets he bought with us and, although we knew it was wrong, we savoured every mouthful.

When she was in a dangerous mood, we learned, through experience, to nurse the situation with great care. It was like treading on broken glass: the slightest slip resulted in bruised skin, hurtful innuendos and a feeling of sadness that haunted our young lives.

As we got older, we should have been able to temper the situation, but years of restraint and conditioning made it difficult for us to resist her authority and she always succeeded in overpowering us. I used to wonder if there was anyone I could confide in. Was there someone we could trust who, most importantly, would believe our story?

I remember one morning being off school because of illness. The shepherd's wife came to the house enquiring after my health, but Auntie did not let her in. I crept to the door and stood on tiptoe behind Auntie's back. I hoped the visitor would notice my sad face. I didn't know what I was expecting her to do – I knew she couldn't take me with her. After a few minutes of conversation, she smiled and left. I wanted to shout after her, I wanted her to help me, but deep down I knew she couldn't. I stepped back into the hall and tried to sneak into the bedroom, but Auntie saw me, grabbed my hair, twisted a few strands round her fingers and threw me outside in my pyjamas. Just as she was about to close the door, the shepherd's wife appeared again.

Auntie's mood changed instantly. 'Oh, there you are!' she said. 'Come inside and not catch cold.'

The lady had dropped her glove on the path and was returning to pick it up.

I quickly went back into my room, where I could hear the two women talking sharply to one another, but I couldn't understand what was being said. When Auntie came back inside, her face was red and covered in beads of sweat. She pushed me across the room, shook me from one corner to the next, and slapped my face several times, spitting hate at me. She threatened to throw me outside for the rest of the day, but because she was afraid of unexpected visitors she locked me in my room instead and refused to feed me until evening.

With Auntie, the verbal abuse was relentless, always at the same intense level. Every day I was reminded that I was good for nothing, that I would turn out to be like my mother. She said that history always repeated itself. I didn't want to believe her; I didn't want her to be right.

She was sneaky in character and took advantage of any situation that might elevate her position in the parish. There was always an alternative motive if we sensed a change in her behaviour, especially if she needed something positive to speak about when the child welfare officer came to visit at the end of summer. As a result of this, I sometimes benefited, which suited me well.

On one occasion, I was invited to join the Brownie Pack and Auntie found herself in a position where she could not refuse. The Brownie meetings were run and organised by prominent people in the parish – the very people she wanted to impress – so she reluctantly let me join in. It was an evening I looked forward to, no matter how badly treated I was on my return home. She always seemed to want to make me feel guilty for doing something I enjoyed or feel sorry for her by telling me that she was unwell and that I should have stayed at home to look after her.

I was eventually approached by the Scout Master from the village and asked if I would like to be a helper with the Wolf Cubs. This I enjoyed very much; I thrived as I gained confidence, learning to control the young boys. It was obvious to my foster mother that I was enjoying this too much and she continued to make me feel guilty, but I kept going to the meetings until I went to secondary school, when I had to stop because of extra homework.

My teacher later suggested to Auntie that I could benefit from the youth club, held in the school hall on a Friday night, and although she did not let me go very often, she had to be seen to be encouraging me. I did enjoy my time away from the croft, although I still desperately wanted Auntie to take an interest in what I was doing, to give me advice on the right way to tackle things and to sympathise when things went wrong, but she showed no interest in anything I did outwith the croft. She loathed activities that brought us pleasure or attention to life inside her house.

One night, while sitting on a tall window ledge in the hall waiting my turn for judo lessons, I began playing with the window cord used to open the top pane. Absentmindedly, I put my head into the loop and continued to talk to my friends. When my turn came, I jumped off the ledge. I don't remember what happened next, but I woke up to the instructor's voice. He was asking me if I was all right and saying he would take me home. My throat was sore and I found it difficult to talk for a few minutes, but I was more afraid of Auntie's reaction to a stranger taking me home than the injury I had just received. I asked him not to report it to the school, reassuring him that I was all right. I had been careless and knew that if Auntie found out I would be punished. She never noticed the red mark round my neck and it soon disappeared. I remember thinking it would have been nice to tell Auntie of my mishap and be reassured, even if it meant being told off in a motherly way, but I knew this was beyond her.

While I remained at primary school, I was given the responsibility of ensuring that my brothers' and sister's homework was completed to a certain standard. I was attacked physically and verbally when they appeared to be struggling. Each mistake was whacked against my back and shouted into my ear. I was dragged to the bedroom and threatened with a stick, the point prodding into my stomach. If there was no visible improvement in their work, she would rant and I was punished severely. She would send a bad report to Glasgow, too. I was then dragged back to the living room, where I personally had to re-do their lessons. This resulted in neat homework, obviously done by someone else, and consequently kept them behind the rest of their class.

Did she want so much control over them that she felt she had to destroy their ability to develop mentally? Was this a deliberate attempt on her part to undermine and weaken their resolve, or was it a form of misguided ignorance?

Correcting their work in this manner stifled any ability to learn and held them at a distance from the teachers at school. Every night she screamed at them and smacked their fingers with a ruler when they couldn't pronounce a word or spell it accurately. She tore their jotters and left them to explain to their teachers why their books were in such a mess. Of course, the teachers did not believe the explanation they gave and the belt or an exercise of one hundred lines was given to do at home, whereupon the whole tangled mess was repeated again and again.

Mary, although developing reasonably well physically, was far behind with the emotional side of her character. She was afraid of many things and did not get the help and support she so badly needed to calm those fears. She refused to go into a car or a van without force and without screaming. I don't know what caused this hysterical reaction, but instead of Auntie trying to calm her down, or maybe going into the car with her to show that there was nothing to be afraid of, she bundled Mary into the back seat and slammed the car door, ordering the driver to lock her in. Most times the car returned home within minutes, Mary still kicking and screaming in the back seat. Auntie apologised, without looking at the visitor, and ushered Mary inside. Once the door was closed we could hear a thud and scramble as our sister tried to escape Auntie's swinging arms. Mary needed help and we were afraid.

She was terrified of getting her hair washed and started to cry every time the basin was put in front of her. Auntie shouted at her to stop, shook her violently and grabbed her head, forcing it down into the water. Mary kicked her legs and struggled for breath as she choked on the soapy water. If Auntie couldn't calm her down, Mary was dragged outside soaking wet, still screaming. The remaining contents of the basin, and often the basin itself, were thrown over her, the bowl bouncing against her head. She was left shivering and sobbing. What pleasure did Auntie get out of this? What was she trying to achieve?

George was always a quiet boy and remained distant for most of his childhood. He managed in his own way to cope with Auntie, although she beat him and manipulated his life to suit her needs. He was afraid to show emotion and kept it hidden from all of us. We never knew what he was thinking or how he was feeling. He needed to protect himself from everyone and everything and seemed lost in his own thoughts and his own agony. Many times I heard him sobbing in the corner by himself. He didn't want sympathy from us – he wanted comfort from a mother who did not exist.

On one of my last days at primary school, I arrived home to see Auntie actually smiling. My siblings were sitting at the table looking reasonably happy – no one was standing in the corner or locked in their bedroom. She was holding a letter from the school stating that I had passed my 11-plus examination. She appeared unusually excited and presented me with a silver charm bracelet. I was handed a pencil and ordered to sit down and write a small note to the welfare officer, telling him of my results and about the present I was given. I was allowed to wear this bracelet only at school dances or whenever someone important came to the house. It eventually vanished and I never saw it again.

These moments of peace, however engineered, never did last long – and the screaming and slapping and accusatory behaviour returned tenfold. Every mistake we made taught us to be more cautious and careful in everything we did or said. We didn't want to be beaten, we didn't want to be spat at and we didn't want to be physically manhandled by Auntie or anyone else.

When I moved up to senior school, my responsibility for the actions of my brothers and sister relaxed a little. I was no longer chastised for their academic failures, but during holidays and weekends things remained the same. If one of us got into trouble, the rest of us suffered too. If Auntie wanted to cause dissention in the ranks, she picked a favourite child for a day. She fawned and pandered, her obsequious behaviour almost sickening to watch. She was determined to cause jealousy and bad feeling, but it didn't work. We knew what she was trying to do and these opportunities to be spoiled and pampered were precious, so we enjoyed them when we could. We stuck together and played her little game the way she wanted it played. We lapped up the few hours of much-needed attention, or, if we were lucky, a couple of days' reprieve from continuous abuse, and waited for the minute when this short period would come to an end. We watched every movement she made and tried to understand what was going on in her mind. When her facial expression changed and her patience ran out, it was time to back away quietly and allow things to return to normal. The time as favourite was over and as an individual we were each soon forgotten.

I always remember every Saturday night Scottish dance music played on the wireless and Robert and I were forced to dance round the room, whether we wanted to or not. Sometimes she made us sing along with the wireless programme brandishing a brush in our hands, performing like an actor on stage. It was as if she was reliving her younger memories in movement of tempo and character through us.

She thumped her stick in time to the music and shuffled about in her seat. The faster her stick moved, the faster we danced. We couldn't stop until she became bored and picked up her newspaper or played with her cats. As long as she seemed happy, we danced until our feet ached. If we kept her calm and didn't speak too much, she remained quiet for most of the evening.

It is sad to say, but we were her slaves, her entertainment and her only release from the stressful existence she led. She used us to satisfy her needs and took full advantage of our mistakes and failures to release the frustrations that pulsated through her body every second of her day.

12

Teenage Years

After the summer holidays of 1960, I started back at the academy. My new school was situated three miles away in the city of Elgin and every morning I caught a bus at the crossroads. A school uniform was essential for my upgrade to the academy and because all pupils would be dressed in a similar fashion I felt at last I would fit in like everyone else.

I had hoped that I would not feel self-conscious about the clothes I wore or the way I presented myself to the world, but Auntie had other ideas. She ordered a long, navy, pleated skirt that reached down to my ankles. I did not want to be different any more; I wanted to be the same – I wanted to be able to relax with my new friends and make a fresh start. I tried to explain this to my foster mother with as much sensitivity as I thought was necessary in the hope that she would understand how I felt, but she eyed me with a strange look and said that I would never be like anyone else: I was a foster child who depended on the charity and goodwill of others; I had no belongings and no relations, and I should be grateful for everything she gave me.

On the morning of the first day of term, I left the house wearing my long skirt. I could feel the material flapping round my ankles and I was sure that everyone would be watching me and laughing at my old-fashioned attire. As soon as I reached the railway bridge, I decided to roll it up at the waistband until the hem reached the top of my knees. It worked and my skirt hung nicely from the edge of my blazer. I looked good. I felt pleased and ready to tackle anything.

The first day of school went well and, when the bell rang at the end of the last period, I reluctantly headed for the bus station and Coxton. On the way home, I stopped under the bridge and adjusted my skirt back to its original length. It had been a good day, I felt like a different person. I had new friends, new teachers and a chance to blend in with the rest of the pupils. I had come to a firm decision: I was determined not to mention the word 'foster' at the academy or anything that might suggest I was different. This was a fresh start – a new me – and I liked it.

During the summer months, the thick band of material round my waist became very uncomfortable. It was hot and stuffy in the classroom and I couldn't remove my blazer without drawing attention to the untidy bulge at my waist. I felt my appearance could indicate a possible lack of parental care and I didn't want to highlight it. I wanted to pretend that everything was all right; I didn't want to be different any more.

I was determined to feel comfortable and keep my skirt short. I had to think of some other way, a more permanent way, of adjusting the length of this skirt. I decided to wait until the holidays arrived, then hide the skirt under my mattress. I hoped Auntie would get so distracted by our presence on the croft that she would forget all about it. Before the autumn term began, a new uniform was ordered from Glasgow. The skirt, when it arrived, was the same colour and design as my original one. It was perfect. I now had a plan that might even work. I was terrified in case she asked me for my old skirt, but she didn't. My idea was to shorten it somehow and wear it under my new long one. I wanted to feel happier in my school uniform and less self-conscious. The next problem was how to get it out of the house without her knowing, and where to hide it.

On my next visit to the village, I put the old skirt under my coat and hid it in an old duffle bag under the railway bridge, along with a pair of scissors, elastic, needle and thread, which I took from Auntie's large sewing box. I had very little experience of using a needle and certainly didn't know how to handle the pleats of a skirt. It was going to be guesswork. I didn't want to destroy this skirt – it was part of my 'new look' plan.

I grabbed every opportunity to go to the village, making time to begin the transformation of my school skirt. I was excited, and scared of making a mistake, as I gingerly cut a large quantity of material from the top of the skirt, trying to keep it even. I turned down a hem and sewed it as neatly as possible. I threaded a piece of elastic through the newly sewn hem and tied the ends together. It took a few days to complete, but I now had a skirt that fitted me perfectly, which I wore under the new, much longer one until I was safely out of sight of the croft.

I removed the long skirt every morning under the shadow of the bridge before I reached the bus stop and school. I kept it in my duffle bag all day until it was time to come home and then I slipped it over my fashionably cut skirt before the croft came into sight. It was a complete success – I never again had to worry about how I looked. The skirt itself kept in reasonably good condition and didn't require ironing; the only problem I had was keeping it clean.

I stored the short skirt under the mattress during the holidays and sneaked it to the woods to wash in the burn. It dried over a branch and before I put it back under the mattress I straightened the pleats. By the start of school, it was pressed beautifully, ready to be smuggled out again. It was still under the mattress the day I left the croft for ever.

My reaching puberty coincided rather dramatically with the death of Marilyn Monroe. I remember at the time seeing her picture in a magazine and wondering how a girl with so much beauty and confidence could take her own life. I was convinced I was ugly – Auntie had seen to that. For me, rather than beauty and confidence, it was uncertainty and an unpleasantness I couldn't understand.

One afternoon, as I arrived home from school, I was immediately locked in my room without any explanation. I couldn't think what I had done wrong – or forgot to do – and it was some time before she came in to see me. She had a pair of my pants wrapped in newspaper. I noticed that there was a smearing of blood on the gusset. I hadn't noticed it before and couldn't recall hurting myself.

Auntie asked me to explain. I couldn't, so she accused me of being with a man. Being rather naive and not understanding the true workings of the human body, I tried desperately to remember if I had walked home with anyone the day before. I mentioned my elderly neighbour and his bike. He had let me pedal as far as the bridge and maybe, I thought, that's when I scratched myself, which would explain the spots of blood on my clothes. I couldn't see any scratches, though. She was furious and accused me of being impertinent and making fun of her. She pushed me down on the bed and pulled off my pants to inspect them, but they were clean. I inched backwards until my back hit the wall, frightened by her body language. She was looking at me as if she did not know me; her hands, pressed down on my shoulders, were numbing my skin. Her eyes stared into mine, her breathing laboured and erratic.

For a few minutes, she hovered above me, her face contorted into a series of deep, troubled frowns. She seemed to be struggling with some unknown trigger, struggling to bring the present back into focus. I lay against the wall quietly afraid of this woman, waiting for her confusion to end, waiting for the quietness to come. I watched the glow from her cigarette fade and die as she inhaled, then she let go of my shoulders and left the room. I was refused supper and went to bed still wondering what I had done wrong.

The next day she gave me a letter to give to my teacher, explaining to me that it was just a message for the headmaster. But during lunchtime the following day, I was called into the nurse's room and asked several questions. Auntie had reported the incident to the school nurse and requested her assistance in handling the situation. It was the first time I had heard of periods or was given any help in understanding the changes taking place within my body. I dreaded the monthly scenario of begging for money to buy what I needed to help me.

The only information I got about the 'birds and the bees' came from sex education lectures at school – at home, the subject was never brought up. It was impossible to discuss the opposite sex with Auntie because she refused to talk about men. Any interest I might have had was severely restricted anyway. I could not interact with children after school because I lived in the country and had to take the first bus home, nor was I allowed to spend time with them during the weekends. In fact, the only chance I had for any conversation was during playtime or when I went to the village for groceries. I found it difficult to make any lasting friendships and often wandered about on my own. It was noted in the school report sent to Glasgow that I was quieter than a young girl of 14 should be. I was afraid to be involved with boys – to let Auntie see me talking to them or to give her the impression that I wanted to be in their company – and afraid of what Auntie would do to me if she found me with one. It was like the forbidden fruit: what one wants and can't get, one wants all the more.

I failed to understand the hormonal changes taking place within me, even though the school nurse had tried to explain things to me. I received no support at home and was left to deal with these changes in my own way.

I began to challenge Auntie more frequently, and my work on the croft became less important. She accused me of being wayward and insolent and wrote this in a letter to the welfare officer, who sent a representative to the croft to give me a lecture on how to behave.

One morning after Sunday school, Robert and I met a brother and sister who had just moved to the area. Their house was situated near the school and we became friends for a short time. The girl took ballet lessons and I was immediately attracted to her. Every time we were in each other's company, I wanted her to dance. She was like the dancers in my comics, but here in real life. I was enthralled. Her brother and Robert got on very well and I was beginning to like this boy very much. I felt attracted to him but because we were not allowed to play with friends after school or at the weekends, I asked him to come up to the croft because I wanted to see more of him. I told him he would have to hide behind the shed while I did my outside work because Auntie did not like visitors. We had fun between jobs, laughing and chatting. I don't know what I expected, but it was good to have company other than that of my siblings. It felt thrilling and exciting.

For a short time, I was happy in the company of this boy and, in between feeding the hens and chopping sticks for firewood, we laughed and chatted, keeping an ear out, listening for sounds of Auntie. Our friendship began innocently enough until we were drawn closer together. He asked me to kiss him and we were so engrossed in the act, we did not hear Auntie creep up behind us. She grabbed the boy by his shoulders and thumped her stick on the ground as if she were training a young puppy. He was terrified. He pushed past her like a frightened rabbit and rushed down the brae, never to return. Auntie dragged me by the hair and threw me over a stone, then pulled down my pants and thrashed me with her stick until I was unable to speak. A first kiss – which most of us remember as an awakening of the first spring of adulthood – became for me a memory of pain and accusation.

After this incident, I thought that the only boy I could marry was Robert and we hugged in agreement like friends for ever and planned a future together with George and Mary as our children.

I was beginning to handle things in a more mature way and this infuriated Auntie. She said I was becoming unpredictable and she distrusted my whimsical nature. She targeted the younger ones with fervour – a bizarre enthusiasm – in an effort to control me. It felt bad enough attending a different school: I did not want them to think I had deserted them totally.

As my first year at the academy came to an end and the school dance was imminent, I began to feel uneasy. I wanted to go, but I knew that I would be the only one in school uniform. Everyone else was making plans about what they were going to wear, but when I asked Auntie if I could wear a dress to fit in, she said she would look out one of my old summer ones. I was a little unhappy about this because all my dresses were in bad condition and I wanted to look pretty like everyone else. I didn't say anything and accepted that I would be wearing a dress instead of my uniform.

As the dance drew nearer I noticed Auntie making alterations to a long pink nylon dress with many layers of petticoats. It looked delicate, but old, and I didn't think anything of it. She spent night after night for at least a week sewing every hem until it was finished. Then after supper one evening she asked me to try this dress on. Like any other girl, I thought it would be fun to dress up and feel special. It fitted me very well, except it reached to the floor and felt more like a gown for a princess. I still did not think it was for me and wondered who was going to wear it.

On the day of my school dance, I got up as usual and, after finishing my chores, I asked if I could dress for my party. Out came the long, flowing pink nylon costume, which she presented to me with a pair of white second-hand sandals. I didn't know what to do. I could not and did not want to tell her that I was embarrassed to wear it and that I would look like something from the olden days. The dress itself was all right and would have been more acceptable if it had been shorter, but no matter how I felt I knew I had to put it on. I arrived at school fluttering in pink embroidered layers of nylon, feeling very self-conscious, wanting to hide under my desk. But by lunchtime the excitement of the day took over and my over-flamboyant outfit was nearly forgotten.

Auntie had put a massive amount of time and effort into the alteration of this dress. I don't know where she had got it from, but at least in her own way she had tried, whether for my benefit or to make a good impression, it really didn't matter.

* * *

As I progressed through high school, I got a chance to go on the annual school trip to Glenmore, a centre with residential accommodation and all sorts of facilities that was used by school parties and other organisations for trips into the Cairngorm mountains. I really wanted to go. I knew that if I asked Auntie myself or handed her a form from the teacher, she would immediately refuse, and I didn't know how to approach her without causing a serious row. I had to make it look as if she was expected to sign the permission form, or if she didn't, she might risk some comment in the school's annual report to Glasgow. I decided the best chance I had was to speak to the headmaster. I explained my situation again and asked if he could write a letter to my guardian requesting my involvement in this outing. He did just that and permission was granted, albeit grudgingly, and under a huge degree of duress. It was the first time I was to attend a senior school activity.

After giving her consent, Auntie had no choice but to pay for the bus trip. For days leading up to the trip, I was reminded that she was doing me a favour by letting me go; I was accused of being selfish; I was repeatedly told how much it was costing her and how I would have to pay her back. She pushed and nipped my arms every time she passed and persistently complained of being ill. How could I leave her without any help, she moaned. How could I be so insensitive?

She refused to provide me with decent walking shoes or a bag to hold my personal items, and gave me absolutely no pocket money. I didn't care: I was actually going. I was leaving the croft for a whole week and I couldn't wait.

During the week away, our first trip to the mountains was initially marred by the fact that I had to wear my school uniform and use my school bag to carry my personal belongings. Everyone else was dressed in warm casual gear, carrying haversacks full of goodies and spare clothes. I felt a bit disappointed and self-conscious; in fact, I stood out like a sore thumb. I felt everyone was looking at me and laughing behind my back.

But the atmosphere was so relaxed that soon I forgot how different I looked. Everyone was having so much fun that no one seemed to notice very much anyway. I could lie on my bed in the dormitory without getting into trouble. I could read a magazine without hiding it under the covers. I could run around with other pupils without looking behind me for approval. It was sheer unnatural bliss.

Food was plentiful, and I was introduced to something with such an incredible taste that I swore if I could manage to come back the next year, I would try and save enough money to buy more: a tube of condensed milk. One of the teachers had bought it from the climbers' shop and had given it to me to sample, or so he said. I think, looking back now, it had been noted that I was never at the shop and probably did not have any money to spend. I lay on top of the bed and squeezed this mixture slowly onto my tongue. It was like nectar: thick, creamy and sweet. I will never forget that taste and nothing has beaten it since.

I revelled in the attention I received when out climbing or walking, and as a result I tried very hard to keep up with the teachers and stay within the front group. I was determined to keep going, even though my legs felt as if they were on fire and the corns on the ball of each foot, which plagued me continually, sent stabbing pains shooting up both my legs as I stepped on the many stones that covered the paths and hillsides. Every time the leading teacher looked round, I was there, plodding on regardless. I could see amusement in his face and I liked it.

Each day I put extra effort into everything I did. I wanted them to like me; I wanted to please them, to think I was worth something. I wanted to hear, 'Well done, you've done good today.' Many nights I was so exhausted by my sheer determination to succeed in everything that I fell asleep immediately after supper.

My behaviour was obviously cause for concern because one morning before we set out the science teacher took me aside and gave me a few words of advice. He suggested I stop trying so hard to please. He said the outing was not a test of endurance but an opportunity to enjoy myself and have fun. I told him that's what I thought I was doing, and he didn't argue, but after thinking about what he'd said I took his advice and slowed down. There was no pressure to excel at anything: enjoyment and companionship *were* the main functions of this exercise. I realised that it didn't matter if I was last or if I failed to keep up with everyone else.

Slowly, I began to relax and chat with the children around me. This in turn allowed me to enjoy the evening singsongs and the various organised activities.

I had been going to bed early every evening because I was so tired but also I had this ever-present feeling of guilt that prevented me from having fun. I felt I had done nothing good to deserve this better life and I couldn't understand why no one else felt the same way.

After talking to the science teacher, I saw that I didn't have to work hard to be liked or spend a whole day working to get a reward, all I needed to do was be myself and let someone else do things for me for a change. It was like a breath of fresh air. I soon realised that life could – and would – be something to look forward to in the future.

Every year from then on, the headmaster wrote a letter, giving me the chance to repeat the experience. My class teacher provided me with second-hand walking shoes and included in the permission form a mandatory requirement for clothes suitable for this type of activity. He insisted in the letter to Auntie that it was a safety issue and stated that the school would not be held responsible if this was not adhered to.

I had experienced a new sense of freedom and one year I used the idea of a school trip as an excuse to get away for a weekend on my own. I did not have a consent form, but after a make-believe story and a lot of expert deception Auntie accepted my ruse. Although she was worldly wise in many things, she was not fully aware of what was happening outside the confines of the croft and it was easy to mislead her at times. Maybe she thought that I would not dare disobey her, or that I did not have the intelligence to make up clever stories.

That weekend I set off on my own, with a duffle bag filled with the necessary bits and pieces for hillwalking. I headed to Lossiemouth beach, six miles away, where I intended to camp for the weekend. I had not given much thought to where I would spend the night, and while walking along I came across some beach huts. I found one open and set myself up for a short stay. As night fell, I could hear the wind whistling along the sands. Seagulls were making strange sounds as they settled down for the night. I breathed in the scent of the sea, inhaling the distinctive freshness, one I had not experienced since the children's home in Dunoon, and it was very pleasing. I couldn't sleep at first, so I walked down to the water's edge. I sat on the beach until late, enjoying the peace and listening to the waves rippling at the water's edge. I watched the darkness of the sky turn the palest blue and watched the dawn silently creep along the rim of the sea, casting an eerie light across the dunes. The blue-tinged shadows of early morning, with the slanting rays of a rising sun, reflected mournfully across the still water. I felt sad and lonely; I was missing my brothers and sister. I wanted to go home, but I didn't want to see Auntie. I was very, very tired.

The sea breeze made me shiver and I knew it was time to go into the hut and rest. I lay and listened to the wind still whistling as it skirted the dunes and the swish of the waves as they gently hit the beach. These sounds acted as a mild sedative and I quickly fell asleep.

I awoke later on in the morning to evidence that I had not been alone. A set of fresh large footprints led directly to and from me towards the half-open door. I realised how stupid I'd been. I wanted to stay and enjoy my freedom a little longer, but I had become scared for my safety and, with very little hesitation, I quickly packed everything back into my bag and walked home. Auntie accepted my explanation of a cancelled trip due to illness in the group and because the money she gave me was still intact she didn't question further. No matter how desperate I got over the years to sample some freedom, I never put myself in the same danger again until I was much older.

My homework increased as I worked towards O Grade examinations and life on the croft was as hectic as ever. I was allocated an hour to finish any written work before being sent outside to work on the croft. Schoolwork was impossible to complete in that timeframe and I spent most of my playtime sitting in the cloakroom working through the curriculum.

I missed my school bus regularly because I hadn't finished my chores on time. After several late appearances, I was summoned to the headmaster's office. He wanted an explanation as to why I was continually missing classes. He was pleasant and understanding during the discussion, and listened patiently as I tried to explain my lack of punctuality. I didn't expect him to believe me, but he reacted with sympathy and compassion. I don't know if he really understood my position – perhaps he didn't know how to deal with the problems I had – but I continued to be late for class and was never called to his office again.

One morning, after arriving particularly late for morning classes, I was hiding among the coat stands waiting for the bell to ring so I could join the next subject, as I usually did, when I became aware of rows and rows of pockets waiting to be picked. Everyone but me seemed to have pocket money and I wanted some, too. It wasn't fair. I convinced myself I was entitled to the odd penny, though I didn't really think I was going to steal anything. For several days, I kept the idea in mind. Then one morning I was so hungry, I persuaded myself that it wasn't really bad, that no one would miss a penny here or there. I was scared but strangely excited as I felt around in this little girl's pocket. Hunger makes you do strange things.

There was a mixture of coins in her pocket and I took enough to buy an egg-filled roll at dinnertime. It was so easy.

I thought I would feel all right about it, but I have never felt so guilty. What was this girl like? Would she get into trouble for losing her money? I had to see her, to see whose pocket I had ransacked. I waited until school was over for the day and stood near her coat. I didn't know her, but I knew I had to pay her back. I could not do this again. It wasn't me. I had just been so hungry, and stealing the money had been so easy.

At the beginning of the following week I replaced the pennies with part of my dinner money. I stood many times in the cloakroom, knowing I could get away with it, but knowing it was wrong and I would never do it again.

On 22 November 1963 – who can forget that date – I was walking down the high street in Elgin during my lunch break, feeling very low and hungry. Being a foster child weighed heavily on my shoulders. I wanted to be normal, to feel different, important. I noticed a large poster on the window of the city's picture house. It was announcing the cancellation of a forthcoming film, *PT109*, about JFK's wartime experiences. Next to it in large letters it read: 'President Jack Kennedy has been assassinated.' I stopped and stared at the headline, trying hard to understand why people did horrible things. Looking around for something to take my mind away from world events and back to the need for self-importance, I noticed several restaurants decked in upper-class splendour. The smell oozing from within was intoxicating and made my stomach rumble. How could I get inside? How could I pretend I was important enough to sit at one of those tables and sample the food? After several minutes' pacing up and down, I acknowledged that my visit would have to wait. I had to plan this well to make it work.

I decided that the only way I could get the money for this project would be to save some of my dinner money. Every Monday afternoon we had to present our week's ration of tickets for inspection and then keep them safe for the rest of the week. Fortunately, by then I was at senior school and arrived home later than the rest of my siblings. With Robert's help, we devised a system where, after showing his tickets to Auntie, he sneaked down to the foot of the brae and gave me the amount I needed to show her. After a few weeks of saving this money, starving myself to death and running errands for the shopkeeper in the village, I was ready.

The next problem was how could I persuade Auntie to let me take my Sunday clothes to school that day. I wanted to look the part and didn't want anything to go wrong. I don't remember the excuse I gave, but it must have been believable because on the day concerned I set off to school with my duffle bag filled with my good clothes: a pale-blue and white woollen dress, a large white brimmed hat edged with a blue ribbon and, to complete the look, a pair of white cotton gloves.

When the dinner bell rang, I changed in the school toilets. I put my duffle coat on to protect me from the November chill and headed for the centre of town. I was getting scared by now and wasn't sure how I would carry this out. Would I get what I was looking for? Would I really feel good? Would I feel important enough to be satisfied with the result? I picked the restaurant that attracted me the most – its large windows draped with heavy lace curtains and, inside, rows of small tables dressed in white embroidered linen, bejewelled with sparkling silver cutlery and pink silk flowers – patiently waiting for the next customer. I stood for a few moments, plucking up enough courage to enter the large double-glazed doors. Once inside, a waitress pounced on me and directed me to a table next to the window. She eyed me with curiosity and handed me the menu. Out of the corner of my eye, I could see the other waitresses peeking round the door. What were they thinking? Did I look out of place? I was the centre of attention – good or bad, I didn't care. I ordered my meal of roast chicken and apple tart and waited.

It was the best and tastiest meal I had had for a long time. I practically swallowed everything whole, I was so hungry. I tried to remember the right cutlery to use and work from the outside in, as Auntie had taught me. I acted politely and as posh as I could for a 15 year old.

It was a success. I paid my bill, put on my white gloves and, elegantly poised, left the restaurant. I felt pleased with myself and headed towards school.

Once back in uniform, I couldn't help smiling to myself for the rest of the afternoon. I felt good, very good. I knew when I went home I would be faced with another onslaught of abuse, but I thought to myself: Today it doesn't matter, today I can close my eyes and remember a day I will never forget, a day I was Lady Muck for an hour and a half.

I didn't need to repeat the exercise: I had fed the inquisitor and satisfied a long-overdue need. It did occur to me, however, that I could quite easily be in danger of developing a split personality, hiding behind the facade of pretend personalities in this make-believe world where I felt safe and comfortable. If I continued in this frame of mind, I would eventually become scared to reveal the real me in case I was ridiculed. My mental well-being would suffer and I would indeed become like my emotionally unstable mother: good for nothing and living in a self-induced fantasy world.

As the seasons passed and the dark nights closed in once more, my walk home from the bus stop was no longer black and lonely. Robert was my companion and he protected me from the unknown dangers lurking in the wider world. Always in the back of my mind on these nights was my experience years earlier when my siblings were still at primary school and I had walked home alone from the bus stop. I had lost the security of their company and was feeling insecure anyway, then one night as I was reaching the bridge, a car came up behind me. I moved over to let it pass, but nothing happened. I quickened my pace and began to feel a little scared as the car continued to creep slowly behind, keeping me bathed in the bright headlights. I reached the top of the road and instead of turning right to head for home, I slid under the barbed-wire fence and into the field. I had to get away from this person, from the uncertainty behind me.

I stumbled across the rough ground, catching my feet on unseen stones, dipping into furrows and holes, and falling over clumps of grass. Was someone still behind me? I was afraid to turn round and look. I thought if I could reach the dark side of the wood, the occupant of the car would lose sight of me.

I could still see the headlights shining into the field as I followed the edge of the wood, desperately trying to get my bearings. I stayed close to the perimeter until my eyes recognised the vague outline of the derelict shepherd's bothy situated near the croft and I knew I was safe.

This experience was hard to deal with. It was difficult to understand why certain people acted like this; why would an ordinary member of the community become unpredictably alien in mannerism and approach? I couldn't speak to Auntie in case she blamed me for this driver's strange behaviour. But was it me? Was everything really my fault? Was it true that bad followed bad?

Her short temper and intolerable impatience remained evident when I tried to ask questions or needed maternal reassurance. Her predicted manipulations of the restrictions she imposed on us were deliberately designed to confuse and torment us.

Christmas 1964 came and went with little celebration. Doors had been opened on the stroke of midnight to let the old year out and the new year in. Robert and George stood outside in the freezing cold with a piece of coal and a large log, ready to re-enter the house after the bells with 'good luck', and Mary as usual was locked in her bedroom because of an altercation earlier in the evening. A second-hand black-and-white television sat on the dresser, broadcasting Andy Stewart and the White Heather Club.

One more year at school for me, I thought, as I sat and watched the flickering screen. Where would I be this time next year?

This television gave us nothing but heartache. We were not allowed to watch any of the programmes unless Auntie wanted to see them. When the set went on the blink and lost the picture, she made us work the buttons back and forth until, if we were lucky enough, the picture returned. All evening we worked on this set while she banged the table and shouted profanities at us, which would be followed by a piece of coal or a splintered log, as she became increasingly annoyed with our failure to find a picture.

Sometimes in the height of her anger, her facial expression was unclear. It was so contorted it was difficult to identify a frown from a smile. When she did smile, I couldn't tell whether it was genuine or sadistic in nature.

The last time I saw her genuinely happy about anything was the day she received the results of my 11-plus exams. Would I do just as well with my O Grades? I wasn't sure. My schoolwork had been falling below its usual standard and I was afraid that she would get very angry if I failed the grades. Months later I would find out.

As my school years came to an end, it was time to visit the careers' officer. I wanted so much to be an art teacher. My achievements in this subject were not brilliant, but above average, and my teacher encouraged me to forge ahead with my selected choice. It was something I really enjoyed doing and I was willing to work hard to achieve success. I relished the absolute freedom of expression displayed in the art class; I appreciated the experience, the active involvement in an activity I loved, without question or restraint; the ability to visually portray on paper my feelings of a particular day. My pictures were full of darkness, crosses and graves when my days were hard and brutal, and light, funny and cartoon-like when Auntie was going through a quiet phase. Art, to me, was a release valve that exploded in pencil and paint. It kept me sane. It was an essential stabiliser in the development of my personality.

Unfortunately, anything I created at home or took back from the academy was taken from me, ripped and thrown onto the fire. The only works that survived Auntie's destruction were a watercolour portrait of the Queen wearing her 'Trooping the Colour' uniform and a black-and-white picture of Winston Churchill. They were displayed on the mantelpiece in my bedroom to be shown to anyone important who came to visit the croft.

Auntie had the old-fashioned idea that art and all its derivatives were activities for the fallen women, or sluts, as she called them. She created her own values, her own importance, and was determined that I was led down the path she thought was right. Her misunderstanding or acceptance of modern values and opportunities forced me down a very different path, one I had not intended or considered.

Her preferred choice of career for me was secretarial work, but my test results in shorthand and typing were not good enough to continue with the subjects and I think she was very disappointed. She had wanted to keep me at Coxton. The only other career she was familiar with was nursing, but the nearest training college for student nurses in the '60s was Aberdeen. I think she knew deep down that once I left the croft I would never return. I think she was afraid of losing control, of what I might say and do once I was free from her suffocating grasp.

During the last few weeks of study before the summer vacation arrived, the local swimming baths ran a competition for all North-east schools to produce a poster to promote their 'Learn to Swim Week' campaign. Several pupils were picked to participate, including myself. I was reluctant to get involved because I knew that my foster mother would disapprove. In addition, if there was any chance of me winning the competition, my name would appear in the local press, which made me nervous. She would be furious at the publicity and the connection with art. She would do her best to make me suffer for going behind her back and misleading her. But because the City Baths were the instigators, it was easy for me to lie by omission. Auntie assumed it was a swimming contest and I did not enlighten her. Each day I took my swimming costume to school to keep up the pretence, never thinking that I could actually have the chance of winning – but I did. Now I *was* scared. What if she came to the ceremony and discovered my deception?

To my immense relief, she did not and I accepted 24 tokens for free entry to the swimming pool. My name did appear in the local paper, but I don't think she ever noticed. For the rest of the time I spent with her, she remained under the impression that I could swim, but I couldn't: I only learned to swim when my own children took to the water.

My poster hung in the swimming enclosure for a few weeks and was then transported to the Royal College of Art for an exhibition. I tried to get it back when I returned to Elgin for a visit some years later and though I was informed by the staff that if I would sketch the inside of their new pool, they would try to source it for me, I returned home to Aberdeen and never followed it through.

Leaving school for the last time was, for me, not a happy event. It had been my only source of contentment: it was there that my efforts to progress were praised and encouraged; it was a place where I could be myself in character and achievement, where I was regarded as normal, where the pencil in my hand became alive and opened the door to the precise art of the wordsmith and the beautiful steady rhythm of iambic pentameter.

As the summer holidays came to an end, I had just returned from the village on my rickety bike, still equipped with the back-wheel guard fixed to prevent long skirts getting caught up in the spokes, when I noticed Auntie walking down the road towards me. This was a strange thing for her to do because she very rarely left the croft or showed any pleasure at the thought of us coming home. I became very concerned. What had I done this time? What was the reason for this unusual behaviour? Whatever it was, I knew it was serious enough for Auntie to leave the security of her home.

As she got closer, I noticed she was actually smiling and waving a brown envelope. She was walking so fast that her straight leg sliced through the grass that grew in the middle of the road, scattering stones to the front and side. The envelope flapped open and she waved the form in my face. My exam results had arrived and I had done better than expected. She was extremely pleased.

Her speech was rapid and constant; she was planning my future, she was eagerly anticipating the praise and admiration she now expected from the child welfare officer. Before supper I was ordered to sit down, handed a pencil and paper, and told to write a letter to the authorities, giving them the good news. She knew it was a positive sign of her success – my efforts were insignificant. As far as she was concerned, she had helped me achieve good academic status and gained points as a successful foster mother.

I was uncertain as to what lay ahead and afraid of the step I was destined to take. I could not get any reassurance from Auntie or any indication that the career choice made for me was the right one. I had so few possessions and could not see any way of getting enough of what I needed with which to leave home.

All my friends were keen to venture into the world of adults and occupations, with the support of their parents, whether to further education or local employment. My nurse training was due to start in January of the following year and I managed to acquire a job in the food factory at Fochabers for the meantime. I needed new clothes and books, and this was the only way I would be able to afford them. I didn't realise that Auntie would take all my pay and give very little back.

I enjoyed my time there and became part of a huge family. For the first few months, I felt so hungry. Auntie did not give me a packed lunch and I was lucky if I could sneak some bread from her cupboard. The amount of food being processed in the factory became too much and I eventually helped myself to raw carrots and cooked chicken pieces selected in bins for their delicious tinned soups. No one seemed to notice or object and it was a lifesaver. I needed the nourishment to help me through the working day – and very often to sustain me on the long walk home. Every morning when I asked for my bus fare, I was given the fare to work but not enough for the return journey. I tried to tell her it was insufficient, but she accused me of trying to deceive her. It was as if she wanted me to get there to earn the money, but it didn't matter if I took all night to get home. It was more than six miles to the croft and, after a hard day's work, walking home was the last thing I wanted to do. By the time I got home, all food for dinner had been removed from the table. Sometimes if I had not managed to help myself at the factory, I had to plead with Auntie to give me a few slices of bread and margarine.

At the end of July 1965, Auntie received a request for my attendance at the Occupational Health Department at the hospital in Aberdeen where my training would take place. They had received a report from my own doctor, which they were not happy with, and I was required to have a medical examination. I was well underweight for 17 and, before they could consider me for the course, they wanted to check if I was fit enough.

I arrived at Aberdeen railway station several weeks later. It was the first time I had travelled any distance from the croft on my own. I made my way to the hospital, where my height, weight and bloods were taken. I was under six stone in weight and was informed by the examining doctor that if I did not put on what they classed as a fighting weight, I would not be able to cope with the long hours of work and intense study needed to succeed. As a result, they would not be able to accept me for the course.

I left the hospital, feeling quite sad. I knew there might be a possibility that I could be turned down, which would spoil any chance I had of leaving the croft. I was desperate: I didn't want to go home, I didn't want to go back to Auntie, but I didn't know what else to do. But maybe I would be accepted for the course and my life would change for ever. I knew if I didn't go home, I would lose the opportunity. I knew it was too good to be true, but at least the possibility was there. I had to go home and wait for fate to play its cards.

On the way to the station, I checked my rail ticket and noticed I could use it any time; it wasn't an ordinary day return. I got excited; I was shaking. The idea of not going home right away appealed greatly. Auntie told me that the hospital might keep me for a few days and accommodation would be provided if required. Could I take advantage of this and get away with it? For how long could I manage to stay without raising concern? At the time, I didn't think of food, shelter or the simple act of cleanliness. There was no problem with the job at the factory because I was part of the casual workforce and could return whenever I was ready. All I needed to do was send a postcard to Auntie to tell her I would be delayed and hope she would not get suspicious and enquire about my whereabouts. I paced the station platform, trying to pluck up enough courage to stay.

I watched the train north leave and wandered out into the streets of Aberdeen. What was I going to do now? I had nowhere to stay and very little money to do anything with. Although scared, I was looking forward to the challenge and was relieved at not having to face Auntie for a while longer.

The sun was shining as I walked up Bridge Street onto Union Street, where I spent some time wandering about looking in all the shop windows. I began to feel quite hungry, so I checked the loose change in my pocket and found enough money to buy a loaf of bread and a packet of cheese triangles. I had a few coins left over and this change would last a few days. I needed to find toilets, I needed to find water to drink and I needed to find a place to stay the night.

The public toilets were situated in a beautiful sunken garden area not far from the main street and with a few pennies stashed away in another pocket, another problem was solved. I couldn't stay in the gardens – it was too open and could be seen from the street above – and as I watched each shop light up for late afternoon trading, I was getting worried. I still hadn't found a place for the night and it was too late to go home.

After a few hours' walking up and down the main street, my feet began to hurt and I was getting tired. I was lonely and I wanted to find a seat. It was beginning to get dark when I noticed a large graveyard with wooden seats, trees and flat gravestones. The entrance was imposingly impressive, so I entered through a large granite-pillared megalithic structure and sat down on one of the benches. Immediately, I felt relief. The ache in my feet subsided and I began to feel better. I opened the paper bag from the baker's shop, broke off a few pieces of soft, doughy bread and ate them, along with two triangles of cheese. I sat among the trees and tombstones, relics of the city's past, beside people who had lived, people I did not know, and I felt safe. I watched people bustling by, wondering if they were all happy with life or if some of them were lonely like me. No one knew I was there, no one cared. I was a tiny person in the corner of a big place: I was lost. I felt the tears well up in my eyes as I thought about Robert, George and Mary. I was missing them.

By now, it was getting much darker and I knew I had to find a place to sleep, but where? Could I stay here, I wondered. Would someone find me and send me home? I moved towards a flat gravestone tucked underneath a very bushy tree, out of sight of the main gates, and waited. A man came in and looked around, as if he was checking the area. I stayed as still as possible, hoping he wouldn't see me, and watched as he slowly walked back onto the street. There appeared to be no one about, so I settled down to sleep on the cold cement stone. I tucked my anorak tight around my waist and pulled up the hood.

It wasn't a cold night, but I felt strange. Unlike in the country, the stars were hidden and I couldn't see the soft clouds against the night sky. The light from the city was too strong. I felt uneasy, remembering my beach hut experience from several years ago, and my confidence wavered. I had done it again. I was a silly, silly little girl.

I must have fallen asleep very quickly, however, because the next thing I knew it was morning and, luckily for me, the place was still deserted. The gates were open, so I ventured onto the quiet streets. I desperately needed to use the toilets, but couldn't risk going too early in case someone suspected something. I did not have a watch, but it seemed very early, so I just went back into the graveyard and ate some more of my soft bread and cheese until I felt it was safe to use the facilities.

I spent another night there, but on the second morning I was wakened by noises coming from the far end of the church. I could hear voices and became paranoid, thinking I had been seen and reported to the police. I gathered my belongings and fled.

I set off down the street and kept walking – I wasn't ready to go home yet. I passed a building that resembled a castle and eventually arrived at the seafront, where I noticed there were several game stalls not far from the beach. It was still reasonably early and holidaymakers were just beginning to filter down to the seaside, so I joined them and felt less conspicuous. I had to find another place to sleep or I would have to admit defeat, whether I liked it or not.

As I walked further along the beach, I noticed some huts. They weren't as neat as the bathers' huts at Lossiemouth, but I decided to check to see if I could use one of them at night. They looked as if they were being dismantled, but I noticed that I could squeeze in between them and shelter quite happily without being seen in the dark. As long as the weather stayed fine and it didn't rain heavily, I would be all right. I convinced myself I would be quite safe for the short time I intended to stay.

My next problem was I had no money left. I was starting to get hungry, too, so I approached a man who was working at the target-shooting stall further along the beachfront and asked if he was looking for someone to help. He looked at me with curiosity and asked if I was still at school. I assured him that I had just left and was looking for pocket money. I explained that I was going to college at the beginning of the year and was looking for a summer job. To my surprise, he took me on, but, to keep things right and legal, he asked if I could bring a relative or friend to confirm my identity. I had no one to ask and was relieved when he did not bring up the subject again. He was very kind and I earned enough money to buy food and spend a penny. I also discovered from one of the stallholders that there was such a thing as public baths, where I could wash. I had tried to bathe in the sea several times, but I could taste the salt all day, plus it was freezing cold and I had never really felt clean afterwards.

I managed to work quite happily for another few days – but it was now nearly a week since I had left the croft. I was starting to feel uneasy: Auntie would be wondering why the hospital was keeping me so long. I sent her another postcard, reluctantly writing that I would be home at the end of the week.

As it happened, my decision came just at the right time. The stallholders started asking questions that made me feel very uncomfortable. One was curious why I wore the same clothes every day, while my boss wondered why I had not managed to produce someone to verify my identity. The woman in charge of the toilets at the beach asked me if I ever went home, and why I was always washing clothes in the sink. I didn't have an answer for any of them and tried to get around it by pretending to be shy, but the seed of doubt had been sown. I had to leave.

It was time to return to Auntie. I had overstayed my time and knew I was close to being found out. I was also afraid that the hospital would contact my foster mother with my medical results before I got home. I was told to expect them in six weeks, so I wasn't overly concerned; I had plenty of time to get back to the croft before I was in serious trouble.

I packed everything into my duffle bag, collected my daily wage and never went back. Surprisingly, I had never been asked for my address and this made it easier for me to disappear. I had confided my story in one of the stallholders whom I had befriended and asked her to explain everything to the man who employed me once I was gone. I was worried in case he would report my disappearance to the police. I never saw or heard of these people again.

I took the next train north, feeling very worried and concerned. What had I done? For a little bit of freedom, I had jeopardised my whole future. If I was found out, my punishment would be instant and traumatic. Even if I had passed the medical, my nursing career would be over and I would be forced to live with my guardian until I was 21. I didn't think I could bear that – please help me, I thought; please, someone help us all.

I saw the croft from the train as it passed over the bridge. From a distance, it was a picture of peace and tranquillity, the perfect place to live, away from the hustle and bustle of life, away from prying eyes, offering a safe and comfortable environment for children to play. I saw it as a prison, a place where children cried all day, were beaten and verbally abused. It was a place where a mother's love was desperately missing.

My legs were shaking as I climbed the brae towards the front door. The geese were out and about as usual, hissing my arrival to Auntie. She appeared at the door and casually acknowledged my presence. No welcome home, I thought, no 'Where have you been?' My worries were all in vain. I should not have been so stressed. I had forgotten that she didn't care very much for me: of course she hadn't been unduly concerned about my absence. She did ask why the visit to Aberdeen had taken so long, and I informed her that more tests were necessary, as my weight was deemed inadequate for my age, which could be detrimental to my ultimate success in my career choice. She appeared uninterested and accepted the explanation as if it were some sort of blasé, non-committal statement of insignificant importance. I tried to emphasise the need for me to put on more weight in the hope that our meals became more substantial, but I knew it would make no difference to the way we were fed. I had to have hope, though.

When I brought up the tiny amount of food we received at mealtimes, she became aggressive and hostile, pushing the table against my legs or pinning me to the dresser. She told me to re-pack my bags and take the next train back to Aberdeen. She knew I didn't have the money to do it and gloated over the control she had. She struck the table with her stick, angry at being accused of deliberate malnutrition. Her attitude towards me remained very abrupt for several days after I returned from Aberdeen. I couldn't do anything right. Every job she gave me had to be re-done several times. If I objected, she would catch my hair, roll it round her stick and pull me in circles round the sheds until I stopped complaining. I was constantly battered with verbal abuse – I wasn't good enough to be trained as a nurse, she yelled. Who did I think I was, anyway?

I was determined not to let her upset me and equally resolute not to let her dampen any enthusiasm I had for a better life.

I went back to the factory and continued to eat as much as I could. Each day I returned from work, dreading the letter from Aberdeen with the results of my medical. I hoped that it would not mention that I had just spent one day at the hospital, rather than the whole week I had pretended to be there.

When the letter finally arrived, however, I wasn't even told what it contained. I was never weighed again and, to my immense relief, I was accepted for three years of nurse training.

13

Escape

I continued to work at the factory until Christmas 1965, when I was invited to take part in the end-of-year pantomime, *Aladdin*. It was an opportunity to have fun and take part in a live performance, to experience the creativity of a wonderful fantasy adventure. I wanted the chance to join in, so I told Auntie about the show and my proposed involvement. I explained rehearsals were held after working hours, meaning I would be late home for supper and my chores on the croft would have to be delayed until I returned. Her attitude was deliberately hostile – as usual, she opposed any activity that might result in my enjoyment. I saw her mental dilemma: on one hand, there was her habitual urge to forbid my involvement in anything fun, while on the other was her deep desire to promote her image of good parenting. The latter won, but every night I came home late, I had to stand outside, rain or shine, until permission was given to enter the croft. The door was locked and sometimes hours passed before it was opened. She would pretend to be ill and did her best to make me feel guilty for not coming home on time. I was glad when rehearsals were over.

The show opened at the end of the week before the factory closed for the festive celebrations. The atmosphere was electric. For my part, I was dressed in a Scout uniform and sang Christmas carols with three other girls. Our make-up was heavy, elaborate and fun. It was an absolute success and I enjoyed every minute. Everyone knew I was leaving to train as a nurse and on my last day at the factory I was presented with a nurse's watch.

When I think back to my time at the factory, I loved every minute of it. I loved the atmosphere and the hard-working characters: their sense of humour; their carefree, yet sensitive approach to life. I was also grateful for the opportunity I had had to improve my health by nibbling on raw carrots and cooked chicken. I was grateful for the social experience and the introduction to the working environment.

That year was my last Christmas and New Year at Coxton. The four of us continued to support one another until the day came when I left the croft for ever. On the morning of my departure, I rose early and ironed all the clothes I was taking with me. I folded them neatly and placed them in my case. I was very excited, although slightly disturbed as I noticed Auntie becoming restless and uneasy. She appeared more agitated than usual, flitting in and out of the room, muttering to herself. I continued to pack everything away and tried not to let her unsettling behaviour affect me.

Once the case was full and I had checked that everything I needed was accounted for, I clipped it closed and placed it in a corner ready to be picked up.

There was a palpable feeling of animosity building up between Auntie and myself. The atmosphere was filling with resentment and intensity. I didn't understand why she was so upset. It didn't make any sense – I expected her to be happy for me, but every time she passed I was aggressively nudged, her nails digging into my shoulder, nipping my skin. As her agitation increased, she shook and clicked her tongue as her cigarette flicked from one side of her mouth to another. Everything I did or said was wrong, and not to her liking.

As the morning progressed, I was beginning to feel less confident about leaving. I was also starting to feel afraid that at the last minute she would find a way to stop me. I could feel the panic rising inside me, and I became more and more anxious to leave – to get out of the house, away from this woman.

These feelings were mixed with more sentimental ones, too. Although I was afraid of her in that moment, I also wanted to speak to her and say sorry for all the bad things I felt I had done over the years. But she wouldn't let me speak. I wanted to hug her and say goodbye, I wanted to get her blessing, but she accused me of insensitivity and indifference. She made me feel guilty for leaving and criticised my selfish behaviour.

I didn't know how to react. I stood quietly in the corner and let her belittle my character and threaten to ruin any chance I had of a better future. Just before it was time to leave for the station, she picked up my case, unclipped it and threw everything round the room. She screamed and shouted, scraping her nails down the living-room door. She said I would destroy everything I touched and ruin everything I tried to do, just like my mother before me. I hadn't earned this chance, nor was I worthy of it. I would destroy her reputation with my failures and when I came crawling back to the croft, I would find a locked door. No one would want me; I would be homeless and destitute. My brothers and sister would not be allowed to speak to me again.

For an instant, I actually believed her. I hesitated and felt everything slipping away from me. I looked from my sobbing siblings to this screaming woman, then at the clock on the mantelpiece. I realised I had to go.

I did not have time to re-pack neatly, so I stuffed everything back into the suitcase as quickly as possible. I was determined not to miss the train and throw away my first real chance of freedom. I hoped, in her own way, that she was going to miss me. I had to feel I was worth something.

I could see her struggling. Her emotions were tearing her asunder. I knew she was afraid to show any affection, to show a weakness that might in some way suggest a failure in how she portrayed herself. She was reacting to the moment in the only way she knew how, with aggression, and using rejection as a weapon. I would like to think she was sad at my leaving; I had given her something of myself over those ten years, something I hoped she would be able to understand eventually.

She did not let me say goodbye to Robert, George and Mary. As I stood in the hallway firmly holding my suitcase, I heard my little sister crying in her bedroom. She was desperate to hold on to the certainty of my presence, to know that I would always be there to comfort her and help her through the days ahead. I knew I had to walk out of this house if I had any chance of a future for myself and, if possible, getting help for my brothers and sister. I was convinced that once I was gone I would be able to do something positive to remove them from this place and this woman.

Emotional turmoil boiled inside my mind as I fought the decision of whether to go or stay. I turned and looked at the empty, cold and dirty fireplace; the fat, well-fed cats; the spoilt orange-and-white dog yapping in the corner; the uncared-for interior, with its smoke-stained wallpaper and dust-covered windows, then into the sad, pleading eyes of my siblings and the overpowering silhouette of a woman I didn't know.

I escaped into the daylight with tears in my eyes. I was stepping into a free, fresh world, one I wanted to explore, but I was desperately wondering when – or if – I would see my family again. It was the saddest day of my life, not because of Auntie or the croft but because I was leaving my sister and brothers behind. I desperately hoped they understood why I had to go. They too would eventually get the chance to leave the croft, but this was my time.

I ran down the brae, past the neighbours' croft. I kept running until I felt safe. I looked back at the house on the hill and burst into tears. My sobs were uncontrollable. I was afraid for Robert, George and Mary; I knew Auntie would treat them with the utmost contempt now that I was gone. Her frustrations would be relieved with bouts of verbal and physical abuse. The next few weeks would be spent in fear of everything she did and said. The slightest mistake or childish disobedience would be pounced on with a brutal deliverance, as she fought to decipher her next move.

I reached the railway bridge for the last time, pulled myself together, took a deep breath and stepped forward more confidently than I had ever done before. I did not want to turn back. It would be a sign of weakness, and I did not want her to win.

I headed under the bridge where I had spent many a lonely hour, consoling myself or eating a small meal to satisfy my hunger, then on to the crossroads, where I had so often caught a bus into Elgin and the railway station. Auntie had given me money for the train fare only, saying that I would get paid at the end of the month. I wouldn't need anything else, as my food and accommodation came off my wages and what was left was enough to last me a month. The money I had earned at the factory to buy my nursing textbooks had somehow disappeared and I would have to depend on my first pay packet to furnish me with the reading material I needed for study.

I settled down in the carriage and watched the croft disappear from view as the train ran south past Coxton and over the bridge. I imagined the chaos in that house – the screaming, the shouting, the sobbing – as I sped past. I tried to forget, as the croft disappeared from sight, focusing on the constantly changing scenery instead. I was the lucky one. I was finally free and going towards what I hoped was a better future. The feeling was intense: I was now able to release fragile emotions without fear of abuse, mockery or rejection. I was determined not to let my past affect any decisions I made. I knew I had to succeed where my mother and father had failed.

I had escaped from Auntie and the croft, and from Social Services, with their scrutinising and biased reporting of the person they thought I was, not the person I had become. All they knew of me came from my foster mother's written account of day-to-day events and the vague reports of the social workers, written in our absence while we were at school. I was never asked for any input or able to defend myself in any way. I was portrayed as being a rather wayward child and not helping in the home. I was aware that everything I said was noted, reported and discussed in Glasgow and not once were my individual views, likes or dislikes given serious consideration. I felt like crying, but tears were difficult to find. Years of conditioning had destroyed my emotional make-up and severely damaged my ability to respond in a way that might ease the pain I now felt. It would take many years to completely heal, to be able to show joy, an excitement for life and trust in the people around me. I closed my eyes, gathered my thoughts and began the journey that lay ahead.

The train pulled into Aberdeen on 17 January 1966, two days before my eighteenth birthday. I was filled with a strange feeling of anticipation, fear and excitement. I caught a bus from Union Street to my destination and arrived at the nurses' home in late afternoon, carrying one suitcase with a change of clothes and some toiletries. I wore a deep-red curled wool coat, which Auntie had acquired from somewhere, a black hat, tartan stockings held up with tape from a liberty bodice and black suede shoes. I was the picture of a very naive girl in a strange city with no one to turn to, dressed in an outfit that resembled the fashion of the early '50s. I was very self-conscious of my looks and deeply worried about how I would be perceived. However, my concerns were unwarranted. I received a generous welcome and quickly became friends with the other students.

Once everyone had settled in and our details were checked, we were shown to our rooms, where we unpacked our suitcases and claimed our beds. We were called to the dining room for tea and sat round a large table, where we began to get to know one another. The atmosphere was buzzing with conversation and full of anticipation for the training that was to come. After the evening meal I began to explore the building – so many rooms, luxury upon luxury, toilets, bathrooms . . . a bath! I couldn't wait to try it out. Bubble bath and perfumed oils were yet to be discovered, but the cocoon of warmth from the half-filled bath embraced my body, soaking into my skin. I could feel every nerve and muscle relaxing, ten years of mental and physical abuse draining into the water around me. It was as if a heavy weight had been lifted from my whole being. I felt cleansed inside and out. I could at last look at myself naked without feeling guilty or bad, and I was able to undress in complete privacy, free from the attentions of others. I was experiencing a freedom I had never felt before, one that I still felt I didn't deserve. This was a different world; it was like being released from a long confinement. I was free to be myself.

It wasn't long before I settled down to the new routine and visits to the wards commenced in earnest. I was on my way, my training had begun in earnest, and I felt scared but proud.

There were inevitably things in this new life that I took time to adjust to. I had to learn not only about a career in nursing, but also how to look after myself and make my own decisions. I was not streetwise and did not know how to interact to any great extent with people of my own age. Having lived in the country, I had only really had dealings with my siblings. School friends were left at the school gates, outside of which interaction was forbidden. I found it extremely hard to join in a conversation – my fellow students talked about family, friends, holidays and what to buy with their pay, and I couldn't reciprocate the conversation – and very often I became embarrassed when I was in a large company of students. I was terrified of saying something wrong and lacked confidence in my own abilities, which kept me in my room when I was not working. It took some time before I was able to settle down and enjoy a close friendship with anyone.

The pace of city life also proved extremely difficult to keep up with, and it was confusing. I didn't know how to handle myself in different environments or understand what I was expected to do when I was off-duty. I had very few possessions and was in awe of the amount of clothes and toiletries that my fellow students seemed to cram into their cupboards. When a friend went home one weekend, I sampled her perfume and applied some of her make-up. I had visions of Auntie appearing at the bedroom door ready to slap my face and call me a slut, a good-for-nothing slut. I ran my fingertips along the row of stylish dresses hanging neatly in her wardrobe. I wanted to try them on; I wanted to own them.

I remember going into town once wearing a beautiful soft-blue dress with white daisies round the collar. I felt good when I was out, but ever so guilty when I returned to my room that evening. It took me a long time to learn about clothes sizes and I kept buying shoes that were too big for me. I didn't even realise shoes came in different sizes! I was buying them on their visual appearance not for the way they fitted my feet. Luckily for me, I was attracted to sling backs and got away with larger sizes without them falling off my feet! It was the same when I went to buy a bra. I had arrived at the home still wearing navy knickers and a white vest. It took my bedroom buddies some time to introduce me to the world of fashion and modern toiletries.

Most of my young life had been spent enshrouded in yesteryear's ideas and traditions and I was not aware of new technology. I found it difficult to adjust to living in a sterile environment. The rules and regulations were completely alien and keeping up with things going on around me was tiring. I couldn't understand things there the way I could at the croft.

But even though it was hard at times to adjust to this new way of life, I knew I had a goal to accomplish. It was extremely difficult to stop looking over my shoulder in case Auntie was there with her stick, but I knew I would become more self-aware, I knew I would succeed in the end. I had to.

I felt I belonged at the nurses' home: I could trust these people not to hurt me. But it was another thing to trust them not to judge me. I did not want the students to know about my past life, so I invented one that seemed believable. I didn't feel bad about the pretence at first. I felt it didn't matter. Coxton couldn't hurt me any more and it was up to me to make a success of my psychological recovery. But soon my stories became inconsistent; I was beginning to contradict myself. Several student nurses began to ask awkward questions and I wasn't a very good liar, so I arranged to meet three of them in my bedroom and told them the whole story. They were very considerate and seemed to understand what I was going through. I never mentioned my imaginary family again: I realised I didn't have to pretend to be someone else to become a better person.

I met my first boyfriend on one of our jaunts into town after college and the brother-and-sister relationship we had lasted for many months. He was a year younger than me and we became the best of friends. He provided much-needed comfort when I was anxious, and was generous with hugs when I felt vulnerable and lost, asking for nothing in return. His loyal companionship played a large part in stabilising my fragile emotional state, but in the end I knew it couldn't last: I had lied to him. I desperately wanted him to like me, so felt I had to pretend. I couldn't tell him the truth about my life as a foster child in case of rejection, so once again I invented a family of my own. Having built the relationship on deceit, I felt he would never trust me again, so I ended it.

One day while walking on the beach, we found a very young rabbit crouched among the sand dunes. It looked so helpless and alone, I convinced my boyfriend to take it back to the nurses' home at Woodend Hospital. I thought I could hide it under my bed. I sourced a large cardboard box, punched several holes in the lid and lined the bottom with shredded newspapers. It was perfect. Every day I saved lettuce and raw carrots from my salad; I bought a cat's collar and a ball of string, and every night when daylight faded I took the rabbit, named Dumpling because of his brown colour, out for a walk round the grassy area at the back of the home or allowed him to run about my bedroom as I studied for my exams. I was happy: I had company, someone to look after and something to hug. I didn't need to face my demons by visiting the nurses' common room.

Things were going well until I received a note from one of the maids who cleaned my room. I had forgotten that she checked the rooms on a regular basis. She made it clear that pets were not allowed and that I would have to find a home for the rabbit as soon as possible. I was devastated, but I knew she was right. When I spoke to her, she offered to take Dumpling. She said her little boy would look after him. I believed her wholeheartedly and handed him over with a heavy heart. I never saw him or the maid again.

My second relationship was just as naive. On our first date, I persuaded this young man to take me home to his parents' house. I really wanted to stay with them, as their daughter. I wanted the family, rather than their son. I possessed a deep-rooted need to belong, which scared me – to the point that I felt tormented by my behaviour. I was yearning for a place where I could settle, a solid home to hold me down: an anchor, if you like. It would be somewhere that I could forget and develop. I yearned for a refuge: maybe it was so I could hide from the world around me. Of course, this relationship did not last. The issues I had about belonging to someone made sure of this.

I think, looking back, I felt very insecure. I remember my feelings of guilt in the company of my boyfriends, thinking Auntie was always watching, accusing me of inappropriate behaviour.

In my innocence, I had thought that once I left the croft, life would become much easier, but still I craved parental affection and fought against the loneliness that lingered around me. I wanted to find happiness, to find someone that wanted me. Since the desertion of my parents, I had been seeking to replicate the closeness I had once shared with them, trying to fill the void they left behind, searching for life to begin again where it had ended so abruptly all those years ago, the day we were taken from our home in Glasgow. During the years with Auntie, I had convinced myself that life could be good, *would* be good. I clung on to the idea that there was someone out there who would love me for myself and treat me with the kindness I felt I deserved, who would reassure me that I was not a failure but a valued member of the human race.

I became more and more frantic with worry as our first holidays came round and all the students in my group began to plan their vacation home. We were expected to vacate our rooms and take up new placements on our return to whichever hospital we were allocated. But I couldn't go home: I had no place to go. I spoke to the Home Sister about Coxton for the first time, explaining why I couldn't and wouldn't return to the croft. She handled my query with a degree of understanding and gave permission to remain in the nurses' home for the rest of my holidays. I spent a lonely two weeks either reading, listening to the wireless in my room or exploring the hospital grounds. Everyone had gone home to their parents: I was lost and very sad. I did not know the other nurses well enough to interact with them and the majority were well into their senior year and settled with friends of their own. At the end of the fortnight, I was glad to see everyone return to the schoolroom and the wards.

The horrors of Auntie's treatment followed me into adulthood and often affected the way I looked at things or how I reacted to different situations. I felt uncomfortable around some of the students who seemed so independent and confident. Many times I was invited to join in their activities or attend some of their parties, but I was content to lie on my bed when I came off-duty and listen to the wireless or read a magazine. It was so relaxing to have time and space to myself. I couldn't explain this to anyone, as they would not have understood. I did not tell them that I had been brought up in a foster home because I wanted to be seen as their equal and not labelled an underdog. Foster children, even to this day, are tarred with the same brush, blamed for everything and accused of all wrongs. They are not usually treated as individuals or listened to sympathetically.

My first room had been in temporary accommodation, designed to help student nurses adjust to life away from home. When our introductory months were over and we were moved up to the main nurses' home at the hospital to begin our training in earnest, the bright lights from the complex disturbed my sleeping pattern. I had grown up with dark nights and dark mornings, especially in winter, the countryside lit by moon, stars and the odd flash of lightning. The lights, shining through my thin bedroom curtains, woke me early in the mornings. I would often be shaking with fear after seeing Auntie's menacing silhouette featured against the window. The vision was so realistic that I could feel her hand pressing down on my chest. I couldn't move; I couldn't breathe. I struggled against the fear of her presence until I was fully awake, then she vanished. I would lie and stare at the ceiling for a long time, trying to erase the image of the face that was still haunting me. I kept telling myself that I was in my own room filled with my own belongings and she could never drag me out of bed in the middle of the night again. I spent time teaching myself to relax and found that if I read before lights out, I slept better. Gradually, the visions slowly disappeared for ever.

Often when sitting in the nurses' common room listening to some of the slow tunes of the '60s, the air filled with sensitive strains, promises of love and bridges over troubled waters, I found it impossible to control my feelings. Sometimes the deep loneliness this music evoked became so unbearable that I had to leave the room and return to my bedroom, where I sobbed for the rest of the evening. I seemed to be full of such a sadness I couldn't get rid of. This depressed state was dragging me down and preventing me from successfully adapting to my new life. I was determined to fight it and so restricted the length of time I spent listening to this music that was affecting me so much, finishing the evening in the home's kitchen with a cup of hot chocolate instead, forcing myself to 'face the music' by speaking to a few colleagues, trying to improve my social awareness.

Most of the comics I had read inside my hut in the woods were *Commando* books given to Robert by a neighbour. At the time, I could not bring myself to read love stories: they always had a happy ending and I couldn't believe that this could ever be true for me. It upset me too much to think that maybe out there a life of kindness and love did exist; it was too far away for me to reach, anyway. However, I began to read books to children in hospital and was able to absorb some of their trust, their absolute belief in happy endings, and in doing so realised that I alone could change the way I felt about myself and other people.

I wanted to use my childhood experiences in a more positive way in the hope that they had given me sympathy to tackle anything. I felt that the ten years I had spent with Auntie on the croft had taught me a lot about the complexities of human nature and how to deal with situations on the spur of the moment. I was very aware of my shortcomings and very self-conscious of my actions, but I did not want to spend the rest of my life feeling sorry for myself. I did not want to blame anyone or any place for my future behaviour. As a result of this closer analysis of my fragile emotional state, I became aware of how I was reacting to authority and I didn't like it.

I remember in my first surgical ward the Sister trying to tell me I was doing a procedure the wrong way and for the rest of the day I sulked, not fully understanding that I was in training to be a nurse and should not have taken her correction personally. By the time my work was finished, I was aware of my immaturity; I felt I lacked wisdom and the emotional development usually found in adults. I had to take control of things and stop judging everyone by Auntie's standards.

One Christmas Eve, I was nursing a seriously ill patient at the city's fever hospital, when the Salvation Army's brass band appeared directly outside the window. They acknowledged my presence and began to play 'Silent Night'. The old sadness surged through my body, tears streamed down my cheeks and I began to lose control. Then I checked myself: what if a relation of this lady walked in and saw me in this state? I was the nurse. I was this lady's protector, her carer, and the one ultimately responsible for her well-being. I was ashamed of my weakness, embarrassed by my emotional instability and painfully self-conscious about my reaction to a beautiful piece of music. From that day on, I decided that, if I was to continue in this profession, I had to pull my socks up and become a much stronger person. I must not forget, however, to retain a degree of compassion, so important when dealing with people in need of care, but I told myself that I had to learn to develop it and use this quality in a more sensitive and positive way.

Before long, I was dealing with other people's experiences and emergencies and, as my character strengthened, I began to understand the right and wrong ways in which people reacted emotionally to different situations. This enabled me to deal with my own feelings and allowed me to handle my personal life in a more mature way.

Several months after leaving the croft, I felt settled enough to turn my attention to finding a way to help the rest of my family. I started by writing a long letter to the Child Care Authorities, giving them details of the abuse still going on in that house and pleading with them to remove my brothers and sister from that place and that woman. They sent a representative to meet me and discuss the problem. I arranged his visit to coincide with my day off and we met in a small café. After listening to my story again, he assured me he would look into the matter but would have to go north to assess the situation for himself. A few weeks later, I received a letter in return, stating that he could see nothing wrong in the way Auntie was handling everything and that my account of events was highly exaggerated. He also said that the rest of the family had settled down greatly since I had left and, in his opinion, I had been the troublemaker all along. He also said at such a late stage in their care, where would they put my siblings? Of course, it was not in the authorities' interest to admit mistakes might have been made, but I was devastated and disappointed. I thought he would have believed me and made things better. I didn't know what to do next. My siblings would feel I had deserted them.

Soon after the social worker's visit to the croft, Robert ran away for the last time and followed me to Aberdeen. His beatings had increased to an unacceptable level, with Auntie continually trying to break his spirit. Each time he ran away, he was brought home by the police and given a lecture on behaviour and responsibility. Life on the croft became so unbearable without the support and company of his big sister that a desperate desire to flee that place of deprivation became his obsession. His chance finally came when he managed to find out where I was staying and he hitched a lift to Aberdeen.

The first I knew of his arrival in the city was when I received a phone call from an office in Aberdeen harbour. He had tried to sign on to the fishing fleet but was underage and a signature from an older family member was required before he could be employed by the company. He had given my name as next of kin and told them I was a nurse at the local hospital. I was asked to come down and sign the appropriate papers, which I did.

It was nice to see him again, to know he had plucked up enough courage to leave Coxton. He was so thin and looked so young. I felt deeply sorry for him, but ever so proud. We hugged and hugged while the man behind the desk waited patiently for our reunion to conclude. Once the papers were signed, I was introduced to a man waiting to speak to me. He said he was a newspaper reporter. When Robert had relayed the story of the croft to his future employer, it had been deemed suitable for publication in the local press, but because of the delicate human content it required my permission and verification before a decision could be made. I verified the details, but could not give permission to run the article. I explained that we still had a brother and sister living there and unless he could give some guarantee that he could in some way help to have them removed from that dreadful place I was unwilling to give him free access. He could not assure me of this and the story was never released.

I did not realise how difficult a task I was asking the reporter to undertake. But by letting the story into the public domain, so many people would have been affected, for better or worse. The good people who had spent ten years trying to help us would have been dragged into the whole fiasco, their quiet lives disrupted by the press. The barrage of public responses would have been equally emotionally disturbing. I was also aware of my foster mother's position, of how things had gone against her, and her ability to cope had been undermined by the lack of support from the people she was employed by.

She told me once that she had applied to foster one child, not four, and that if the authorities had not persuaded her to take four children, she might have been able to adjust better to the role of mother. For the first time, I felt sorry for her. I couldn't change the past, and I didn't know how to improve the future.

As it was, four unwanted children had been sent north to a small croft in Morayshire for the chance of a better life, to be part of a happy and well-adjusted family unit. For ten years, we struggled to survive, trying physically and mentally to understand Auntie and all her rules, desperately seeking the family environment we were promised when we left the children's home. This dream fell apart the moment we set foot inside that croft. We were too young to see or notice the difficulties Auntie had in understanding another generation. The system and the adults to whom we had been entrusted believed everything Auntie told them without question. They ignored our pleas for help and left us to fester in an unsuitable and regimented environment.

Robert spent several successful years trawling the North Sea and gained his First Mate's Certificate. I was often afraid for him, my little brother tossing about on the wild seas. We kept in regular contact and took every opportunity to discuss our experiences at Coxton. Each conversation played a major part in healing those times, and the bond we developed over the ten years spent on the croft is just as strong today as it was then.

Life was very hard for Robert. As a consequence of the lack of control in his life and the loneliness he suffered, he struggled with alcohol and behavioural problems for many years. His knuckles bore his frustrations, the raw, skinned sores evidence of walls and houses he had hit in a bid to release his emotions, to cause himself pain, to let the tears and the curses be heard in a world that didn't seem to care. It was a cry for help. He yearned for guidance and maternal love in a bid to wipe Auntie from his memory, to end once and for all the abuse still befuddling his mind. He eventually moved south, to England, where he met his understanding wife and had several children. He suffers badly today from severe health problems, mostly the result of years of beatings, mental abuse and extreme starvation. The family has grown up now and, although he is disabled, he enjoys a quiet life with his wife and grandchildren.

Once Robert and I had left Coxton, it wasn't long before Mary and George followed, each in their own way. Mary continually ran away when the pressure at home became too much. Time after time, the police brought her back to the croft, her accounts of abuse dismissed and ignored. No consideration was given to any attempt by her to explain her disruptive behaviour. The police did challenge Auntie, but she insisted that she was the injured party, suffering abuse at the hands of her two remaining foster children. She didn't want to file a complaint, though, because, in her opinion, she was more than able to handle the situation. It didn't matter how many times Mary absconded, any investigation relating to this repeated incident was never set in motion.

It was one final event that ended Mary's time on the croft for ever. After a few angry words being spoken between the two women, Auntie as usual trapped Mary between the wall and a chest of drawers. She began a frenzied attack, beating Mary incessantly with my hockey stick. The violence and vehement criticism was so severe that George rushed into the house and tried to stop her. He was forced to intervene when Mary shouted that her arm was broken. It took several minutes to prise the stick from Auntie's tight grip, her knuckles bone-white with rage.

George ran outside and threw the stick as far as he could away from the house. He was determined to end the attack on his sister once and for all. Enough was enough. Mary reacted instantly. She ran down the brae and did not return until the police brought her home later that evening. Owing to her injury and her state of mind, she was immediately removed to a young women's hostel, where she was assessed and diagnosed as emotionally unstable. She was barely 16, her mind irreversibly damaged, her emotions in permanent chaos. She found life unbearable and was unable to get anyone to believe what she had endured at Coxton. She was later admitted into psychiatric care in the Glasgow area, where she stayed for a couple of years. I tried to keep in touch, but all my letters went unanswered. We had deserted her and I think she thought we did not want her any more. She shut down emotionally and detached herself from the family.

I was in the last year of my nurse training when I met my late husband. The thought of marriage and a home to call my own was inviting, and after a short three-month courtship we decided to go ahead with a wedding. I had no parents to hold me back and I was desperate to commit to a loving and caring relationship.

The wedding went smoothly and I was welcomed into my new husband's family. I was amazed at the number of presents I received from people who had known me for such a short time. I had very few belongings and each gift was gratefully appreciated, all of them helping to decorate and furnish my first home – the one I had dreamt about while sitting in a hessian-clad hut shivering with cold and suffering from hunger.

One present, a set of pans, given to us by friends of the family, caused me some confusion. Although I was very pleased with my present, I couldn't understand why such an influential and intelligent couple (one a headmaster, the other a teacher) would give us pans they had used themselves. The inside was covered in black film, which I thought was a sign of use. I spent the next month scrubbing them with steel pads and wire mesh until my husband noticed what I was doing and explained that it was a non-stick coating. It was the first time I had seen anything like that – a hangover from my years at the old-fashioned croft. I felt naive and stupid and utterly vulnerable. I wanted to run away and hide. I'd shown a lack of intelligence, perception and, worst of all, common sense. I was emotionally drained and needed to react in a humorous and silly manner to rescue my self-respect.

I remember taking a walk down the main street in Aberdeen the day after we returned from honeymoon. My new husband, whom I didn't know very well at the time, pointed to two men sitting on a bench, one bearded, strumming a guitar. This man was wearing a black donkey jacket, a polo-neck sweater and desert boots, a common sight in the '60s. My husband proceeded to walk towards the young man, pulling me rather reluctantly behind him. 'I can't stand lazy bums like that,' he shouted. 'I'm going to kick him hard and wake him up to the real world.'

I was horrified, and suddenly unsure of this man I had known only for a short time. As we approached the two men, the bearded youth looked up. To my relief, he gave us the biggest, cheekiest grin I have ever seen in my life. They greeted each other warmly, as only the closest of friends would do. This young man was to become a great friend, my son's godfather and much, much more in the years to come.

Every time he came to visit, he bounced into the house and bulldozed into the kitchen like a friendly grizzly bear. His huge grin and cheery character filled the room with excitement and anticipation. He was always hungry. He had discovered education in the mid-'70s and was determined to go to college and acquire qualifications for entry into art school, but, not being entitled to a grant, money was scarce. His first comment when he arrived at the house was always, 'Is it fishfingers or beans tonight?' Then, with a glint in his eyes, 'Or both?'

At the beginning of my marriage, I followed my husband everywhere. Every time he turned round or went to the bathroom, I was there. He didn't understand how desperate I was to keep him near me. Just like the shepherd all those years ago on the croft, I was afraid that he would tire of my company and ask me to leave. I couldn't believe he actually wanted me in his life, that he was prepared to accept me and my idiosyncrasies.

I was aware that he had recently broken off an engagement and was afraid that he might have reacted on the rebound, that I was in some way a compensatory choice. I yearned to tell him about Coxton and Auntie; I wanted him to understand why I was acting this way and hoped he could help me adjust to this new life, but I didn't know where to start. I know he found my behaviour unsettling: one day, he sat down beside me and asked me to stop following him around. He said I was trying too hard to please him and he was finding it quite suffocating. I knew I had to relax. I had to accept my new environment and my position in this family and work with the people around me.

Nine months later, I gave birth to my honeymoon baby, a beautiful baby girl. I couldn't believe she was part of me – a miniature me – a perfect bundle of love. A year later, we moved into our first real home.

Motherhood was a great stabilising influence in my life. I developed a strong maternal instinct and was determined that I would never neglect my children, nor would they ever be starved of love and affection. I did not want them to feel the loneliness and sadness I had experienced throughout my childhood. What did unnerve me at times were the routine visits by health visitors to the house to check on the welfare of my children. I had flashbacks to Coxton and the child welfare officers from that time. My greatest fear was that they would think I was a bad mother and take them from me. I remembered Auntie saying that history always repeated itself.

I realised I had to extinguish these ghosts by going to Coxton and showing Auntie that I was a capable mother. I wanted to prove her wrong. As our car drove up the brae, I began to shake inside. The building hadn't changed; the geese and hens were still scraping round the sheds. The same green door opened to the sound of the engine and Auntie shuffled out, still in her tartan slippers. Her hair bore the shape of hurriedly removed curlers. She appeared nervous, but invited us into the dark interior. A teapot sat on the kitchen table, warm and shrouded in a knitted cosy. She spoke to my children and my husband and nodded in my direction. The children were impressed by the amount of animals and gave her the nickname 'the Lady and the Pussycats'. She was kind to them and gave my little boy a knitted doll dressed in the uniform of a soldier from the Boer War. Changed days, I thought, as we ended the visit and headed for the car. I had left her a very important message: I hadn't turned out like my mother after all.

On the way home, my husband told me that Auntie had noticed that I was not wearing any make-up or nail varnish and had complimented him on doing a good job by keeping me respectable and under control. He was amused by her comments and had wanted to tell her that I was an independent person in my own right, but he didn't. Although I smiled at him and treated it as a light-hearted comment, I felt angry inside. What right had she to judge me now? She had nothing to do with me. She still couldn't see me for the person I had become. Even becoming a good mother did not seem to be enough for her. She still didn't trust me or allow herself to think that I might succeed at something over which she had no control.

After some thought, I realised that her opinion didn't matter any more. I no longer had to justify my actions nor was I afraid of her. I settled down to the journey home and listened contentedly to the happy chatter of my three children filtering through from the back seat of the car. I couldn't help smiling. I felt I had conquered another demon – one of many that had haunted us during our stay at Coxton.

I still couldn't speak openly to my husband about the past. There didn't seem to be enough hours in the day to look after my three young children and find a spare minute for serious personal discussions. However, as time progressed, I settled down to life as a mother and a wife, coping with a husband I rarely saw, learning to play with my children.

Then one day, out of the blue, I received a letter from an aunt I didn't know existed. It was a detailed account of how my mother had died of a broken heart and how hard her life had been since her children were put into a home. She wrote several times, repeating the same thing over and over again, and in one enclosed my mother's wedding ring. Every letter mentioned the sad life this woman had led – not once was there mention of us four small, abandoned children. It was as if we never existed; it was as if she was speaking to a stranger.

After numerous letters and phone calls, I became suspicious of this person and her many stories. Each so-called experience involving me didn't ring true. She seemed to be forgetting that these were my memories too: they were of my mother and the things we did together. Although she presented herself as a caring relative, whenever I mentioned my brothers and sister her mood changed dramatically. It was obvious she did not want to talk about them and felt awkward when their names were mentioned. I wondered, was this my mother contacting me? And, if so, why was she pretending to be someone else – was she so afraid of me? I was beginning to feel a little overwhelmed at the thought.

After a long discussion with my husband, I decided to find out once and for all. The next time she phoned, it took me just a few seconds to pluck up the courage to ask.

'Are you my mother?' I said.

There was an eerie silence at the end of the line. Some time elapsed before she spoke. In the meantime I was thinking: will she hang up, or deny everything and stick to her story? At last, in a quiet voice, she admitted that I was her daughter. I could feel the hairs rise on the back of my neck, though I could not distinguish the fear I felt from the excitement. Could I really welcome this woman as my mother – this woman, now a stranger, who had abandoned me and my siblings and left us in the hands of an unstable carer? Could I really accept this person as part of my family?

Warning bells rang in my head as I tried to come to terms with what was happening. Our conversation was short and guarded. The pretence was shattered, the deception ended, the truth was out. The number of phone calls increased throughout the next few weeks and I sensed a growing confidence in her voice. She wanted to meet. I reluctantly agreed but remained uncertain as the day grew near. My husband and I drove to the station to meet her. I couldn't think straight: I knew nothing about her, I wasn't sure if I was doing the right thing, what had she been doing all the years we were in need of her, why had she left it so late to find me . . .? I had thought she was dead and that was why she couldn't come for us.

I remembered the day at the children's home when she had walked out of our lives without a backward glance. Was she coming back to haunt me or lay some claim to my children? I felt I had moved on from those days and I didn't need her any more. She could never be my mother, I knew that, but maybe she could be my friend. What I couldn't say to anyone was that I had longed for this moment for many years: I had yearned for this mother as a lost child yearns for home, comfort and attention. The feeling of neglect and abandonment had remained desperately real for such a long time and my heart ached to hear words of comfort from a mother whom I had once loved.

I had kept my story inside, believing I couldn't tell my husband how I really felt because he would not understand or believe me, but at that moment I looked into his eyes and saw a depth of feeling I hadn't noticed before. Everything about him in that instant was clear and immediate. I didn't have to say anything. I knew whatever decision I made here and now would be supported by him.

The train drew into the station and I scanned the crowd for a familiar face. I vaguely remembered what she looked like, but 20 years had passed since last being together. But I knew her immediately. Although older, she was still the small, bespectacled woman from my past, though her smile seemed cold and false. I felt a chill in my bones as I moved towards her. She embraced me lightly and I felt nothing. I thought I could rekindle the warmth and the longing I had for this woman, this mother I had so yearned for all my childhood, but she appeared confused. She attempted to take my hand, then presented me with a small blue-and-white hand-knitted hat and scarf that would have better fitted a six-year-old child. I tried to introduce my husband, but she looked through him with a glazed expression. She did not see this man as part of me. I was her little girl of six and she seemed to expect me to go with her. I was devastated. I watched her scan me with a vague expression, clouded by a strange misunderstanding, as she was forced to face her past demons. I could see her struggling to mentally fill in the missing years and she was failing miserably. I felt like walking away, but I couldn't leave her in such a pathetic state.

Against our better judgement, we invited her home to meet her grandchildren. She remained very quiet in the car and I could see her staring at me in the mirror. I realised she was still lost in her own world of turmoil and chaos. She wanted to start again where she had left off, as a mother with a little girl to look after. She could not cope with the lost years and was unable to understand my transition from child to adult, wife and mother. My husband and children did not exist in her world: they were visitors to be pleasant to and nothing else.

I did my best to make her welcome. This stranger sitting beside me in my own house was my mother, the woman I had so desperately wanted to find over the years to explain to me the desertion of my parents. This was our mother, the one Robert and I cried for all these years ago in the children's home, who we called out for when we were thrown outside into the cold night. She had left me behind in 1954 and it felt as though she was still there in her mind. I could see she was mentally leaving me again and this time I was relieved.

We spent a quiet evening talking about nothing in particular and after breakfast next morning we drove her back to the station for her journey south. I felt sorry for her. She was unaware of times past and the need for a healing process for both of us. She was unable to see the present as it was and couldn't accept that I didn't want to go with her. I wasn't the little girl she remembered. I wondered if she would stop searching for me now and hoped somehow that she had found some kind of closure to her nightmares. Today she was the lost one: I had to let her go. It was the last time I saw or heard from her until I was informed of her death ten years later in 1987.

By the mid-'70s, I felt confident enough to try and help my little sister. My children were no longer at the baby stage and were looking forward to meeting their auntie. My husband and I applied for, and were granted, permission to take Mary home from the psychiatric hospital for the Christmas holidays. We hired a car and travelled south to collect her. She was so happy to see us, and the first visit went so well, that we repeated it again the following year. At the end of each visit, however, she became increasingly agitated and upset at the thought of returning to the hospital, and one year we did not have the heart to take her back. We applied to have her discharged into our care and permission was granted. She lived with us for nearly two years until her behaviour became impossible to control. It became increasingly difficult to deal with the ups and downs of a troubled young woman and share her with my three children under five.

Every time my husband tried to help her, she crouched down in the nearest corner, expecting to be beaten. We tried very hard to sympathise with her, and she tried so hard to adjust to normal life, but the damage to her mental health was so severe that we were forced to request the help of the family doctor and, with the assistance of the right people, got her admitted to a hospital in Banff just north of Aberdeen. She settled down well into her new environment and I was able to visit her regularly. After several years of intense therapy, she recovered enough to manage her own flat, albeit supervised and supported by an excellent team of workers. She took an overdose in the early '80s, and though she survived, when I visited her in hospital, I had never seen her so low in spirit. She felt used by everyone, she was past caring.

Since the age of three, when Auntie was forced into her life, her mind had forever been in turmoil with the world around her. Now approaching 40, the will to fight against abuse and adversity had burned out. There was nothing left, she was finished. After I left the hospital, she signed herself out and walked about 50 miles to her flat in Banff.

Our meetings after that were filled with a sadness that was

devouring her whole existence. I saw her mentally slipping away from life and from me. Her phone calls became more desperate, her worries took on a magnitude out of all proportion. She phoned one evening to tell me she loved me. It was our last conversation. Several days later, she died. Her death certificate stated natural causes. She had given up the ghost, but she was now at peace.

Auntie had destroyed this little girl, this young woman who had never known what love was. I wrote down the words to 'Nobody's Child', a song we often sang at Coxton, and placed it on a wreath at her graveside.

Robert, George and I stood quietly at her open grave, arms linked, with thoughts of Coxton and Auntie. We remembered the beatings, the screaming, the starvation. What a waste of life: a sad life, a life without love. Mary was lying in a cold box, her brothers and sister standing feet above, wanting to hug her, to take her home. We turned and walked away and returned to our families.

My husband died suddenly just before Mary's death. He was a lovable rogue, one of the best bar-room philosophers I have ever met, a Peter Pan who didn't want to grow up, afraid of any responsibility, whether it be domestic or financial. He was a fun dad, drunk or sober, lost in time and adventure. I had spent most of my spare hours alone: at times, the house felt so empty when the children were asleep. I longed for the company of my husband, but I was being selfish. My time was my own: I could lie on the settee and watch television, read a book, relax or do nothing. This was my home, my environment and my place of refuge. It was better than Coxton, where I was beaten, pushed, manipulated and controlled, where peace did not exist. At least when my husband was in the pub, I could have a cup of tea and listen to the wireless without being dragged onto the floor.

My husband's pay packet was emptied in the pub and I was forced to return to nursing to make ends meet. Night duty was a blessing – I was at home, albeit in bed, when school holidays came around and my children were safe. These years were hard, bringing up a family, keeping the debts as low as possible, trying to hold down a full-time job. It was exhausting and lonely at times. I felt that perhaps my obsessive behaviour at the beginning of our marriage had forced distance in our relationship. I told him about Coxton many times and he tried to listen, but I think he was afraid for me, afraid of my memories. I know he loved me, but I also know that he could not deal with my inability to get terribly excited about anything. He couldn't understand that I didn't know how. He felt safer hidden amongst beer mugs and beer drinkers. He was a poet at heart, always lost in his own imagination.

George was the last to leave the croft after enduring months of increasingly irrational behaviour from Auntie. Her emotional outbursts continued on a daily basis and eventually pushed him to the limit of his tolerance. Conditions became so bad that he couldn't even sit in peace to drink a cup of tea without being bombarded with verbal abuse. She continually harassed and tormented him, trying to blackmail him by saying that if he stayed with her he could inherit the croft but if he decided to leave, he would have nothing and nowhere to go. She taunted him with the neglect of his parents and told him that he was still as worthless now as he had been when he had first arrived. She showed him no sympathy or compassion and George just couldn't take any more. The cup of cooling tea hit her face, splashing against a half-smoked cigarette, the soggy shreds of tobacco dripping onto her apron and sliding slowly towards the dirty wooden floor. He told her that he did not want her croft: it was a stinking, filthy place and not fit for decent habitation. He watched the tea drip from her long nose and into her mouth. He had tried to speak to her and reason with her, but she wouldn't listen. She hissed abuse and screamed incessantly. He knew this was the end. He couldn't take any more. A lifetime had passed since he had arrived at this place, a lifetime of starvation and severe neglect. He was four years old then and wanted to trust everyone. This trust had been beaten out of him and he had nothing left to give.

He headed for the door and out into the fresh air.

He returned that night because he didn't know where else to go, but the door was locked. The final decision to leave had been made for him. He turned and walked away for the last time.

He worked in a store in Elgin and for several weeks he slept rough, wherever he could rest his head for the night. He slept under hedges, on park benches and in a caravan until the loneliness became too much. He decided to head for Aberdeen, where my mother-in-law looked after him until he found work as a greenkeeper on a local golf course, with live-in accommodation. He entered into an unsuccessful marriage, which shattered his confidence so much that he packed up and headed further north, where he acquired another similar post. He worked for some time until his health deteriorated due to poor nourishment in early childhood and years of sustained beatings. He now lives quietly with his son and a partner. He spends quality time with his daughter and grandchildren among the beautiful Highlands of Scotland, never asking for anything he feels he doesn't deserve and unselfishly giving help to anyone who needs it.

From the earliest days at the croft, Auntie had showed no

compassion, sympathy or kindness without calculating how it would return to her advantage. Day after day we woke with the birds, sweltering in a croft as hot as an oven in summer, but freezing to death in an icebox in winter, our hands raw and scratched with overwork, our backs aching from a weariness that permeated to the centre of our bones, a permanent, insatiable hunger for sustenance: it was finally at an end. Many evenings we had stood outside, shivering in the pouring rain, often dressed only in our pyjamas. Hours would pass sometimes before Auntie let us back inside and the rest of the day was spent listening to her sharp tongue or ducking every time she passed us. We were very unhappy and longed for a hug or some form of comfort. We didn't want to stay with this woman – she was cruel and unkind – but there was no one to confide in and no one to turn to for help. We had to live day-by-day, week-by-week, trying to make sense of her methods and understand what she was asking us to do. I was too young to realise that Auntie might also be regretting taking on a large family that was proving too much for her and that she, too, had no one to confide in or ask for advice. She was left alone to work it out for herself and she knew she was failing miserably. I think she also knew that the authorities would not be willing to take us back. They would have found it practically impossible to re-foster four children and keep us together as one unit. My siblings still cannot find sympathy for her actions today, but my experience with people in a nursing environment gave me the ability to question her abnormal behaviour and try to analyse the cause and effects. The mental and physical scars, for me, disappeared a long time ago, but for my younger siblings they are still visible.

The loss of Mary still haunts us, and our regret that maybe

we could have done more to help her will stay with us for the rest of our lives; but each of us had to solve our own problems and rid ourselves of the effects those ten years had on our separate lives.

It is not a perfect life, but the basic values and instincts, regarding the survival of the human race, should always be reflected in the way our young are protected and nourished, no matter what country, race or economic climate we live in.

Like a flower, a child should blossom
safe within a world of care.
Never lend them to the stranger
who will strip their future bare.
Like a flower, she gives us beauty.
Like a stem, he turns her head.
Pluck them from the perfect picture,
then there's only ghosts instead.
Like a flower, a child should flourish,
growing stronger every day.
Take the life that flows inside them,
and the sunshine fades away.

As the years passed, I heard that our foster mother was taken into long-term care after electrocuting herself when trying to boil a kettle of water, ironically breaking her arm in the process. The croft was in a state of filth and disrepair, and she was unable to care for herself safely. Her cleanliness was so lacking that the row of metal rollers that always hung round the foot of her hair had to be cut off. It was a sad end to what should have been a cosy family unit. If our placement had been treated sympathetically by Auntie and the authorities, we would not have allowed her and her croft to lapse into this serious state of neglect.

Not long after that incident she suffered a stroke and I went up to see her. We had very little to say to each other and I noticed tears seeping from her eyes, following the lines of her weathered face. This time she was the vulnerable one, this time she was alone. I bent down and kissed her, something I had never been allowed to do. She touched my hand and whispered, 'Thank you.' I didn't visit her again until her second stroke, after which followed pneumonia. She was dying in front of me: I wanted to protect her, to forgive her, but I couldn't. I still felt bitterness towards her for the way she had treated us all.

That was the last time I saw her alive. Several months later, I was informed of Auntie's death and my youngest daughter and I went north to her funeral, so that I could close this chapter of my life once and for all. I did feel sorry for her, having to spend her remaining years in a residential home with no one but the staff to care about her.

The church was empty when we arrived and she was lying in an open casket. We both went up to see her and, although I knew it was wrong, I had this strange compulsion to grab hold of her nose. Whether it was because I was nervous at seeing her again or I just wanted to make sure she was really gone, I'm not certain, but I had to grab it and it made me feel much better.

My daughter said nothing for a moment, then she took hold of my hand and whispered, 'It's all right now, Mum. It's over.' I watched her coffin being carried to the graveyard on the shoulders of men who did not know her and I was handed a cord when it was time to lower her into the ground. I should have felt sad for her, but I remember feeling as cold as the ground she was entering.

Would she be forgiven for what she did to us? I hoped so because I could only try to understand her loneliness. It would be a new dawn and the sun would rise without her. In my dreams, she will be at peace, but in those of my brothers she will be in hell.

Coxton, as it Is Today

On my final visit to Coxton, I stepped over the threshold into my past and was faced with a bleak picture of desertion, neglected decor and ruin. It was lifeless and strangely quiet. I felt as if some part of me was still hiding within its walls, begging to be set free. Time and moisture had retained the murky grey dampness I remembered so well. The stones and mortar were tumbling in places as if baring Auntie's soul to the elements and to the strangers she hated so much. Inside sat the broken enamelled sink with its solitary tap spitting dirt into the discoloured basin; a deep grey net curtain, once white, still hiding the forbidden food cupboard, now empty, hung in protest at our intrusion; a discarded metal basin, now rusted and upside down on the last crocheted rug that was dying of decay, portrayed a stark image of abandonment. It was empty of all her personal things except a small hair roller hugging the base of a chipped tiled fireplace. There was no evidence that any child had ever lived there. I breathed in the mildewed dust and was immediately transported back to a time and place I wanted to forget. It was the first time I was able to enter that house without fear of retribution. I felt sad for the effect this episode had had on me and my family, and what it eventually did to Auntie. I looked over to where the wood used to be: the essential background to my conception of this place was gone and I realised that I didn't know this place at all. Everywhere I looked held a bad memory. The old monkey puzzle tree that always sat outside our bedroom window had fallen down and was lying in a sad mangled state. I shut the green wooden door for the last time and imprisoned the past for eternity.

I walked down the overgrown brae, once full of geese, hens and ducks, cats chasing one another round in circles, a quiet black-and-white collie dog following me everywhere, and four young children hiding in corners or behind sheds afraid to move in case they received a beating, desperately looking and hoping for someone to love them. I should have left a trail of angry memories behind, but I felt strangely at peace. There were tears in my eyes – tears for my siblings and all they had suffered, tears for our lost childhood.

A pigeon cooed from the corrugated-iron roof, a last farewell, a tribute to all animal life that roamed the fields and enclosures. I had done my duty, as the eldest child, to Auntie and to the croft. It was time to go home to my children.

It was the end of an era and one I wanted to forget. I had done my best to try and cope with my memories of the croft and, in a way, I felt that I had succeeded. The treatment we had received had changed our formative years and marked our lives forever, but for me the ghosts from the past hadn't bothered me in adulthood as much as I had thought they would.

I have spent my life making excuses for Auntie, telling myself that she must have had a good reason for the way she acted, and somehow this has proved to be almost a comfort, or at least enough reason to explain what took place at Coxton. It is very easy to forget when I am speaking to my siblings today that there were brighter moments in amongst the dark ones. They have been deeply scarred by their experiences, while I have laid to rest those nightmares. I had no control over what happened to each one of us at any moment at the croft, and I know that I can't change the past, but I was determined at the very beginning to learn from our experience and make myself a better person because of it.

I still find it difficult to accept help easily. I feel that I don't deserve it, and I am not happy unless I manage to finish what I have started without assistance. It is as if I am still searching for encouragement and praise, continually hoping I don't receive criticism. I do believe that if you are taught as a child that you don't deserve love or praise, it's very hard to accept affection in later life and take reasonable criticism without either feeling that you have to prove yourself or becoming defensive with every move you make.

The way I deal with these feelings has improved over the years and with the help of my nursing experience, my devoted family and my loyal friends, I have become a better and stronger person.

It had been a bad year for me: my husband had died suddenly in front of me and I couldn't save him. Now Auntie was gone, too. The uncertainties of the past crept back, the guilt I had felt at Coxton was nagging at my soul. I needed to talk to someone, but no one was there. I needed to hug someone, but no one was around. My children had turned to their friends for comfort to help them through the dark times – they were afraid that they would hurt me further by involving me in their heartache. So I found myself alone, trying to understand the last few months.

It felt as if Auntie had come back to haunt me. Her screams and shouts woke me up in the middle of the night. I wanted to hide and shut out the world, get rid of the mental pain I was in. I felt as if I was that little lost girl again, standing in a cold Glasgow tenement crying for her mother to come home. My work began to suffer and instead of working with patients and staff I hid for short periods in the X-ray department's dark room. I felt safe there, as if no one could hurt me any more.

After many absences, I was referred to the hospital psychiatrist, who attempted to sympathise with my problems. I was still struggling six months later, when I got an unexpected visit from the bearded young man of twenty years ago. I was hanging out some washing when the back gate opened. I hadn't seen him for some time and it was nice to see his cheeky smile again. He had not heard from me since the death of his friend and my husband, and had become concerned for my welfare. He wanted to know how I was coping and if he could help in any way.

'Hi, there,' he said in a chirpy voice, one I knew so well. 'Is it fish fingers and beans tonight?' We laughed at the memory. It was good to see him again – I dropped everything and ran for a bear hug. 'I'm here to take you out for a wee while, if the kids don't mind. It will do you good.'

I grabbed my jacket and we headed into town. We talked for hours and I could feel the old me bursting through the shadows. I felt the clouds I'd been living under for the past six months drift away. Our evening passed quickly and we arranged to meet again a few days later. Mike looked down at me before he left that night and something in his eyes made me feel safe. It was enough for the moment.

We discovered that we had a lot in common and felt relaxed in each other's company. Most importantly, we still liked each other. The relationship developed into marriage and, with 23 years of togetherness to date, and many adventures under our hat, he has remained my soulmate, my protector and my best friend. I always knew there was someone out there for me: someone with a sense of humour, someone who would hold my hand, cuddle me and take an interest in me. I have found this someone in Mike, my bearded friend of the '60s, my king of all kings. He has helped me to step beyond my limits of self-doubt and move away from the fears of the past. He gave me a confidence that I never thought I could have, and the ability to look at life in a different and philosophical way. Mike has opened my mind to a new, confident me and in turn has encouraged the writing of this book.

The guilt of the past has finally been laid to rest. The nightmares that haunted me in the years at Coxton and beyond have vanished. Mike and I do everything together and are rarely apart. Our days consist of endless conversations on anything and everything; our faces ache with laughter, and each day the love and trust we have in each other grows stronger and stronger. Life has exceeded my wildest expectations. I am now loved and cherished as never before. I have a devoted husband, adoring children and four lively grandsons. Coxton is a fading memory, one I will never truly forget, but one that doesn't hurt any more.

Bring in the sunshine,
drive away rain.
Bring out the laughter
and ease all our pain.
Give us, the young ones,

a chance to grow old.
Feed all our hunger,
keep us in wonder
away from the cold.
Make all our bad times
turn into good.
Solve all our problems
if only you would.
Take just a moment
to notice our day.
Give us a reason,
find us the freedom
for children to play.
Safely together,
safely beside you.
We'll travel for ever
on an ocean of blue.
Someone to hold us,
someone to guide us,
whenever the wind blows
and whispers our name.

Author's Note

In writing this book, it has never been my intention to point the finger of blame at anyone or any institution involved in the tragedy of my lost childhood, nor did it occur to me to look for compensation for the years I spent in an abusive foster home with my siblings.

When I sat down to begin this book, I found myself looking back through a long, dark, misty tunnel of mixed emotions and sparse information, where early memories reeked of lost childhoods and disturbed minds: an old spinster woman, lonely in her small croft, desperately seeking company; a family of four young children removed from their home and forced to live with this woman who had absolutely no concept of how to bring them up. Healing my mind and putting those children's ghosts to rest has taken many years of soul searching.

Since leaving the croft in 1966, after ten years of mental and physical abuse, I have blamed everyone from my parents and the child welfare officers to my foster mother and latterly the complete ignorance of everyone involved; but in setting down this account of events and putting them into perspective, I have managed to come to terms with everything and everyone.

I have the full permission of my brothers to use their real names. In doing so, they feel they finally have a chance to tell their story to a world that has never believed them. In their minds, keeping some form of personal identity relative to the horrendous events detailed in this book proves that their attempts to ask for help were truly justified. For them, it gives a sense of relief being finally able to put to rest the nightmare of their childhood.

All poetry included in this book has been written by me and I feel it is necessary to create the atmosphere of a time when writing poetry in a homemade hut in the woods was my only emotional release.

Many of my early years are a blur in my memory. However, due to the passionate yearning of my younger brother Robert to find an answer to the questions surrounding our parents, a few of the neighbours still living in the same street in Glasgow were able to describe events and the circumstances of our childhood and thereby give us a clearer picture of our early years. The help and memory-awakenings of old school friends and neighbours at the croft have also added substance to the true sequence of events that took place.

The love and respect of my three children and the pleasure of seeing my four grandchildren thrive much-loved within a caring environment has strengthened my need to put pen to paper and close this book once and for all.

Without the love and support of my devoted second husband and the ultimate patience shown, as he listened to and read my manuscript over and over, I would not have completed this exercise – an exercise that has served as an important therapeutic conclusion.

Author's Note

My last poetic creation is dedicated to this beautiful man, as a special thanks for taking hold of my life when the days were dark and desperate after the death of my first husband and for making me a more sensitive and confident person.

Michael,
if the wheel of fortune
had stopped before my time,
I'd have lost a dear companion,
a special friend of mine.
He sweeps away my darkness
encased within his arms,
provides a blend of comfort,
found deep within his charms.
If I couldn't touch him,
or hold him close to me,
my life would have no meaning,
my dreams would not be free.
My reason for existing
would disappear from sight,
to leave a vacant presence,
a dying flame of light.
If I'd never met him,
or found his soothing smile,
my path would be uncertain,
without his certain style.
There'd be no morning sunrise,
no music in the air.
There'd be no time to listen,
if Michael wasn't there.